Ghost Ranch and friends

a cookbook

Rebecca Martinez
Foodservice Director

Rebecca Morgan
Editor

Original Watercolor and Cover Design
by
Pomona Hallenbeck

GHOST RANCH
CONFERENCE CENTER
GHOST RANCH
HC 77 - BOX 11
Abiquiu, NM 87510-9601

ISBN 0-9652025-0-X $15.00

Printed in the United States of America

First Edition 1992
Second Edition 1996

About Ghost Ranch

Ghost Ranch is...

an education and mission center of the Presbytrian church,
welcoming people of diverse faiths and racial and cultural origins

a center for learning and empowerment
preparing women, men and children to grow spiritually,
strengthen community, and give transforming service
to church and world

a respectful neighbor in historic Northern New Mexico,
offering with love what it has to give
and accepting with grace what it needs to receive

an advocate for the care of the earth and its resources,
living and teaching harmony with all of God's creation

an open space for body, mind and spirit,
offering beauty, encounter and growth

a gift of hospitality and healing
shared joyfully with all who come

a community of rest, re-creation and renewal
serving God and people of questing faith:
keeper and mender of creation and communities,
seeker and servant of peace and justice,
light, leaven, salt and neighbor
in an uncertain world.

Mission Statement, 1992

A word from Rebecca Martinez

It has been my pleasure to serve as the director of food services at Ghost Ranch for almost 20 years. The kitchen staff and I work very hard to prepare for our guests the most nutritious and attractive meals possible. Many changes have occured over the years as we have become more health conscious and interest has grown in regional foods. We are using more fresh produce than ever before, only lowfat dairy products, and vegetable oils instead of animal fats.

We want people to feel welcome when they come to the dining hall and satisfied when they leave after a meal. People are strangers to us only until they step through the dining hall door. After that, they are our guests and friends.

Pansa llena, corazon contento.
After a meal the heart is full.

Introduction

Over the years, especially during the busy summer months, guests at Ghost Ranch often ask the kitchen staff for recipes: posole, those wonderful enchiladas, a special bread or cookie, the green salad dressing... The idea for a Ghost Ranch cookbook began as a response to these requests.

As the project got under way, we decided to include memorable recipes from Ghost Ranch friends and staff: Julie Stevens' "Trail Ride Sourdough Biscuits," Joan Boliek's "Hypocrites" from the Christmas tree outing, "Molly's Red Chile Sauce" and Ruth Hall's "Spicy Nut Coffee Ring." We began collecting favorite family recipes, including many traditional foods of northern New Mexico.

Rebecca Morgan (formerly 'Becca May) is the editor and driving force behind *Ghost Ranch and Friends*. In the fall of 1991, she conceived the idea of expanding the cookbook to support the Farm to Market Project (FTM), of which she was the director. FTM has supported local beef and produce growers with technical information, and provided a readily accessible market at the Ranch and its Santa Fe counterpart, Plaza Resolana. The "More Friends" addition of this edition of the cookbook includes a number of recipes featuring fresh foods from these local providers.

In addition to recipes from the Ranch kitchen, staff and neighbors, contributions were solicited from Compadres who are friends and supporters of the Ranch and Plaza Resolana. (Note: the Spanish "*compadre*" means godparent.) The recipes, along with the wonderful stories that came with them, give a picture of the richness of this place and the extraordinary people who come here.

Eating is more than a physical event. Sharing food is a mental, emotional and spiritual ritual of caring, fellowship, respecting tradition and awakening memories. "This recipe has been a family favorite for three generations. I'm happy to share it with my Ghost Ranch family," wrote one contributor. "Whenever I make this recipe, I remember good times with family and friends," says another.

The first edition of *Ghost Ranch and Friends* quickly sold out. So, the kitchen continued to get requests for recipes, and there are numerous inquiries about the cookbook at the Ranch Trading Post. Now, the cookbook is back by popular demand!

Many of the people who participated in the first edition are in different places. Rebecca Morgan left her position as Assistant Foodservice Manager (changed her name from 'Becca back to Rebecca once she and Rebecca Martinez were no longer working together in the kitchen), and is now Marketing Director of Contract Business.

Paul Ryer, who assisted Rebecca Morgan on the first edition, is now in Cuba. Paul's and Deborah Hunter's excellent technical work on the original manuscript made revisions and additions easy. Compadre volunteer Anne Hunt, had a big part in editing the first edition. Her persistence and willingness to act as production coordinator got the second edition off the press. There was never any question about using the beautiful watercolor Pomona Hallenbeck did for the original *Ghost Ranch and Friends*.

Dean Lewis, Floyd Trujillo, Mimi Tharp, Chad and Joan Boliek, and Jim and Judy Shibley have retired from Ghost Ranch staff duties, but we see them from time to time in the dining hall. These and other former staff members will be remembered when we prepare their recipes.

We've added a special section, "More Friends," to this edition as a way of including some of the new faces at the Ranch: Julie Jordan - chef and kitchen volunteer extraordinaire, Jean Richardson, Philip and Carol Ruth Geissal, Mary Martinez (who isn't really new), and Gary Salazar.

We never got Tom Guiles' recipe for barbeque, but we do appreciate his help with the financial and business end of the cookbook. Thanks, too, to Philip and Carol Ruth Geissal and the National Ghost Ranch Foundation, and Ghost Ranch director, Joe Keesecker, who encouraged this project from the very beginning.

Phoebe and Arthur Pack, who gave Ghost Ranch to the Presbyterian Church, put together a small recipe collection in the 1930s. The introduction expresses the hospitality of Rebecca Martinez, her talented kitchen staff, and all who contributed to this cookbook:

> *"Herein no claim is made to originality or to first invention. Some of these very dishes in similar form may be found in standard cookbooks or in other privately printed brochures. The secret of many a menu lies rather in its suitability to time, place and mood -- in the homelike touch and in the prideful care with which it is presented to the hungry guest.*
>
> *Food without the personal friendly talk and Nature's best backdrop may never please the palate half so well.*
>
> *We know that it is the combination of all these elements which has pleased you here. We know, too, that the senses of taste and smell have the power to awaken pleasant memories, and if such recollections may be brought back through the medium of the printed words and measures which follow, then we are well satisfied."*

In the first edition of *Ghost Ranch and Friends*, Rebecca Morgan writes:

"Editing this book has been a wonderful experience. The things I found most enjoyable were hearing from over 200 compadres, talking with people from the communities around Ghost Ranch and listening to Rebecca [Martinez] as she cooked, telling me about her childhood in Canjilon with her grandmother and her years here on the Ranch. My hope for this book is that the reader will find not only some delicious foods to prepare, but also a sense of what a 'magic place' Ghost Ranch really is."

Contents

Appetizers & Beverages

Vegetable Dip

Carl and Jean Soderberg
Albuquerque, NM

1	cup mayonnaise
1/4	cup curry powder
2	tablespoons chili sauce
2	tablespoons grated sweet onion (optional)
1	teaspoon red tarragon vinegar
1/2	teaspoon Lawry's seasoned salt
1/8	teaspoon dried thyme
	Dash white pepper

Mix all ingredients in a small bowl. Cover and chill. (Makes 1 cup.)

Hot Artichoke Dip

Nancy Deever
Plaza Resolana volunteer

1	cup Parmesan cheese
1/2	cup mayonnaise
1/2	cup sour cream
1	teaspoon Tabasco sauce
1/8	teaspoon chili powder (hot or mild)
1	can artichoke hearts, drained, chopped (about 14 oz.)
	Triscuits, flatbread, whole wheat crackers

Mix cheese, mayonnaise, sour cream, Tabasco and chili powder in a medium bowl. Stir in the artichoke hearts. Pour into a small casserole dish. Bake at 300°F for 30 minutes or until bubbly.

Note: May substitute low-fat mayonnaise and sour half & half. If doubling recipe, use only 1 1/2 cups Parmesan cheese.

I first had this dip in a Northwoods cabin off the Gunflint Trail in Minnesota. The outside temperature was -22° but this dip warmed us up!

Quick & Delicious Artichoke Dip

Ghost Ranch

2	cans artichokes in water, diced
1	cup mayonnaise
1	cup Parmesan cheese
1	can green chilies, diced

Blend ingredients, heat until warm.

Hot Spinach and Artichoke Dip

Marjorie Moeser
Toronto, Canada

1/4	cup white wine
1	clove garlic, finely chopped
1	package creamed chopped spinach, thawed (10 oz.)
3	whole artichoke hearts, drained, coarsely chopped
4	ounces Gruyere or Swiss cheese, grated (about 1 cup)
	Corn chips (white, blue or regular) for dipping

Place wine and garlic in a small, heavy-bottomed saucepan. Bring to
boiling over high heat. Reduce heat and add spinach. Stir in artichokes
and cheese. Continue cooking over low heat until bubbly. Spoon into
bowl and serve, surrounded with chips. (6 to 8 servings.)

Artichoke Squares

Ghost Ranch

4	eggs
1/2	pound cheddar cheese, grated
1	bunch green onions with tender green tops, chopped
1	clove garlic, minced
6	soda crackers, crumbled
2	jars marinated artichoke hearts (6 oz. each)
	Salt and pepper
	Pinch of parsley
	Dash of Tabasco

Saute onion and garlic in oil from the artichoke hearts until soft. Beat eggs. Combine all ingredients. Pour into 8 x 8 well-oiled pan. Bake at 325°F for 35-40 minutes. Don't cut until cool. Better if refrigerated and warmed when ready to serve. (Makes 36.)

Cheese Crackers

Jane Higbie
Indianapolis, IN

3	cups flour
1	teaspoon salt
1	teaspoon sugar
1	teaspoon dry mustard
1	teaspoon paprika
1	pound sharp cheese, grated
1	cup butter or margarine (2 sticks)

Combine dry ingredients in a medium bowl. Cut in cheese and butter with a pastry blender or 2 knives until mixture is crumbly. Form into 2 rolls, about 1-1/2" in diameter. Refrigerate, wrapped in plastic wrap or waxed paper. Just before serving, slice into circles, about 1/4" thick. Bake in 350° oven until firm and lightly browned, about 10 minutes.

Note: Rolls may be frozen, then thawed in refrigerator and baked when needed.

From a cookbook prepared by members of the Ridge Church, Accra, Ghana in 1972.

Ruth Hall's Cheese Roll

Ruth Ann Newby
Lubbock, TX

2   tablespoons soy sauce
1   package cream cheese (8 oz.)
2   tablespoons sesame seeds
         Crackers

Pour soy sauce over cream cheese in small bowl. (Add more soy sauce, if necessary to coat completely.) Cover and marinate in refrigerator overnight. Toast sesame seeds in oven or skillet until slightly brown, watching carefully so they do not burn. Shape cheese into a log or ball and roll in the sesame seeds. Serve with crackers.

We first met Ruth and Jim in Hobbs, NM in the late 1940's. We enjoyed their friendship and hospitality there and at Ghost Ranch. Ruth was a great cook!

Cheese Bubble

Pam Mattson
Tulsa, OK

1   pound very sharp Cheddar cheese, grated
1   large red onion, finely chopped (3/4 to 1 cup)
2   cups mayonnaise
         Tortilla chips

Combine cheese, onion and mayonnaise in medium bowl. Bake in 3-quart casserole at 350°F until puffy, 20 to 30 minutes. Drain any oil that collects on the top. Serve hot with tortilla chips.

Brie Cheese Loaf

Sharon Gourley
Winnetka, IL

1   round loaf French bread
1/4   cup butter or margarine, melted (1/2 stick)
1/2   teaspoon minced garlic (1 small clove)
8   ounces Brie cheese, cut in chunks

Cut a large ring in the top of the bread. Remove center in one piece, if possible, leaving a bread shell; set aside section of bread that has been removed. Combine butter and garlic; brush some on inside of shell. Put Brie into shell. Cut reserved bread section into serving-size pieces; brush bread pieces on all sides with remaining garlic butter. Place bread slices and filled bread shell on baking sheet. Bake at 400°F; remove bread slices as they brown. Cook until Brie is melted, 15 to 20 minutes. To serve, dip toasted bread slices into melted Brie; when gone, tear off pieces of loaf.

Chutney Cheddar Cheese Dip

Jan and Wil Hufton
Saginaw, MI

1	package cream cheese (8 oz.)
4	ounces Cheddar cheese, cut into pieces
1 1/2	tablespoons sherry
1/4 to 1/2	teaspoon curry powder
3/4	cup Major Grey's chutney
2	green onions with tender green tops, chopped
	Crackers

Place cream cheese, Cheddar cheese, sherry and curry powder in food processor bowl. Process until combined. Remove and form into a round, flat shape on a plate (like a round cake layer). Top with chutney; sprinkle with green onions. Serve with crackers.

Life of the Party

Midge Cavin
Santa Fe, NM

2	packages cream cheese, at room temperature (3 oz. each)
2	teaspoons milk
1	tablespoon prepared horseradish (or more to taste)
	Cauliflower flowerets, celery and carrot sticks

Mix cream cheese and milk until smooth; stir in horseradish. Cover and refrigerate. (Best made a day or two ahead.) Serve with vegetables.

Chunky Onion Dip

Ghost Ranch

8	ounces cream cheese
1/3	cup Bermuda onion, chopped
1/3	cup chili sauce
3	tablespoons mayonnaise
1/4	teaspoon Worcestershire sauce

Mix and chill ingredients. Makes 1 1/2 cups dip.

Big Game Clam Dip

Michael Chamberlain
Plaza Resolana, Santa Fe, NM

2	packages cream cheese, at room temperature (8 oz. each)
2	cans chopped clams, juice drained and reserved (6 oz. each)
1/4	cup mayonnaise
1	tablespoon Worcestershire sauce
1/8	teaspoon chili powder (or more to taste)
	Chips or vegetable crudites for dipping

Mix cream cheese, drained clams, mayonnaise, Worcestershire sauce and chili powder in a medium bowl with a hand mixer. Beat in half of the reserved clam juice. Add enough of the remaining clam juice to obtain desired texture for dipping (thinner for chips; thicker for vegetables).

Michael, along with his wife Kathleen Jimenez, is co-director of Plaza Resolana, Ghost Ranch's Santa Fe center.

Dill Sour Cream Dip

Ghost Ranch

1/2	cup sour cream
1/2	cup mayonnaise
1/4	teaspoon white pepper
8	sprigs fresh dill

Combine ingredients in food processor or blender. Process until blended. Makes 1 cup of dip.

Deviled Eggs

Ruth Livingood Auld
Claremont, Ca

8	hard-cooked eggs, cut in half lengthwise
2	tablespoons prepared mustard
1	tablespoon mayonnaise
1	teaspoon curry powder
1	teaspoon prepared horseradish sauce
1/2	teaspoon salt
2	tablespoons vinegar
	Paprika, parsley, chutney

Remove yolks from eggs: reserve whites. Place yolks in small bowl. Mash yolks with fork; stir in mustard, mayonnaise, curry powder, horseradish and salt. Mix in vinegar. Fill egg whites with yolk mixture. Garnish with paprika, parsley or a dab of chutney. (16 servings.)

Tortilla Roll Ups

Ghost Ranch

1	dozen flour tortillas
2	packages cream cheese, softened (8 oz. each)
1	can chopped green chile (4 oz.), drained
1	package sandwich ham slices (2 oz.), diced—or thinly sliced prosciutto

Mix chile with cheese, add ham. Spread to edges of tortillas. Roll tightly, cover with plastic wrap and refrigerate for 30-60 minutes. Slice in 1 1/2" pieces. (Makes 60 bite-size pieces.)

Caponata

Ann Picaro
Santa Fe, NM

1	medium eggplant, diced (about 1 lb.)
1	medium onion, chopped (about 1/2 cup)
1	medium zucchini, diced (about 1 cup)
1/3	cup chopped green bell pepper
2	cloves garlic, crushed
1/3	cup corn or olive oil
1	can tomato paste (6 oz.)
1/2	cup pimiento-stuffed green olives, sliced
1/4	cup water
2	tablespoons wine vinegar
1 1/2	teaspoons sugar
1	teaspoon salt (optional)
1/2	teaspoon dried oregano
	Dark bread

Add vegetables and garlic to hot oil in a large skillet or dutch oven. Cook over medium heat for 10 minutes. Add remaining ingredients except bread. Cover and simmer 15 to 20 minutes. Serve with dark bread. (6 to 8 servings.)

editor's note: Ann is the mother of Ghost Ranch's Willie Picaro. Willie is the ranch's environmental guru.

Mexican Quiche Appetizer

Ghost Ranch

1/2	cup butter
10	eggs
1/2	cup all purpose flour
1	teaspoon baking powder
	Dash of salt
1	can green chile, chopped (8 oz.)
2	cups cottage cheese (16 oz.)
4	cups Monterey Jack cheese, grated (1 lb.)

Melt butter in a 9 x 13 inch baking pan. Set aside. In a large mixing bowl beat eggs, add flour, baking powder and salt and mix well. Add melted butter, leaving the pan buttered. Add chilies and both cheeses. Mix together and pour into baking pan. Bake uncovered at 350°F for 45 to 60 minutes. Test for doneness with a knife. Be sure quiche is set and knife blade comes out clean when inserted in center. Cut into bite-size squares while hot, but allow to cool slightly before removing from pan. This may be baked and frozen; reheat covered with foil.

Vegetable Pizza

Barbara Decker
Hutchinson, KS

2	packages refrigerator crescent rolls (8 oz. each)
1	package cream cheese, at room temperature (8 oz.)
1	cup mayonnaise
1	teaspoon dried dill weed
1/2	teaspoon onion powder
1/2	teaspoon garlic powder
1/3	head cauliflower
3	carrots
2	stalks celery
6	radishes
1/2	green bell pepper
3	single stalks broccoli

Make crust by spreading rolls flat and patting together to cover the bottom and sides of an ungreased jelly roll pan, 15-1/2 x 10-1/2 x 1". Bake at 350°F until light brown, about 10 minutes (do not overbake!). Cool completely.

While crust is cooling, mix cream cheese, mayonnaise, onion and garlic powders. Reserve. Chop raw vegetables into uniform size, about as big as a pea; combine. When crust is cool, spread with cream cheese mixture. Top with chopped vegetables. Gently pat vegetables into cream cheese mixture. Cover with plastic wrap or foil and refrigerate overnight. To serve, cut into 1-1/2" squares. (Makes 70 squares.)

Stuffed Mushrooms

Peggy Grant
Abiquiu Elementary School

16	large mushrooms
1/4	pound butter
1/2	cup fine dry bread crumbs
2	eggs, lightly beaten
1	tablespoon parsley, chopped
1	tablespoon onion or chives, minced
	Salt and pepper to taste
	Parmesan cheese
	Beef broth

Remove stems of mushrooms, scrape them and chop fairly fine. Wipe mushroom caps with a damp cloth. Heat 2-3 tablespoons of butter in a skillet and saute the chopped mushroom stems lightly. Mix these with the bread crumbs, eggs, parsley, chives, or onions and 1/2 teaspoon each of salt and freshly ground black pepper. Brush the mushroom caps with melted butter and arrange them, cup side up, on a buttered baking dish. Fill each cup with some of the stuffing, sprinkle with grated Parmesan cheese, dot well with butter and add a little broth to the pan to keep them from sticking and burning. Baste during the cooking with additional butter to keep the mushrooms moist. Bake 15-20 minutes at 375°F.

Several years ago I began bringing stuffed mushrooms to our staff Christmas potluck at Abiquiu Elementary School. Recently, as we have needed more and more mushrooms, fellow teacher Ninfa Martinez has been joining me. Actually, she's been doing most of the work. I also pay my tax preparer with stuffed mushrooms.

Crab Cheese Dip

Ghost Ranch

8	ounces American cheese, shredded
8	ounces Chedder cheese, shredded
3/4	cup milk
2	teaspoon lemon juice
1	can crab meat, drained and flaked (7 1/2 ounces)

In saucepan, slowly heat and stir cheeses and milk until melted. Stir in lemon juice. Add crab, heat. Transfer to chafing dish. Suggested dippers: French bread, cherry tomatoes, artichokes.

Ghost Ranch Salsa

Ghost Ranch

1	can whole tomatoes, not drained (16 oz.)
1/2	medium onion, chopped (about 1/4 cup)
6	green jalapeño peppers, seeds and stems removed, minced
1	clove garlic, minced (or 1 tsp. garlic salt)
1/4	cup chopped cilantro
1	medium green bell pepper, chopped
	Salt to taste
	Tortilla chips for dipping

Crush tomatoes by hand or with a blender. Combine ingredients. Serve warm with tortilla chips or use as a sauce. Store covered and refrigerated.

Note: Take care when handling hot peppers. Use rubber gloves and avoid contact with the eyes.

Chili Con Queso

Ghost Ranch

1	cup onion, chopped
2	tablespoons shortening
1 1/2	cups tomatoes, drained
2	cans green chile (4 oz. each), chopped
1/2	tablespoon pepper
2	pounds Velveeta cheese, cubed
3-4	cloves garlic, diced

Saute onion until transparent. Add all except cheese to onion. Simmer until blended, then cool. Melt cheese over low heat, add to above and blend. Serve in chafing dish to keep warm while serving.

Cheese Fondue

Winifred Noyes
Santa Fe, NM

2	cups French bread crumbs from day old bread (without crusts)
1 1/2	cups milk
1 1/2	cups sharp Cheddar cheese, grated
1	teaspoon salt
	Dash of paprika
1	tablespoon butter, melted
3	egg yolks, beaten
3	egg whites

Pour milk over bread crumbs, add salt and paprika. Add butter and egg yolks. Beat egg whites until stiff and fold into mixture. Pour into buttered souffle dish. Set in pan of hot water, bake 1 hour at 325-250°F.

Chili Relleno Dip

Jan and Wil Hufton
Saginaw, MI

3	large tomatoes, peeled, seeded and chopped
4	green onions with tender green tops, sliced
1	can chopped black olives, drained (4 1/4 oz.)
1	can chopped green chilies, drained (3 oz.)
2	tablespoons olive oil
1 1/2	tablespoons vinegar
1	teaspoon garlic salt
	Salt and pepper to taste
	Tortilla chips

Combine ingredients (except salt, pepper and chips) in a medium bowl. Season with salt and pepper to taste. Serve with tortilla chips for dipping.

Ham Balls

Nola Scott
Ghost Ranch staff

2 1/2   pounds ground smoked ham
2   pounds ground lean pork
1   pound ground lean beef
3   eggs
2   cup milk
3   cups graham crackers, crushed

Sauce:
2   cans tomato soup (10 3/4 oz. each)
3/4   cup vinegar
2 1/4   cups brown sugar
2   tablespoons dry mustard

Combine sauce ingredients and set aside. Combine meat, eggs, milk and crackers; form into balls. Place in shallow baking dish. Pour sauce over ham balls. Bake 1 hour at 350°F. (Makes 80.)

Chicken Wings

Ghost Ranch

1   cup soy sauce
1/2   cup oil
1/4   cup honey
1   clove garlic
15-20 chicken wings

Combine soy sauce, oil, honey, and garlic. Pour over chicken wings. Marinate overnight. Bake at 450°F for 40 minutes; turn after 20 minutes.

Pickled Shrimp

Lila C. Smith
Oklahoma City, OK

2 to 2-1/2   pounds shrimp in shells
1/2   cup chopped celery leaves
1/4   cup mixed pickling spices
1   tablespoon salt
2   cups sliced onions
8   bay leaves

Pickling marinade:
1 1/2   cups vegetable oil
3/4   cups white vinegar
3   tablespoons capers with juice
2 1/2   teaspoons celery seed
1 1/2   teaspoons salt
3 to 4   drops Tabasco sauce

Cover shrimp with boiling water in medium saucepan. Add celery leaves, pickling spices and salt. Cover and simmer 5 minutes, until shrimp are pink. Drain, peel and devein under cold water. Layer shrimp, onions and bay leaves in a shallow, non-metallic baking dish. Combine marinade ingredients and pour over the shrimp mixture. Cover with plastic wrap and refrigerate at least 24 hours. Spoon marinade over shrimp occasionally. Remove bay leaves before serving. Will keep in refrigerator at least a week. (10 to 12 servings.)

I've been serving this dish for over 30 years. Until now, I've shared it with no one but my daughter, Susan. Perhaps it is time to let others know about it, although I'd just as soon not everyone in OKC had it!

Peppered Pecans

Jan Wolverton
San Pedro, CA

1/2	cup sugar
1	teaspoon Kosher salt
1	teaspoon coarsely ground black pepper
1	cup pecan halves

Combine sugar, salt and pepper in a small bowl; reserve. Heat a large, heavy skillet until hot. Add pecans. Cook and stir until pecans are brown, 1 to 3 minutes. Some may get very brown, but don't let this intimidate you — they're the best!) Add half of the sugar mixture. Cook and stir until sugar melts. Remove the skillet from the burner if it begins to get too hot. Add the rest of the sugar mixture and stir until the sugar melts. Separate nuts with 2 forks and spread on buttered foil to cool. As they cool, you can break apart larger clumps.

A friend, Rikki Kalzonzes, gave us a small package of these wrapped in gold mylar as a small Christmas gift. Try this special salad: On a watercress base, put a fresh, peeled, cored pear (one per salad). Sprinkle with Roquefort cheese and a good vinaigrette dressing. Top with peppered pecans.

Magnificent Margaritas

Karin Kelley
Walnut Creek, CA

1	can frozen limeade, thawed (6 oz.)
1	limeade can tequila
1/2	limeade can triple sec
1/2	limeade can water
	Ice

Place limeade, tequila, triple sec and water in blender container. Blend on high speed for a few seconds. Remove and reserve. Fill blender container with ice. Add limeade mixture and blend until smooth.

A favorite of the Kelley-Wolverton-Hill clan!

Mint Bed Mint Juleps

Phoebe and Arthur Pack
former owners of Ghost Ranch

"Did you ever try to turn out a dozen or more mint juleps in one batch? The theory of julep making is usually regarded as a deep, dark and personal secret. Some do it one way and some another, but this idea works and is extremely popular during that half hour on our screened porch before supper.

Not more than half an hour before use, pick about 6 fresh sprigs of mint for each glass and set aside the prettier half of the sprays for final garnishing and decoration. Wash the rest of the mint under the faucet and pick off the leaves and terminal buds only into a bowl. Add for each person to be served 1 dessert spoon of maple syrup, half a jigger of water and 2 or 3 jiggers of Bourbon whisky. Mix thoroughly, slightly crushing the mint. Dip out with a ladle so as to take the mint leaves, too, and divide equally among the desired number of metal julep glasses. Then fill the glass to the brim with crushed ice (a hand-cranked crusher is the thing for ice cubes), garnish with 3 sprigs of the previously selected mint and serve. Any frost previously found on the party will settle on the glasses."

This recipe appeared in Recipes from the Ghost Ranch, *published in the 1930's. The Packs owned and operated the ranch as a guest facility before giving it to the Presbyterian Church in 1955.*

Fresh Mint Old Fashioned

Phoebe and Arthur Pack
Former owners of Ghost Ranch

"This is for those who disdain to use fruit in the good old standard refresher...Take a cube of sugar and rub it hard on an orange until the sugar absorbs some of the oil from the peel. Put this in an old fashioned glass, add a dash of Angostura Bitters and 1 jigger of whiskey. Muddle until the sugar is dissolved. Then take a couple of young stalks of fresh mint and peel the leaves off into the glass. Crush thoroughly with the whisky and sugar, add another jigger of whisky, stir and add an ice cube or two. Decorate with one young sprig of mint."

Sangria del Sol

'Becca May
Ghost Ranch staff

6   bottles red wine (750 ml each)
5   cups orange juice
2 1/2 cups lemon juice
        Sugar to taste
        Slices of oranges, lemons, limes

Combine slightly chilled liquids with sugar. Stir until sugar dissolves. Serve with fruit slices. (18-20 servings.)

I use only Santa Fe Vineyards' Tinto del Sol for this recipe but any fairly dry red will do.

Banana Punch

Jessica May
Albuquerque, NM

4   cups sugar
6   cups water
2-2 1/2 cups orange juice (juice of 5-6 oranges)
        Juice of 3 lemons
5   ripe bananas, mashed
1   large can of pineapple juice (64 oz.)

Make syrup of sugar and water. Mix with juices and bananas. Freeze in shallow container. When ready to use, thaw slush (takes quite a while). Dilute with equal amounts of 7-Up or club soda. (Serves 30.)

Hot Spiced Apricot Nectar

Mozelle Neill
Midland, TX

3	cups water
1/2	cup sugar
10	whole cloves
2	whole cinnamon sticks
3	cups apricot nectar
2	cups freshly brewed tea
1/4	cup lemon juice

Boil water, sugar and spices together in a medium saucepan for 5 minutes. Remove spices. Add remaining ingredients and heat. Serve warm. Keeps well in refrigerator. (10 to 12 servings.)

Spice Tea Mix

Betty Sterrett
Escondido, CA

2	cups orange beverage crystals (such as Tang)
1	package unsweetened lemon-flavored Kool-Aid (optional)
1	teaspoon cinnamon
1/2	teaspoon cloves
1 1/2	cups instant tea
1	cup sugar

Mix and store in a covered jar. To serve, mix 1 teaspoon (or to taste) in a cup of hot or cold water.

Santa's Cocoa

Judy Shibley
Ghost Ranch staff

1	box powdered milk (8 quart size)
1	pound box powdered cocoa mix
1	cup confectioners sugar
1	cup coffee creamer (8 oz.)
1	tablespoon salt, if desired

Mix ingredients thoroughly in large bowl. Store in airtight container. Use 1/3 cup mix to one cup hot water. Makes lots!

Breads

Honey Whole Wheat Bread

Anna Shoemaker
Greeley, CO

2	packages active dry yeast
2 1/4	cups warm water, divided (105 to 115°F)
1/3	cup honey
1/4	cup vegetable shortening
3	cups whole wheat flour
1	tablespoon salt
3 to 4	cups all-purpose flour
	Butter or margarine, room temperature
	Whole wheat flour or rolled oats for topping

Dissolve yeast in 1/2 cup of the warm water in a large mixing bowl. Add honey, shortening and remaining warm water. Stir until shortening melts; add whole wheat flour and salt. Beat until smooth with electric mixer, adding enough all-purpose flour to make dough easy to handle. Turn onto floured surface; knead until smooth and elastic. Put dough in greased bowl; turn greased-side up. Cover and let rise until double, about 1 hour. Punch dough down. Divide in half and form into two loaves. Place in 2 greased loaf pans, 9 x 5 x 3". Brush with butter or margarine. Sprinkle with whole wheat flour or rolled oats. Let rise until double, about 1 hour. Bake in 375°F oven until deep golden brown, 40 to 45 minutes. Remove from pans and cool on wire racks. (Makes 2 loaves.)

This recipe came from the back of a sack of whole wheat flour. My husband likes it so well I bake it about every 2 weeks, and rarely buy bread from the store. I use the same recipe for making hamburger buns for a picnic with our children, grandchildren and friends.

Whole Wheat Bread

Louise Ford
Grand Prairie, TX

4 cups whole wheat flour, divided
1/2 cup non-fat dry milk
1 tablespoon salt
2 packages dry yeast
3 cups water
1/2 cup vegetable oil
1/2 cup honey
1 cup unsweetened apple sauce
4 to 4 1/2 cups all-purpose flour

Combine 3 cups of the whole wheat flour, the dry milk, salt and yeast in a large bowl of electric mixer. Heat water, oil, honey, and applesauce in small saucepan over low heat until warm (125°F). Pour warm mixture over flour mixture. Mix at low speed 1 minute, then at medium speed for 2 minutes. By hand, stir in remaining whole wheat flour and enough all-purpose flour to form a stiff dough.

Turn dough onto floured surface and knead about 5 minutes. Put dough in a greased bowl; turn greased-side up. Cover and let rise in a warm place until double, 45 to 60 minutes. Punch dough down. Divide into 4 equal parts. Shape each part into a loaf by patting the dough into a rectangle, then rolling up jelly-roll fashion. Place in 4 greased 9 x 5 x 3" loaf pans. Cover and let rise until double, 30 to 45 minutes. Bake at 375°F until loaf sounds hollow when lightly thumped, 40 to 45 minutes. Remove from pans and cool on wire racks. (Makes 4 medium or 3 large loaves.)

I have made this bread for 17 years. It makes wonderful toast.

Fabulous White Bread

Patrick McNamara
Corrales, NM

1	package dry yeast
1/2	cup warm water (105 - 115°F)
1	cup skim milk
1	cup sour cream
1/2	cup buttermilk
6 or more cups all-purpose flour	
1/4	cup wheat germ
2	tablespoons sugar
1 1/2	teaspoons salt
1/4	teaspoon baking soda

Dissolve yeast in warm water in small bowl. Mix skim milk, sour cream and buttermilk in a small saucepan; heat until warm (not hot), stirring constantly. Pour milk mixture into a large mixing bowl. Add 2 cups of the flour and the yeast mixture; stir well. Add wheat germ, sugar, salt and soda. Cover and let rise in a warm place for 1/2 hour. Stir dough down and add enough flour to make a soft dough. Turn onto a floured surface and knead, adding flour, until dough is soft but no longer sticky. Put dough in greased bowl; turn greased-side up. Cover and let rise until double, about 1 hour. Punch down dough. Divide in two. Form into 2 loaves. Place in greased 8 or 9 x 5 x 3" loaf pans. Cover with plastic wrap and let rise until double, about 40 minutes. Bake at 375°F for 30 to 35 minutes. (Makes 2 loaves.)

I was looking for a white bread that tasted different but didn't have a lot of fattening ingredients. I experimented and this is what I came up with. It tastes rich, but isn't a killer for anyone who's dieting.

Green Chile Bread

Ghost Ranch

2	packages yeast
1/2	cup warm water
1 3/4	cup milk, scalded
1/3	cup sugar
1/3	cup shortening
1	tablespoon salt
6-7	cups flour
2	eggs, beaten
3/4	cup cornmeal
1 1/2	cups hot green chile, diced

Soften yeast in water. Combine next 4 ingredients. Stir until lukewarm and shortening is melted. Add 2 1/2 cups of flour. Beat until smooth. Add yeast, eggs and chile. Beat until smooth. Add cornmeal and remaining flour to make soft dough. Knead until smooth. Place in greased bowl; cover and let rise until double. Punch down. Divide into thirds. Place in 3 greased 8" pans. Cover; let double. If desired, tops may be brushed with milk and sprinkled with cornmeal. Bake at 375°F 40-45 minutes. (Makes 3 loaves.)

Communion Bread

Ghost Ranch

4	cups all-purpose flour
1/2	cup sugar
2	teaspoons baking powder
2	tablespoons margarine
1 1/3	cups milk, divided

Mix flour, sugar and baking powder in large bowl. Cut in margarine with a pastry blender or 2 knives. Add 1 cup of the milk. Slowly add remaining 1/3 cup milk until dough holds together. (You may not need all of the milk.) Rough into a rectangle 10 x 15" and place in a greased jelly roll pan. Bake at 375°F until firm but not brown, about 15 minutes. Cut while warm. Wrap in foil to prevent drying. (Makes 325, half-inch pieces with a 3 x 5" piece left over in one corner for the minister to break during the service.)

Greenwood Inn White Bread

Judy Hoffhine
Bexley, OH

2	cups milk
1/3	cup sugar
1/3	cup margarine
1	cake compressed yeast
1/4	cup warm water (105 - 115°F)
6	cups sifted unbleached white flour

Heat milk, sugar and margarine just to boiling in a small saucepan. Cool to lukewarm. Dissolve yeast in warm water; add to milk mixture. Put flour in a large bowl and add milk mixture. Mix with a spoon and your hands until well blended. Turn onto a floured surface and knead until it feels like satin, about 10 minutes. Put dough in a greased bowl; turn greased-side up. Cover and let rise in a warm place until double, about 1 hour. Punch down dough. Knead again briefly. Divide into 2 parts. Place in 2 greased loaf pans. Let rise again until double, about 45 minutes. Bake at 350°F until golden brown and loaf sounds hollow when tapped, about 45 minutes. Remove from pans and let cool on wire rack. (Makes 2 loaves.)

When I was a child, every summer our extended family would trek over to Phillips, Maine to eat Emma and Vincent York's silky smooth white bread. Mrs. York always told her husband to knead gently to stimulate the gluten and get the bubbles out, not to use this time as his morning work out! To this day, we treat this bread with special care and enjoy it immensely. It makes the best toast ever!

Sourdough Bread

David Morrison
Ghost Ranch staff

Sourdough starter:
2	cups whole milk, sour
2-3	cups flour
2-3	cups water

Bread:
1 1/2	cups sourdough starter
3	cups whole wheat flour
	A little white flour
2	cups water
2	tablespoons sugar
2	teaspoons salt

To make starter: Mix sour milk with equal amounts of flour and water (1-2 cups each). Cover lightly with clean cloth, leave at room temperature for 3 days. Add 1 cup flour, 1 cup water. Let sit out overnight, again lightly covered, until it bubbles and smells sour. Store starter in refrigerator, using at least once a week. As you take some out, return equal amounts of flour and water to keep starter going.

Mix bread ingredients and let rise overnight. Add enough white flour to make modestly stiff dough. Shape into 2 loaves, let rise 20 minutes. Bake for 30 minutes at 400°F.

Crispy Flat Bread

Wendy Fox
Oklahoma City, OK

1	loaf frozen bread dough, thawed (1 lb.)
1/2	cup chopped onion (1 medium onion)
2	tablespoons butter or margarine
1/4	cup grated Parmesan cheese

Let dough rise until double. Roll out dough to fit a greased 10 x 15" baking pan. Saute onion in butter until tender. Spoon onion over dough, pressing into the dough. Sprinkle with cheese. Bake at 400°F until golden and crisp, about 20 minutes. (7 to 8 servings.)

Irish Soda Bread

Lucy Smith Fleming
Libertyville, IL

4	cups unbleached white flour
1/2	cup sugar
1	teaspoon baking soda
1	teaspoon cream of tartar
1	teaspoon salt
1/2	cup raisins, rinsed in hot water, drained
1/2	cup butter or margarine, melted
1 3/4	cup + 1 tablespoon buttermilk

Mix dry ingredients in a large bowl. Add raisins and stir to coat with flour mixture. Mix butter and the 1 3/4 cup buttermilk and add to dry mixture all at once. Add more flour if dough is sticky or more milk if it is too dry. Turn onto a floured surface and knead for a few minutes. Shape into 2 loaves. Place on greased baking sheet. Flatten slightly. Brush with the 1 tablespoon buttermilk. Score top of loaves with a sharp knife, making a "x." Bake at 350°F until golden brown, 50 to 60 minutes. (Makes 2 loaves.)

I often give this bread to friends at Christmas. For a more festive look, I replace the raisins with candied fruit (e.g., cherries, pineapple). I was at the Ranch in 1960 as a member of the college summer staff. I have many wonderful memories of that "special place."

Dilly Bread

Ghost Ranch

1	package dry yeast
1/4	cup warm water (105 - 115°F)
2	tablespoons sugar
1	tablespoon instant dehydrated onion
1	tablespoon butter, melted
2	teaspoons dill seed
1	teaspoon salt
1/4	teaspoon baking soda
1	cup cottage cheese, warmed
1	egg, beaten
2 1/2	cups all-purpose flour
	Melted butter and salt for topping (optional)

In large bowl, dissolve yeast in warm water. Stir in sugar, onion, 1 tablespoon butter, dill seed, salt and baking soda. Combine cottage cheese and egg; add to yeast mixture. Mix well. Add flour and knead into a ball. Cover and let rise in a warm place until double. Punch down and form into a loaf. Place in greased loaf pan. Let rise 30 minutes. Bake at 350°F until golden brown, about 40 minutes. Brush with melted butter and sprinkle with salt, if desired. (Makes 1 loaf.)

Potato Rolls

Ghost Ranch

2-2 1/2 cups	potatoes, mashed
4 1/2 - 4 3/4	cups flour
1	package yeast
1	cup milk
1/2	cup shortening
1/2	cup sugar
1	teaspoon salt
2	eggs

Mix 2 cups flour with yeast; bring milk, shortening, sugar, and salt to 115°F. Melt shortening, stir in mashed potatoes. Add potato mixture to flour and yeast. Add eggs to all. Beat on low for 30 seconds. Scrape sides down. Beat 3 minutes on high. Add remaining flour to make soft dough. Put in oiled bowl, turn once. Refrigerate for several hours to a few days. Roll out, shape, let rise 20-30 minutes. Bake at 375°F for almost 20 minutes. (Makes about 35 rolls.)

"Birdseed" Bread

Anne Hunt
Hawthorn Woods, IL

3/4	cup honey
3	packages dry yeast
3	cups warm water (105 - 115°F)
1/4	cup vegetable oil
4 1/2	cups whole wheat flour
1	tablespoon salt
1	cup + 2 tablespoons millet
2 to 3	cups all-purpose flour
1	egg beaten with 1 teaspoon milk

Dissolve honey and yeast in the warm water in a large bowl. Let stand 5 minutes, or until bubbly. Stir in oil, 3 1/2 cups of the whole wheat flour, and the salt. Cover and let rise in a warm place until double, about 1 hour. Stir in remaining 1 cup whole wheat flour, 1 cup of the millet and enough all-purpose flour to make a dough that is stiff and pulls away from the sides of the bowl. Turn onto a floured surface and knead until dough is smooth and elastic. Put dough into greased bowl; turn greased-side up. Cover and let rise in a warm place until double, about 1 hour. Punch down dough; let it rise again until double, about 1 hour.

Punch down dough. Cut in quarters. Shape each piece into a round loaf. Place on greased baking sheet and let rest, covered, for 20 minutes. Brush with egg mixture and sprinkle with the 2 tablespoons millet. Bake at 350°F until brown and loaves sound hollow when tapped on the bottom, about 30 minutes. Cool on wire rack. (Makes 4 small loaves or can be divided into larger loaves.)

This recipe is adapted from one that is made by Jerome's restaurant in Chicago. The little round loaves are always among the first items to sell at Lincoln Park Presbyterian Church's annual St. Nicholas Faire. Millet is included in many wild bird food mixes, hence the recipe's nickname. It is available at health food stores.

Feather Rolls

Ghost Ranch

2	cups milk, scalded
1/2	cup butter
1/4	cup sugar
3/4	teaspoon salt
1	package yeast
2	eggs, well-beaten
3-4	cups flour

Add butter, sugar and salt to hot milk. When lukewarm, add yeast and, when dissolved, eggs and enough flour to make dough stiffer than cookie dough. Beat thoroughly. Cover, let rise until light. Fill buttered muffin tins 2/3 full. Let rise until pans are full. Bake 30 minutes in 375°F oven. (Makes 2 dozen rolls.)

Pumpkin Nut Batter

Ghost Ranch

6	eggs
4 1/2	cups sugar
1 1/2	cups vegetable oil
1	large can pumpkin (29 oz.)
5 1/4	cups flour
1 1/2	teaspoons salt
1	tablespoon baking soda
1/2	tablespoon allspice
1/2	tablespoon cloves
1	tablespoon cinnamon
1 1/2	cups nuts, chopped
3/4	cup raisins

Beat eggs in a large bowl. Add sugar, oil, and pumpkin. Mix thoroughly and set aside. In a separate bowl combine dry ingredients; add to pumpkin mixture and stir until just moistened. Stir in nuts and raisins. Grease and flour pans. Recipe makes 12 cups batter, enough for 4 loaves, 12 mini-loaves, 4 layers for cake, or 4 dozen muffins or cupcakes.

> Loaves: bake at 350°F for 1 hour 10 minutes for large, 40 minutes for minis.
> Muffins: bake at 350°F for 25 minutes.
> Cake: bake at 350°F for 30 minutes, cool for 10 minutes before taking from pan.
> Cupcakes: bake at 350°F for 25 minutes.

Lemon Bread

Ghost Ranch

1/4	cup butter
1/4	cup shortening
1	cup sugar
2	eggs, beaten
	Grated rind of 1 lemon
1/2	teaspoon salt
1	teaspoon baking powder
1 1/2	cups flour
1/2	cup milk

Frosting:
	Juice of 1 lemon
1/4	cup powdered sugar

Cream sugar, butter, and shortening. Add eggs, beat; add lemon rind. Combine dry ingredients. Alternately add milk and dry ingredients to butter mix. Bake 1 hour at 350°F in greased loaf pan. (Makes 1 loaf.) Combine juice and sugar to make frosting, pour over bread while hot, then remove from pan.

Orange Bread

Grace Hessel
Waverly, OH

	Peel of 2 oranges, white part removed, cut into thin slivers
4	cups boiling water
3/4	cup sugar
1/4	cup water
1	cup milk
2	eggs
2 3/4	cups sifted bread flour
2 1/2	teaspoons baking powder
1/4	teaspoon salt

Pour boiling water over orange peel; drain. Combine orange peel, sugar and 1/4 cup water in small saucepan. Bring to boiling and cook to the consistency of corn syrup. Cool. Beat milk and egg in a medium bowl; add cooled syrup with orange peel. Combine and sift dry ingredients; add gradually to orange mixture. Beat until smooth. Pour into greased 6 x 10 x 3" loaf pan. Bake at 350°F for 30 minutes. (Makes 1 loaf.)

This loaf can be made in smaller sizes. I sometimes add nuts or sesame seeds.

Zucchini Bread

Joanne Jennings
Bozeman, MT

2	cups grated zucchini
1	cup oil
2	eggs
3/4	cup sugar
1	tablespoon vanilla
1 1/2	cups all-purpose flour
1 1/2	cups whole wheat flour
1	teaspoon baking soda
1	teaspoon cinnamon
1/4	teaspoon baking powder
	Nuts, raisins, dates (optional)

Combine and beat zucchini, oil, eggs, sugar and vanilla in large bowl. Add dry ingredients. Stir in nuts, raisins or dates, if desired. Pour into 2 greased loaf pans. Bake at 325°F for 1 hour. Remove from pans and cool on wire rack. (Makes 2 loaves.)

Even gardening at 4,800' gives one a bonus of zucchini! I grate it and freeze it in 2-cup containers for bread throughout the year. Zucchini bread is good to carry hiking or cross-country skiing.

Spicy Pineapple-Zucchini Bread

Ghost Ranch

3	eggs
1	cup vegetable oil
2	cups sugar
2	teaspoons vanilla
2	cups zucchini, coarsely shredded (unpeeled)
1	can crushed pineapple, drained (8 1/4 oz.)
3	cups flour
2	teaspoons baking soda
1	teaspoon salt
1/2	teaspoon baking powder
1 1/2	teaspoons cinnamon
3/4	teaspoon nutmeg
1	cup walnuts, chopped

With mixer, beat eggs to blend. Add oil, sugar, and vanilla; continue beating until mixture is thick and foamy. Stir in zucchini and pineapple. Combine dry ingredients, add nuts. Gently stir into zucchini mixture just until blended. Divide batter equally between 2 greased and flour-dusted 5 x 9" loaf pans. Bake at 350°F for one hour. Cool 10 minutes, turn out on a wire rack.

Date Nut Bread

Helen Rethmel
Alamogordo, NM

1 1/2	cups chopped dates
1	cup chopped nuts
2 1/4	teaspoons baking soda
3/4	teaspoon salt
1/4	cup margarine
1	cup + 2 tablespoons boiling water
3	eggs
1 1/2	cups sugar
1 1/2	teaspoons vanilla
2 1/4	cups all-purpose flour

Combine dates, nuts, baking soda, salt and margarine in medium bowl. Pour boiling water over the mixture and let it stand for 20 minutes. Beat eggs in large bowl. Add sugar and vanilla. Gradually add flour; beat until smooth. Add date mixture into flour mixture; stir just until blended. Pour into greased loaf pan or several small round cans. Bake at 350°F (375° for high altitudes), about 1 hour or until done.

Lil's Cherry Slice Bars

Marion Sweet
Verona, WI

2	cups butter (no substitutions)
1 3/4	cups granulated sugar
4	eggs
1	teaspoon vanilla
3	cups all-purpose flour
1 1/2	teaspoons baking powder
1/2	teaspoon salt
1	can cherry pie filling (21 ounces)

Glaze:

1 1/2	cups sifted confectioners' sugar
1 to 2	tablespoons milk or water

Cream butter and granulated sugar with electric mixer in large bowl until light and fluffy. Add eggs, one at a time, beating well after each addition. Add vanilla. Sift dry ingredients together; add gradually to creamed mixture. Reserve 1 1/2 cups batter; spread remaining batter in greased jelly-roll pan (baking sheet with sides). Spread cherry pie filling over batter. Plop on remaining batter. Bake at 300°F for about 45 minutes; cool. To make glaze: Combine confectioners' sugar and milk or water in small bowl to spreading consistency. Spread glaze over cooled cake. To serve, cut in bars.

Banana Sour Cream Coffee Cake

E. Louise Hermanson
Berkeley, CA

1/2	cup vegetable shortening
1	cup sugar
2	eggs
1	cup mashed banana (about 2 bananas)
1/2	teaspoon vanilla
1 1/2	cups sour cream
2	cups all-purpose flour
1	teaspoon baking powder
1	teaspoon baking soda
1/4	teaspoon salt

Filling:

1/2	cup chopped nuts
1/4	cup sugar
1/2	teaspoon cinnamon

Cream shortening and sugar in large mixer bowl on high speed until light and fluffy. Reduce speed and add eggs, banana and vanilla. Fold in sour cream. Sift together and add dry ingredients. Combine ingredients for filling in a small bowl. Sprinkle half the filling in the bottom of a greased 8 x 10" baking pan. Spoon half the batter evenly over the filling; repeat. Bake at 350°F for 45 minutes. (6 or more servings.)

This recipe was in the <u>New York Times</u> in the '40s. We were separated from family during years of seminary training, and overcame our isolation and loneliness by sharing homemade breads with folks in the neighborhood and the tiny congregation we served. Whenever I make this bread, I regain that sense of fellowship—the household of faith.

Cranberry Coffee Cake

Joan Becker
Pittsburgh, PA

1/2	cup butter or margarine
1	cup sugar
2	eggs
2	cups all-purpose flour
1	teaspoon baking soda
1/2	teaspoon baking powder
1/2	teaspoon salt
1	cup (8 oz.) sour cream
1	teaspoon almond extract
2	cups crushed fresh cranberries
3	tablespoons orange juice
1/2	cup sliced almonds

Glaze:

3/4	cup sifted confectioners' sugar
1	tablespoon warm water
1/2	teaspoon almond extract

Cream butter and sugar with electric mixer in large mixer bowl. Add eggs. Combine dry ingredients. Reduce speed and add dry ingredients alternately with sour cream. Add almond extract. Put a third of the batter in a greased bundt or tube pan. Combine cranberries and orange juice in a small bowl. Swirl a third of the cranberry mixture (about 2/3 cup) into the batter in the pan. Repeat two more times with remaining batter and cranberry mixture. Sprinkle top with sliced almonds. Bake at 350°F for 50 minutes. Let cool for 5 minutes. Remove from pan and drizzle with glaze. (Makes 12 or more servings.)

To make glaze: Mix all ingredients in small bowl until smooth.

Rhubarb Coffee Cake

John and Barbara Decker
Hutchinson, KS

1/2	cup margarine
1 1/2	cups granulated sugar
1	egg
1	teaspoon vanilla
2 1/2	cups all-purpose flour
1	teaspoon baking soda
1/2	teaspoon salt
1	cup buttermilk or sour milk*
3	cups chopped, trimmed rhubarb
1/2	cup packed brown sugar
1/2	cup chopped nuts

Sauce:

1/2	cup butter or margarine
1	cup sugar
3/4	cup evaporated milk
1	teaspoon vanilla

Cream margarine and granulated sugar in large mixing bowl until light and fluffy. Beat in egg and vanilla. Sift dry ingredients and add alternately with the milk, beating well after each addition. Fold in rhubarb. Pour into greased and floured 9 x 13" pan. Combine brown sugar and nuts and sprinkle over the batter. Bake at 350°F for 45 minutes. Serve warm with sauce. (12 to 16 servings.)

To make sauce: Combine all ingredients in a small saucepan Bring to a boil. Boil for 3 1/2 minutes. Remove from heat and beat until light and smooth. Serve warm.

* To make sour milk, add 1 tablespoon lemon juice or vinegar to 1 cup warm milk; let stand 5 minutes.

Almond Coffee Cake

'Becca May
Ghost Ranch staff

1	package dry yeast
1/4	cup warm water (105 - 115°F)
1/4	cup + 1 teaspoon sugar
4	cups sifted all-purpose flour
1	teaspoon salt
1/2	cup butter or margarine (1 stick)
1/2	cup vegetable shortening
3	egg yolks, beaten
1	cup warm milk

Filling:

2	packages (8 oz. each) cream cheese, at room temperature
2	egg yolks
1/2	cup sugar
2	teaspoons almond extract

Dissolve yeast in warm water with 1 teaspoon of the sugar in a small bowl. Let stand about 5 minutes or until bubbly. Mix flour, the remaining 1/4 cup sugar and the salt in a large bowl. Cut in the butter and shortening with a pastry blender or 2 knives. Add 3 egg yolks and milk to yeast mixture; stir into flour mixture and mix well. Put dough in greased bowl; turn greased-side up. Cover and refrigerate overnight.

To make filling: Beat all ingredients in medium bowl until light and fluffy; reserve. Remove dough from refrigerator. On floured surface, cut dough into 3 parts. Roll each part into a rectangle, 1/4" thick. Spread about 3/4 cup of the filling on the center third of each rectangle. Fold sides over the center and pinch ends to seal. Place on greased baking sheets. Let rise 1 hour. Bake at 350°F for 35 minutes. (Makes 3 coffee cakes.) *Note: may drizzle with powdered sugar and milk glaze.

I use the egg whites to make Forget 'em cookies. (See cookie section for recipe.)

Aunt Bertha's Coffee Cake

Marion Sweet
Verona, WI

1	package dry yeast
1/4	cup sour milk, (105 - 115°F)*
1	cup milk
1/3	cup butter
1/4	cup sugar
1/2	teaspoon salt
1	egg, well-beaten
1	cup raisins, plumped in hot water, drained
3 3/4	cups all-purpose flour

Topping:

1	cup sugar, divided
1	heaping teaspoon cornstarch
1	cup sour cream or evaporated milk
2	tablespoons butter
3/4	teaspoon cinnamon

Dissolve yeast in sour milk. Heat the 1 cup milk just to boiling. Remove from heat and add butter, sugar and salt. Let cool to lukewarm. Add dissolved yeast and the egg. Add raisins and enough flour to make a moderately stiff batter. Cover and let rise in a warm place until double, about 2 1/2 hours. Spread in greased 9 x 13" pan, about 1/2" thick. Cover and let rise again.

To make topping: Combine 1/2 cup of the sugar, the cornstarch, sour cream and butter in a small saucepan. Heat to boiling. Spread topping over batter as it rises. Sprinkle with cinnamon and remaining sugar. Bake at 350°F for 20 to 30 minutes. (Makes 1 coffee cake.)

*To make sour milk, add 1 teaspoon vinegar or lemon juice to warm milk. Let stand 5 minutes.

This recipe was originally called "Jewish Kaffee Küchen." It was renamed after Aunt Bertha got it from a neighbor.

Ruth Hall's Spicy Nut Coffee Ring

Nola Scott
Ghost Ranch staff

1	cup warm milk (105 - 115°F)
1/4	cup sugar
1	teaspoon salt
1/4	cup margarine or butter, at room temperature (1/2 stick)
1	package dry yeast
1	egg, slightly beaten
3 3/4	cups sifted all-purpose flour
4	tablespoons margarine or butter, melted (1/2 stick)
	Powdered sugar icing
	Chopped nuts for topping

Filling:

1/2	cup sugar
	Finely chopped nuts (Ruth liked pecans)
	Cinnamon

Combine warm milk, sugar, salt and margarine in a large bowl. Add yeast and stir until dissolved. Add egg. Stir in flour, 1 cup at a time, until dough is easy to handle. Turn dough onto floured surface. Cover and let stand 10 minutes. Knead until smooth and elastic (approximately 8 minutes). Put in greased bowl; turn greased-side up. Cover with a damp cloth and let rise in a warm place until double, about 2 hours.

Punch dough down. Roll out on floured surface into an oblong, 1/4-inch thick, about 12 x 24". Cut in half lengthwise. Brush surfaces with 2 tablespoons of the melted margarine. Sprinkle with cinnamon mix. Roll up tightly, beginning at the wide side of each oblong. Seal well by pinching edges of dough into rolls. Place seam-side down in 2 greased 8" ring molds. With scissors, make cuts almost through the rings at 1-inch intervals. Brush cuts with the remaining melted margarine. Cover with a damp cloth and let rise in a warm place (85°F) until double, 35 to 45 minutes. Bake at 350°F for 30 to 35 minutes. Remove from pan; drizzle while warm with powdered sugar icing and sprinkle with chopped nuts. (Makes 2 coffee cake rings.)

A long-time Christmas tradition at Ghost Ranch! For many years, Ruth Hall made a ring for every ranch family during the holidays. Ruth and Jim Hall came to Ghost Ranch in 1961 when Jim was named director of the ranch and stayed until Jim's retirement in 1987. The Halls extended hospitality to thousands of people during their years at the ranch, and were people with a vision: Ruth's love of paleontology provided a sound basis for what has become the Ruth Hall Museum of Paleontology and Jim's enthusiasm and commitment to the ranch and the surrounding communities is reflected in the direction Ghost Ranch continues to take.

Refrigerated Cinnamon Rolls

Ghost Ranch

1	package yeast
1/4	cup warm water
4 1/2	cups flour
1	teaspoon salt
2 1/2	cups sugar
1	cup shortening
1	cup milk, scalded
3	eggs, slightly beaten
4	teaspoons cinnamon
1	stick butter, melted

Dissolve yeast in water. Mix together flour, salt and 1/2 cup sugar. Cut in shortening with a knife, then mix it in with fingers until mixture resembles coarse crumbs. Add milk, eggs, and yeast. Mix well (dough will be sticky). Cover bowl and refrigerate dough overnight. Mix together remaining sugar and cinnamon. About 3 hours before baking, divide dough in 2 equal portions. Knead each portion on a lightly floured surface until dough is smooth and elastic. Roll out each portion of dough to a large rectangle about 1/8 inch thick. Brush butter on surface of dough; sprinkle cinnamon sugar on each rectangle. Roll dough fairly tightly, starting from long side. Cut each roll into slices about 2 1/2 inches wide. Place slices about 1" apart in two well-greased 9 x 13 baking dishes. Cover pans with damp cloth. Let stand in warm place about 1 1/2 hours until double. Bake at 375°F (350°F for glass pans) for 25 minutes. Glass dishes seem to give more volume to rolls. Ice rolls if desired with powdered sugar frosting. (Makes 2 1/2 dozen rolls.)

Cinnamon Rolls

Gertrude Anderson
Boulder, CO

1	package dry yeast
3 1/2	cups all-purpose flour, divided
1/4	cup granulated sugar
1	teaspoon salt
1 1/4	cups warm milk (120°F)
1	egg
1/4	cup oil

Filling:

2/3	cup packed brown sugar
6	tablespoons (3/4 stick) butter or margarine, at room temperature
1	teaspoon cinnamon
	Powdered sugar icing

Combine yeast, 2 cups of the flour, the sugar, salt, milk, egg and oil in a large mixer bowl. Beat with electric mixer on low speed for 1 minute, then beat at medium speed for 3 minutes. Stir in enough of the remaining flour to form a soft dough. Cover and let rise in a warm place until double. Divide dough in half. Roll each half to a rectangle, 8 x 16". Mix ingredients for filling in a small bowl. Spread half of filling on each rectangle. Roll up like a jelly roll, beginning with the long side of the rectangle. Cut each roll into 16 pieces. Lay rolls flat on greased baking sheets. Bake at 375°F for 20 to 25 minutes. Drizzle with powdered sugar icing. (Makes 32 rolls.)

Hot Cross Muffins

Ghost Ranch

1 2/3	cups flour
2/3	cup sugar
2	teaspoons baking powder
3/4	teaspoon cinnamon
1/2	teaspoon salt
1	egg
1/3	cup vegetable oil
2/3	cup evaporated milk
3/4	cup raisins
1/4	cup powdered sugar
1 1/2	teaspoons milk

Sift flour, sugar, baking powder, cinnamon, and salt into medium bowl. Make a well in center of flour mixture. Beat together egg, oil and evaporated milk. Pour into well. Stir with wooden spoon just until flour is moistened. Stir in raisins. Spoon into buttered muffin tins, filling cups 2/3 full. Bake in 400°F oven about 20 minutes. Remove from tins and cool 5 minutes. Combine powdered sugar and milk. Drizzle over tops of muffins to form a cross. Serve warm. (Makes 12 muffins.)

A good treat for Easter morning.

Blue Corn Blueberry Muffins

Mary E. Johnson
Windsor, CO

1	cup blue cornmeal
1	cup all-purpose flour
1/3	cup sugar
2	teaspoons baking powder
1/2	teaspoon baking soda
2	eggs
1	cup sour cream
1/4	cup vegetable oil
1	cup blueberries, washed and patted dry

Mix dry ingredients in a medium bowl. Beat eggs, sour cream and oil together in a small bowl; add to flour mixture and stir just until moistened. Stir in blueberries. Fill paper-lined muffin tins 1/2 to 2/3rds full. Bake at 400°F for 25 minutes. (Makes 12 muffins.)

Max Roybal, santero carver and teacher with the Festival of Crafts, introduced me to blue corn seed from the Isleta Pueblo. We grow and grind the blue corn used in this recipe under the guidance of San Isidro, patron saint of the farmer and carved by Max.

Pineapple Nut Upside-down Muffins

Marta Rivera
Ghost Ranch staff
Canjilon, NM

1/4	cup firmly packed brown sugar
2	tablespoons margarine or butter, melted
12	pecan or walnut halves
1 1/4	cups flour
3 1/2	teaspoons baking powder
1	teaspoon salt
1/3	cup sugar
1 1/2	cups bran flakes cereal
1	can crushed pineapple, undrained (8 oz.)
1/4	cup milk
1	egg
1/4	cup vegetable oil
1/2	cup nuts, coarsely chopped

Combine brown sugar and margarine. Portion scant teaspoons into each of 12 greased muffin cups. Place nut half in each. Stir together flour, baking powder, salt, and sugar. Set aside. Measure bran cereal, pineapple and milk into large mixing bowl. Mix well. Let stand about 2 minutes. Add egg and oil. Beat well. Stir in chopped nuts. Add flour mixture, stirring only until combined (batter will be thick). Portion evenly into muffin cups. Bake at 400°F for about 25 minutes or until browned. Invert onto serving plate. Serve warm. (Makes 12 muffins.)

Simple Muffins

Karen Zabreskie
Sun City, AZ

1/3	cup shortening
1/2	cup sugar
1	egg
1	cup milk
2	cups all-purpose flour
3	teaspoons baking powder
1/2	teaspoon salt

Cream shortening and sugar. Add remaining ingredients and stir just until mixed. Fill paper-lined muffin tin cups half full. Bake on top rack of oven at 400°F for 20 minutes. (Makes 12 large or 30 small muffins.)

Whole Wheat Orange Muffins

Philadelfia Leyba
Rebecca Martinez' grandmother

1/2	cup margarine
2	eggs
1	cup sugar
3/4	cup milk
1	cup all-purpose flour
1	cup whole wheat flour
1	teaspoon baking soda
1	cup raisins
1	orange rind, grated

Cream shortening, egg, and sugar together until well blended. Add flours, baking soda, and milk. Mix all together, add raisins and orange rind. Mix only until ingredients are moistened. Fill muffin tins 2/3 full, bake at 350°F until golden brown, about 25 minutes.

Rebecca's grandmother would make muffin tins out of evaporated milk cans split in half. They would grease the cans with lard—no no-stick spray in those days!

Raisin Bran Muffins

Helen L. Wright
Coshocton, OH

5	cups all-purpose flour
2 1/2	cups sugar
5	teaspoons baking soda
2	teaspoons salt
1	box raisin bran (10 oz.)
4	eggs, beaten
4	cups buttermilk (1 qt.)
1	cup vegetable oil

Sift first four ingredients into a large bowl. Add remaining ingredients and mix, just until combined. Fill paper-lined muffin tin cups 1/2 to 2/3rds full. Bake at 350°F for 20 to 25 minutes. Batter keeps, covered, in refrigerator for 8 weeks. Remove from refrigerator 20 minutes before baking. (Makes 3 quarts of batter. Each quart makes about 24 muffins.)

Holiday Muffins

Camilla L. Cave
Dodge City, KS

2 1/2	teaspoons baking soda
1	cup boiling water
1/2	cup butter or margarine (1 stick)
1	cup sugar
2	eggs
2 1/2	cups all-purpose flour
2	cups All-Bran cereal
1	cup 40% Bran Flakes
1	teaspoon baking powder
2	cups buttermilk
3/4	cup chopped pecans
3/4	cup chopped pitted dates
3/4	cup raisins

Dissolve baking soda in boiling water; let cool completely. Cream butter and sugar with electric mixer in large mixer bowl until light and fluffy. On low speed, add remaining ingredients and the baking soda mixture. Fill paper-lined muffin tin cups 1/2 to 2/3rds full. Bake at 375°F, 30 to 35 minutes. (Makes 3 dozen muffins.)

At Christmas time I give a dozen of these muffins to each of my neighbors and friends.

Bran Muffins

Joan Boliek
Ghost Ranch staff

2	cups boiling water
4	large-size shredded wheat biscuits, broken into pieces
3/4	cup shortening
1 1/2	cups sugar
4	eggs, beaten
5	cups whole wheat or all-purpose flour (or a mixture)
4	cups All Bran cereal
5	teaspoons baking soda
1	teaspoon salt
4	cups buttermilk (1 quart)
8	ounces (about 1 1/2 cups loosely packed) raisins

Pour boiling water over shredded wheat; let stand 5 minutes. Cream shortening and sugar with electric mixer in large mixer bowl until light and fluffy. On low speed, add eggs, and remaining ingredients, including the shredded wheat mixture. Cover and refrigerate overnight. Make just what is needed in paper-lined muffin tin cups, filled 1/2 to 2/3rds full. Bake at 400°F for 15 minutes. Batter will keep in refrigerator up to 2 months. (Makes 60 muffins.)

Blueberry Muffins

Nancy Gee
Miami, OK

1/2	cup vegetable oil
3/4	cup sugar
1	egg
1	cup milk
2	cups all-purpose flour
3	teaspoons baking powder
1/4	teaspoon salt
1	teaspoon vanilla
3/4	cup blueberries, washed and patted dry

Mix oil and sugar in a medium bowl. Combine egg and milk and add to sugar mixture. Sift dry ingredients and add to the batter. Stir in vanilla and blueberries. Fill paper-lined muffin tin cups 1/2 to 2/3rds full. Bake at 350°F for 20 minutes. (Makes 12 large muffins.)

When Bob ran for Congress, we printed recipe cards which were distributed in packets. In the first printing, the blueberries were left out of the recipe!

Ghost Ranch Gingerbread

Ghost Ranch

1	cup shortening
1/4	cup sugar (optional)
2	eggs
2	cups dark molasses
2	cups boiling water
4 1/2	cups flour
1 1/2	teaspoons baking soda
1	teaspoon ginger, ground
2	teaspoons cinnamon
1	teaspoon salt

Preheat oven to 325°F; grease 9 x 13 baking dish. Cream together shortening, sugar and egg. Blend in molasses and water. Measure dry ingredients and sift together into bowl. Beat until smooth; pour into pan. Bake 50 minutes. Serve warm, cut into squares and top with whipped cream. (15 servings.)

Scottish Oat Scones

Elliott H. Sweet
Verona, WI

1 1/2	cups all-purpose flour
1 1/4	cups quick-cooking rolled oats
1/4	cup sugar
1	tablespoon baking powder
1	teaspoon cream of tartar
1/2	teaspoon salt
2/3	cup butter or margarine, melted
1/3	cup milk
1	egg, slightly beaten
1/2	cup raisins or currants

Combine dry ingredients in large bowl. Add melted butter, milk and egg. Stir just until dry ingredients are moistened. Stir in raisins or currants. Shape dough into a ball on a floured surface. (The dough will be very soft.) Gently pat it into circle, 1/2" thick and about 8" in diameter. Cut into 8 or 12 wedges (or cut with a round cutter). Place on a greased baking sheet. Bake at 400°F until light golden brown, 12 to 15 minutes. Serve hot with butter and strawberry preserves or honey, but the flavor is so rich and oaty, they really need nothing but butter. (Makes 8 to 12 scones.)

Four Penny Survival Biscuit

Dorothy Kearney
Kokomo, IN

1/2	cup soy flour
1/2	cup whole wheat flour
1/2	teaspoon baking soda
1/2	teaspoon baking powder
1/2	teaspoon salt
1/2	cup brown sugar
1/4	cup sugar
2	tablespoons honey
1	tablespoon lecithin
2	tablespoons non-fat dry milk
1/2	cups shortening, scant
1	egg
1/2	teaspoon vanilla
1	cup combination of the following: pulverized coconut, nuts, or wheat bran
1	cup quick oats, crushed slightly
	Cornmeal

Sift together dry ingredients. Cream together sugars, honey shortening, egg and vanilla. Combine creamed ingredients with dry ingredients and stir in coconut (nuts or bran) and oats. Pat dough into an 11 x 20" cookie sheet using enough cornmeal to prevent hands from sticking to dough. Bake at 325°F for 15 minutes. Cool and cut into wafers. (Makes 32 wafers.)

This recipe is called "Four Penny Survival Biscuit" because 4 cents is about what it costs to make each biscuit Over 2.5 million of these biscuits have been sent by Church World Service to Ethiopia where nearly three million people face starvation. The biscuits are 20% protein, 53% carbohydrates and about a dollar's worth of biscuits provides a malnourished child with 1,300 calories and a chance for survival. Consider using this recipe for a meaningful communion service, serve during coffee hour or other community gathering.

Buttermilk Country Biscuits with Ham

Tom and Betty Mainor
Oak Park, IL

2	cups all-purpose flour
1	tablespoon baking powder
1	teaspoon sugar
1	teaspoon dried thyme
1/2	teaspoon ground ginger
1/4	teaspoon baking soda
1/4	teaspoon salt
1/4	teaspoon ground nutmeg
1/8	teaspoon freshly ground black pepper (or to taste)
5	tablespoons vegetable shortening
1/2	cup minced cooked ham
2	tablespoons minced green bell pepper (optional)
3/4	cup buttermilk
2	tablespoon margarine or butter, melted

Combine dry ingredients in a large bowl. Cut in shortening with a pastry blender or 2 knives until mixture resembles coarse meal. Stir in ham and green bell pepper. Gradually stir in buttermilk until mixture holds together. Gather into a ball with hands. Knead once or twice on lightly floured surface. Pat into a rectangle about 3/4" thick. Cut into circles with floured 1 1/2" cutter. Gather and reform dough until all has been used. Place about 2" apart on a baking sheet; brush tops with melted margarine. Bake at 425°F until puffed and golden, about 12 minutes. (Makes about 30 biscuits.)

Wonderful with mustard and thin slices of baked ham!

Peppery Biscuits

Honor Lyons
Plaza Resolana

1	cup unbleached white flour
1/2	cup whole wheat flour
1	tablespoon baking powder
1/2	teaspoon ground black pepper
2	tablespoons minced lean ham or trimmed prosciutto
1/2	cup buttermilk (1 or 2 tablespoons more, if necessary)

Combine white and whole wheat flour, baking powder, salt and pepper in a medium bowl. Stir in ham or prosciutto. Whisk buttermilk in a large measuring cup; pour over flour mixture. Toss with a fork until mixture begins to form a mass. If too dry, add 1 or 2 more tablespoons of buttermilk. Turn the dough onto a lightly floured surface; knead gently. Press into a 7" square pan. Cut into 25 squares. Remove squares and place on a baking sheet, coated with non-stick vegetable spray, leaving about 1" between squares. Bake at 400°F until golden brown, about 15 minutes. Serve warm. May be made day ahead and reheated. (Makes 25 biscuits.)

Blue Cornbread

Ghost Ranch

1	cup blue cornmeal
1	cup whole wheat flour
2	teaspoons baking powder
1/2	teaspoon baking soda
1/2	teaspoon salt
1	egg
2	cups buttermilk
1/4	cup honey
1/4	cup oil

Combine dry ingredients. Combine liquids, add to dry ingredients. Mix until moistened. Bake in a 9 x 9" heated, oiled pan at 350°F for 40 minutes.

Mexican Cornbread

Judy Shibley
Ghost Ranch

1/2	cup bacon drippings
1	cup yellow cornmeal
1	can cream-style corn (17 oz.)
1	cup milk
2	eggs, slightly beaten
3/4	teaspoon salt
1/2	teaspoon baking soda
5	jalapeño peppers, seeds and stems removed, finely chopped
1	medium onion, finely chopped (about 1/2 cup)

Pour 1/4 cup of the bacon drippings into an 8-10" iron skillet. Combine remaining ingredients and pour into skillet. Bake at 450°F until brown, 20 to 25 minutes. The cornbread may appear not well done in the center, but it will be firm when it cools. (10 to 12 servings.)

Cornmeal Mix

Ginny Graham
Durango, CO

4	cups all-purpose flour
2/3	cup sugar
1/4	cup baking powder
1	teaspoon salt
1	cup vegetable shortening
4 1/2	cups yellow cornmeal (1 1/2 lbs.)
1 1/2	cups non-fat dry milk

Sift flour, sugar, baking powder and salt into large mixer bowl. Cut in shortening with pastry blender, 2 knives, or electric mixer on slow setting. If using mixer, scrape beaters often. Beat in cornmeal and then the dry milk. Store in cool, dry place for up to 6 months.

For 10 medium pancakes or 6 large waffles:

2 1/2	cups mix
2	eggs, slightly beaten (or 1/2 cup egg substitute)
1 1/2	cups water

For cornbread or muffins:

2 1/2	cups mix
1	egg, slightly beaten (or 1/4 cup egg substitute)
1 1/2	cups water

Pour into 12 greased muffin pans or 10" greased iron skillet. Bake at 425°F, 25 minutes for cornbread and 15 to 20 minutes for muffins.

For tomato pot pie:

4	large tomatoes, chopped
1	tablespoon chopped green bell pepper
1/2	teaspoon salt
1/4	teaspoon pepper
1 1/2	cups mix
1	egg, slightly beaten (or 1/4 cup egg substitute)
1/2	cup milk
1/4	cup shredded Cheddar cheese

Place tomatoes and green bell pepper in greased 1 1/2 to 2 quart casserole. Sprinkle with salt and pepper. Mix remaining ingredients and pour over tomato mixture. Bake at 400°F for 20 to 25 minutes.

editor's note: Jane Hanna sent us this story: "Ginny and Chuck Graham's recipe for cornmeal mix has been a favorite at the ranch for a long time. One year Ginny made up a large batch for the annual trailride. It was taken up the mountain, with all the other nonperishable food and supplies, several days prior to the departure of the trail riders. When we arrived at our campsite, it was quickly recognized that bears had been into the kitchen tent. Among the many things missing was every crumb of Ginny's cornmeal mix. We gathered that the mother bear and her two cubs liked what they found because they returned to our camp every day."

Sopapillas

Ghost Ranch

2	cups warm water (105 - 115°F)
1	package dry yeast
1	teaspoon sugar
2	cups all-purpose flour
2	cups whole wheat flour
2	teaspoons salt
1	teaspoon vegetable shortening
	Vegetable oil for frying, heated to 400°F
	Honey

Rinse a medium bowl with hot water; combine warm water, yeast and sugar in the warm bowl. Let stand until bubbly. Mix flours, salt and shortening in a large bowl. Stir in yeast mixture. Cover and let stand in a warm place for 15 minutes. Turn dough onto lightly floured surface. Roll to 1/4" thickness and cut into squares about 4" in diameter. Cook in hot oil until light brown and puffed. Drain on paper toweling. Serve with honey. (Makes 15 sopapillas.)

Baking Powder Sopapillas

Criselda Dominguez
Ghost Ranch staff
Abiquiu, NM

4   cups flour
2   teaspoons baking powder
1   teaspoon salt
4   tablespoons shortening
1 1/2   cups lukewarm water

Mix salt, baking powder, and flour in large mixing bowl. Work in shortening until distributed evenly. Add lukewarm water, mix well, working dough until smooth. Cover. Let stand for 20 minutes. Roll out on floured board to 1/8" thick. Cut in 3 to 4 inch squares. Fry in deep hot oil until golden brown on both sides, turning once. Test oil by dropping small piece of dough in hot oil to golden brown.

editor's note: Since 1975 Criselda has been a community worker in Abiquiu for Ghost Ranch. In the late 1960's Criselda was part of a nutrition program sponsored by New Mexico State University. The program was designed to help educate young homemakers about better nutrition. Criselda and others from the community put together a small cookbook with recipes having ingredients that most families would have in their cupboards. "No fancy stuff," said Criselda. "Just wholesome, good food."

Whole Wheat Flour Tortillas

Rebecca Martinez
Ghost Ranch staff
Canjilon, NM

2   cups all-purpose flour
1   cup whole wheat flour
2   tablespoons vegetable oil
2   teaspoons baking powder
1   teaspoon sugar
1   teaspoon salt
2   cups water, warm

Mix all dry ingredients. Add oil, mix well. Gradually add water to form dough. Knead slightly. Dough should be fairly firm. Break off plum-sized pieces, roll to 1/8-1/4" thickness. Cook on a grill or on a skillet.

Breakfast

Breakfast 68

Ghost Ranch Granola

Ghost Ranch

1/2	cup vegetable oil
1/2	cup honey
1/2	cup peanut butter
6	cups rolled oats
2	cups coarsely chopped walnuts
2	cups shredded coconut

Mix oil, honey and peanut butter in a large saucepan. Cook over low heat until melted. Add rolled oats, walnuts and coconut and stir until evenly coated with peanut butter mixture. Spread in large shallow baking pans. Bake at 325°F, 15-20 minutes stirring once, until golden brown. Watch carefully as it burns easily. (Makes 10 cups.)

Note: Add dried fruits, or substitute pecans, if you wish.

Easy Granola

Evelyn King
Chattanooga, OK

15 1/2	cups regular rolled oats
2 1/2	cups flaked coconut
2	cups wheat germ
2	cups chopped pecans
1 1/2	cups firmly packed brown sugar
1	cup sunflower kernels
3	teaspoons salt
1 1/2	cups vegetable oil
2/3	cup water
3	teaspoons vanilla
1	cup raisins

Combine first 7 ingredients in very large bowl. Combine oil, water and vanilla in medium bowl; pour over oat mixture. Toss gently to coat. Spread in a large roasting pan or on several jelly roll pans. Bake at 250°F for 35 to 40 minutes, stirring frequently. Stir in raisins. Store in air-tight containers. (Makes about 28 cups.)

Hine's Health Breakfast

Jim Hine
Tucson, AZ

2	cups water
2	tablespoons wheat or rice bran
2	tablespoons oat bran
2	tablespoons couscous
2	tablespoons grits
1	teaspoon margarine
1/4	teaspoon salt or Mrs. Dash

Bring water to a boil in a small saucepan. Add remaining ingredients. Reduce heat, cook 3 to 5 minutes. In microwave, cook about 3 minutes on high power. For a side dish, substitute broth for the water. (2 to 3 servings.)

I put this together hoping it would reduce my cholesterol, and it did.

Kelly's Corn Cakes

Vada Cain
Portland, OR

1	cup yellow corn meal
1	cup raw wheat germ
3	tablespoons sugar
1/2	teaspoon baking powder
1/2	teaspoon vanilla (optional)
1/8	teaspoon salt (optional)
1/3	cup vegetable oil
2	eggs
2	cups buttermilk
	Butter or margarine, maple syrup or yogurt

Combine dry ingredients in medium bowl. Make a well in the center and stir in the oil, eggs and buttermilk. Stir just until mixed. Cook on lightly oiled electric grill, skillet or griddle until tops begin to bubble. Turn and cook until done. Serve with butter or margarine, syrup or yogurt. (4 servings.)

What a way to start a day! Super GO power lasts until one can get a dinner posole fix at the Ghost Ranch Dining Hall!

Blue Corn Pancakes

Brian K. Johnson
Santa Fe, NM

1	cup blue corn meal
1/2	cup flour
1/2	ounce freeze-dried eggs*
1/2	ounce low-fat dry milk powder*
2	tablespoons sugar
2	teaspoons baking powder
1	teaspoon salt
1	cup water*
2	tablespoons vegetable oil
	Syrup

Combine dry ingredients in medium bowl. Store in plastic bag until camping trip. In camp, at sunrise, add water (boiled or treated to kill Giardia) and oil. Add additional water, if necessary, to achieve proper consistency. Cook in a large oiled skillet over backpack stove or on a griddle over two backpack stoves. Pan is hot when a drop of water dances on the surface. Serve with syrup. (4 servings. May be increased for larger parties.)

* For home use, substitute one whole egg and 1/2 cup milk. Add with water, reduced to 1/4 cup.

I am one of the backpacking seminar leaders at Ghost Ranch. During a September 1991 trip near Ghost Ranch with 23 Sierra Clubbers, the blue 'cakes were served up a few feet from the Continental Divide Trail. Los Ojitos (springs) provided the water. We viewed Ojitos Canyon, Mesa de las Viejas, and Mesa los Indios as we stood within the boundaries of the Chama River Canyon Wilderness with steaming pancakes under our noses.

Pancake Mix

Ghost Ranch

Mix:
9	cups flour
3	cups nonfat dry milk
1/3	cup baking powder
1/4	cup sugar
2	teaspoons salt
2	cups solid shortening or margarine

Combine dry ingredients in large bowl. Cut in the shortening with a pastry blender or two knives to a cornmeal-like consistency. Store in an airtight container in a cool place, up to 6 months. (Makes about 15 cups)

Pancakes:
1 1/2	cups mix
1	egg, lightly beaten
3/4	cup water

Combine ingredients. Stir just until mixed. Cook on hot skillet or griddle coated with non-stick vegetable spray, using 1/4 cup for each pancake. Turn when surface bubbles. (About 10 pancakes)

Mike's "Light" Pancakes

Mike and Elaine Fry
Newville, PA

4	eggs
1	cup milk
2	tablespoons salad oil
1	cup flour
1	tablespoon sugar
4	teaspoons baking powder
1/2	teaspoon salt
1	teaspoon baking soda

Beat eggs in medium bowl. By hand, beat in remaining ingredients in order listed. Cook on hot oiled skillet, griddle or grill. Turn pancakes as soon as they are puffed and full of bubbles. Cook on other side until golden brown. (Makes 10 pancakes, 4" in diameter.)

Cholesterol Fighting Pancakes

Beth Marvel
St. Joseph, MO

2/3	cup oat bran
2/3	cup non-fat dry milk powder
1/2	cup flour
2	teaspoons baking powder
1	cup + 2 tablespoons water
1/2	teaspoon vanilla
1	tablespoon sunflower seeds (optional)

Combine dry ingredients in medium bowl. Make a well in the center and add water and vanilla. Stir just until mixed. Cook on hot skillet, griddle or grill coated with non-stick vegetable oil spray. Sprinkle each pancake with a few sunflower seeds, if desired. Turn when pancakes begin to bubble. (2 servings.)

I created this recipe to eliminate the egg and fat from pancakes. They are good sprinkled with Molly McButter and apple butter.

Fruit Pancake Topping

Marlea Gruver
Jobstown, NJ

1	can sliced peaches in syrup, juice drained and reserved (8 3/4 ounces)
1/2	cup apricot preserves
8	maraschino cherries, drained, cut in half
2	tablespoons butter or margarine
1	teaspoon lemon juice
1/8	teaspoon vanilla
2	small bananas, cut in 1/4 slices

Combine peaches, 1/4 cup of the reserved syrup, the preserves, cherries, butter, lemon juice and vanilla in medium saucepan. Heat to boiling, stirring occasionally. Reduce heat. Stir in bananas; heat until hot. (Makes about 2 cups.)

Cheese and Egg Souffle

Nancy Deever
Plaza Resolana volunteer

5 to 6	slices buttered white or whole wheat bread, cut into cubes
3	cups (about 3/4 lb.) grated Cheddar cheese
5	eggs, slightly beaten
2	cups milk
1	teaspoon dry mustard
	Salt and pepper to taste

Alternate layers of bread and cheese in a lightly buttered baking dish. Combine eggs, milk, mustard, salt and pepper in a medium bowl. Pour over bread and cheese mixture. Cover and refrigerate overnight. Bake in 350°F oven until edges are very brown, about 60 minutes. A glass baking dish will take less time.

24 Hour Egg Omlette

Ghost Ranch

5	slices buttered bread, cubed
3/4	pound longhorn cheese, grated
8	eggs, beaten
2 1/2	cups milk
1/2	teaspoon salt
1/2	teaspoon dry mustard
3/4	pound sausage, browned

Place bread cubes in buttered 9 x 13" glass baking dish. Sprinkle with cheese. Beat milk, eggs, spices. Pour over bread. Top pan with sausage. Cover with foil and refrigerate overnight. Bake uncovered 1-1/2 hours at 350°. Be sure it is "set" before cutting. (12-14 servings.)

Egg Casserole

Martha A. Gillespie
Fort Worth, TX

2	cups seasoned croutons
1 1/2	cups shredded cheese (about 6 oz.)
6	eggs, beaten
2	cups milk
1/2	teaspoon dry mustard
1/4	teaspoon onion powder
1/2	teaspoon salt
1/8	teaspoon pepper

Arrange croutons evenly in 8 x 10" or 6 x 10" baking dish. Sprinkle with cheese. Combine remaining ingredients in a medium bowl and pour over the croutons and cheese. Bake at 350°F until brown, 25 to 30 minutes. (6 to 8 servings.)

For a brunch or buffet, I add 4 ounces of drained chopped green chilies and 1 cup chopped, cooked ham. I double or triple the recipe for a large crowd.

Sausage and Egg Casserole

Gertrude Anderson
Boulder, CO

2	pounds pork sausage, browned, drained
12	slices bread, crusts removed, cubed
10	eggs, slightly beaten
2 1/2	cups milk
1	tablespoon Worcestershire sauce
1	teaspoon dry mustard
	Salt and pepper to taste
2 1/2	cups shredded cheese (about 10 oz.)
1	small jar pimiento, drained (2 oz.)

Arrange sausage and bread cubes in layers in a 3-quart casserole. Combine eggs, milk, Worcestershire sauce, mustard, salt and pepper in a medium bowl. Pour over sausage and bread. Sprinkle with cheese; dot with pimiento. Cover and refrigerate overnight. Bake at 350°F for 1 hour.

Sausage Fondue

Karen Zabreskie
Sun City, AZ

8	slices bread, crusts removed, cubed
2	cups shredded sharp cheese (8 oz.)
1 1/2	pounds link sausage, browned, drained, cut in thirds
4	eggs
2	cups milk, divided
1	tablespoon dry mustard
1	can cream of mushroom soup (10 3/4 oz.)

Place cubed bread in bottom of lightly greased 8 x 10" baking dish.
Sprinkle evenly with cheese. Arrange sausage over cheese. Beat eggs
and 1 1/2 cups of the milk in medium bowl; add mustard and pour over
bread and sausage mixture. Cover and refrigerate overnight. Next day,
mix soup with the remaining 1/2 cup milk; pour over bread mixture.
Bake in a pan of water at 350°F until set, about 1 hour. (8 to 12 servings.)

Cheese Grits

Ghost Ranch

1 1/2	cups quick-cooking grits
6	cups water, boiling, no salt
3	eggs, beaten
3/4	stick margarine
1	pound cheddar cheese, grated
1	tablespoon savory salt
2	teaspoons salt
2	dashes Tabasco sauce
	Paprika

Cook grits in water until thick; add other ingredients. Bake 1 hour at
275°F in 9 x 13" greased pan.

May add 1 small can green chiles for extra zip.

Trail Riders Special Sour Dough Biscuits

Julie Stevens
by way of Wes Adams, outfitter

1	gallon (or so) sourdough starter (see recipe below)
12	cups, or so, flour (about 5 lbs.)
2	cups cream or 1 1/2 cans evaporated milk
6	teaspoons (1 small palm) salt
3	tablespoons baking powder(4 small palms)
1/2	cup warm water
3/4	cup sugar
	Shortening or oil for dutch oven

Mix the starter as usual. Get a large pan, like a big dishpan ... metal won't hurt at this stage. Dump a large part of a sack (5#) of flour in dry pan. Pat out and up sides to form a large well in center. This keeps the pan easier to clean and the amount of flour desired can be stirred in. The least amount of flour used - but enough to hold the dough together and form a ball readily rolled out - the better, and more moist the final product. Pour starter into well...just dump in starter - stir in cream or evaporated milk [I enrich with extra powdered milk, dissolved in the least amount of warm water possible] , sugar (some is needed in the rising process), a small palm of salt, add about 4 small palms of baking powder - shake the baking powder can well. (A tip from Wes that really helps.) Kinda stir it down into the middle of the starter and add a little water. Really fizzes and foams, but does the trick. Let stand a while, now and again stirring it down into the starter. Then mix well until adequate flour is mixed in. Turn out on floured board, table or what-ever. Knead energetically for 5 minutes or so - should be a soft ball - not sticky, kinda smooth and soft like a horse's nose!

Roll out dough 1" thick or a little less. Cut generously with a can or small glass, flour the rim. Carefully dip top in hot grease, i.e. just flip'em thru the grease and turn them upright in the HOT heavy (cast iron is necessary with open coals) baking pan. Don't crowd 'em in too tight. They do expand some. Set aside to raise 5 to 30 minutes in a warm place before baking. When they start to look done, turn one over with a fork or remove and open to check for doneness. ENJOY! ENJOY! We have learned when using a heavy cast iron oven (with lid) and coals from a wood fire it takes about 15 to 20 minutes. It is essential to remove coals from the fire and place separately on the ground. Put dutch oven on top of coals and also heaping coals on top of lid. Yep, it takes lots of wood to produce adequate coals depending on the type of wood.

When using a conventional oven, I suggest heating the dutch on top of the stove first and baking in a hot oven, 450 to 475 degrees.
(Makes 50-60 medium size biscuits.)

High Country Sourdough Pancakes

1-1 1/2	cups milk powder
1	teaspoon salt
4 - 6	eggs
3	tablespoons oil
1-2	teaspoons soda or so
8-12	cups starter, or so
2-3	teaspoons baking powder, or so

Mix milk powder in just enough warm water to dissolve it, about 1/4-1/2 cup. Mix together dissolved milk and beaten eggs. Add starter to mixture only when the griddle is very nearly hot then add salt, soda, baking powder, and oil. Stir well as egg mix is reluctant to integrate with the starter. Once all is together the batter will slowly thin while waiting to be cooked. Stir in enough starter to make up what is needed. Water can be added to the desired consistency, but be careful. The thicker the batter the longer cooking time is required. Spread thin coat of oil on grill between each batch. Keep the griddle hot but do not let it overheat.
(Makes 40-60 pancakes.)

Sourdough Starter

1	package yeast dissolved in 4 cups warm water - Stir in until smooth.
2 1/2	tablespoons sugar
4	cups flour

Mix all ingredients, with a wooden or plastic spoon, until smooth in a large crock or wide mouth plastic jug. Allow air to freely flow and place in a warm spot. Never let metal touch the starter itself. Let rise until very light and slightly aged, 24 to 48 hours; do not let the mixture, now called a sponge, get too sour or become chilled. Once the sponge has matured add enough flour and warm [not hot] water to make a batter with the consistency of thick gravy. For large recipes a 1 or 2 gallon plastic jug with wide lid is very good. The starter is very elastic and stirring in the flour can be difficult. Pour in water first and stir until thin then add the flour, beating heartily. Always save back plenty of starter when making the product to ensure rapid replenishment. I keep 1 to 2 gallons of batter/starter on hand for trail ride pancakes every other day and for the biscuits, the more it can age the better. At home, the starter can be stored in the refrigerator and reactivated before use by adding warm water and flour for the amount desired and placing in warm spot for 8-10 hours.

If the batter/starter seems not to be bubbly or active, set near the heat or the fire - not too close to cook or burn the container - stirring in a palm full of sugar will also help. In the mountains or in cold weather insulate the jug, set in the sun to "work" the starter and keep warm. For the most part, the sponge is used in place of flour rather than as a proportion with flour, as many other sourdough recipes suggest.

The trail ride sourdough had its beginnings with Wes Adams, our first outfitter in the Pecos. Wes's mother was a baker in the Clovis area early in the century and the story goes that her original starter was used by Wes. He was quite the showman and thoroughly enjoyed burning the fruits of diligent wood cutters and splitters in a dramatic 6 foot towering inferno "to assure an ample supply of coals" for the long awaited sourdough biscuits. Initially the Ghost Ranch Ride only had Wes's sourdough production for the last night's dinner. During the Pecos Rides I discovered that Wes's cook for his commercial rides, Lyndal Bolinger, was a friend from my home town of Cheney, Kansas. After the Pecos was closed to large trail rides Ghost Ranch moved its ride to Colorado with other outfitters and, tiring of 'gooy' pancakes, I introduced the idea of sourdough pancakes to Jim Hall. He agreed only if we took back-up pancake mix. With coaching from Lyndal and guidance and encouragement from Jessie Fitzgerald, sourdough was born again. Since 1982 refinement of technique and spirit is a result of many able assistants and lots of trial and error. We invite you to do the same. The more you use it, the better it gets!

May your starter be bubbly at any time of need.

Breakfast 80

Salads

Summer Chicken and Ham Salad

Ghost Ranch

2	cups cooked chicken, diced
3/4	cup cooked ham, diced
3/4	cup Swiss cheese, diced
2	hard-boiled eggs, chopped
1	cup chopped celery
3	tablespoons green onion with tender green tops, sliced
1/2	green pepper, chopped
1	tablespoon pimiento
2/3	cup mayonnaise
1/2	teaspoon poultry seasoning
1/4	teaspoon dry mustard
1	tablespoon lemon juice
3	cups lettuce, shredded

Combine chicken, ham, cheese and eggs in a large bowl. Make dressing out of mayonnaise and seasonings. Toss together, cover and refrigerate. At serving, add lettuce. (Serves 4 - 6.)

Broccoli Salad

Mildred E. Koper
Jenkintown, PA

1	large bunch broccoli, flowerets only
5	slices bacon, cooked until crisp, crumbled
1/2	small onion, minced (about 2 tbs.)
6	ounces shredded Cheddar cheese (about 1 1/2 cups)
2/3	cup raisins

Dressing:
1/2	cup mayonnaise
1/4	cup sugar
1	tablespoon vinegar

Combine broccoli, bacon, onion, cheese and raisins in a large bowl. Mix ingredients for dressing and pour over broccoli mixture. Toss to coat. Cover and refrigerate at least 2 hours before serving, stirring several times. (6 servings.)

Broccoli-Raisin Salad

Carolyn Jones
Exeter, CA

2	bunches broccoli, separated into flowerets; tender stems sliced
1/2	cup raisins, plumped in hot water, drained
1/4	cup dried minced onion
1	pound bacon, cooked until crisp, crumbled

Dressing:
1	cup mayonnaise
1/3	cup sugar
2	tablespoons white vinegar

Combine broccoli, onion, raisins and bacon in large bowl. Mix ingredients for dressing and pour over broccoli mixture. Cover and refrigerate. (6 to 8 servings.)

Spinach Salad

Joan Arnold
Basking Ridge, NJ

Dressing:
1	medium onion, chopped (about 1/2 cup)
2/3	cup sugar
1/3	cup oil
1/3	cup vinegar

Salad:
2	packages fresh spinach washed, dried (10 oz. each)
1/2	pound bacon, cooked until crisp, crumbled
6	hard-cooked eggs, chopped
2	cups herb stuffing mix (Pepperidge Farm preferred)

Combine ingredients for dressing in small bowl; cover and refrigerate at least 24 hours before using. Combine spinach and dressing in large bowl. Add remaining ingredients and toss gently. (12 servings.)

A favorite at Basking Ridge Presbyterian Church suppers.

"Shoe Peg" Vegetable Salad

Jean K. Wiant
Estherville, IA

Dressing:
1	cup sugar
3/4	cup vinegar
1/2	cup vegetable oil
1	teaspoon salt
1	teaspoon pepper

Salad:
2	cans shoe peg (white) corn, drained (11 oz. each)
1	can French-cut green beans, drained (14 oz.)
1	can peas, drained (14 oz.)
1	jar diced pimiento, drained (2 oz.)
1	cup chopped green onions with tender green tops
1	cup chopped celery
1	cup chopped green bell pepper (about 1 large green bell pepper)

Mix ingredients for dressing in small saucepan; heat to boiling. Remove from heat and cool. Combine vegetables in large bowl; pour dressing over vegetables and toss. Cover and refrigerate at least 6 hours. Keeps well. (10 to 12 servings.)

Marvelous Tucson Salad

Jane Gibbs Neve
Tucson, AZ

1	bunch spinach, washed, dried, cut up
1	head cauliflower, cut up
3	green onions with tender green tops, chopped
1	pound bacon, cooked until crisp, crumbled
1	cup mayonnaise
1/4	cup sugar
1/3	cup Parmesan cheese

Layer spinach, cauliflower, onions and bacon in that order in 2-quart glass bowl or casserole. Mix mayonnaise and sugar in small bowl and spread on top. Sprinkle with cheese. Cover and refrigerate several hours. Toss before serving. (8 to 10 servings.)

editor's note: Jane was on the Ghost Ranch college staff in 1961.

Ghost Ranch Spinach Salad

Ghost Ranch

1	pound fresh spinach
1	cup pecans
12	ounces dry curd (cottage cheese without the liquid)

Dressing:
1	cup sour cream
1/2	cup sugar
3	tablespoons vinegar
1 1/2	tablespoons mustard
3-4	tablespoons horseradish
1/2	teaspoon salt

Wash and dry spinach; tear into pieces. Add curd and pecans. Put in plastic bag until ready to use. Mix ingredients and refrigerate dressing. Just before serving pour dressing over spinach mixture. (8 generous servings.)

Mixed Vegetable Salad

Mimi Tharp
Ghost Ranch staff

Salad:
1	package mixed frozen vegetables (20 oz.)
2	cans red kidney beans, washed and drained
1/2	cup green pepper, chopped
1/2	cup onion, chopped
8	stalks celery, chopped

Dressing:

2	tablespoons all purpose flour
1 1/2	cups sugar
1	cup vinegar
2	tablespoons prepared mustard

Cook frozen vegetables 10 minutes; drain well. Add remaining vegetables. Combine flour, sugar, and vinegar in saucepan. Cook over medium heat until thick. Stir in mustard. Pour cooled dressing over vegetables and refrigerate.

Indian Carrot Salad

Anne Hunt
Hawthorn Woods, IL

1	tablespoon vegetable oil
1	tablespoon lime juice
1/2	teaspoon ground cumin
1/2	teaspoon ground cinnamon
1/4	teaspoon salt
1/2	teaspoon minced garlic
4	cups sliced, cooked carrots
1/4	cup wheat sprouts or cooked wheat berries

Whisk oil and lime juice together in large bowl. Whisk in cumin, cinnamon, salt and garlic. Stir in carrots. Cover and refrigerate until cold. Serve chilled, garnished with wheat sprouts. (Makes 8 servings.)

My business partner, Mary Abbott Hess, is co-author of The Art of Cooking for the Diabetic (Contemporary Books, 1988). The incredible thing about the recipes in the book is that everyone, not just people with diabetes, loves them. In this book, Mary combines her talents as registered dietitian and fabulous cook!

Potato Salad

John Barney
Santa Barbara, CA

5 or 6	white potatoes, boiled, peeled
6	hard-cooked eggs
1	medium red onion, chopped (about 1/2 cup)
3	stalks celery
12	pimiento-stuffed green olives
2	tablespoons juice from green olives
1	can chopped ripe olives (4 1/2 oz.)
1	jar sweet pickle relish (8 oz.)
1	pint salad dressing, Miracle Whip preferred (2 cups)
	Salt
	Paprika

Cut potatoes in quarters lengthwise, then slice. Place potatoes in large bowl. Slice the hard-cooked eggs; remove 8 yolk slices for garnish. Chop remaining eggs and add to potatoes. Stir in onion, celery, 8 sliced green olives and the ripe olives, pickle juice and salad dressing. Add salt to taste. Garnish with reserved egg yolk slices, 4 green olives cut in half, and a dash or two of paprika. Cover and refrigerate at least 6 hours. (6-8 servings.)

Aunt Tumis' Coleslaw

Joann Williams
Bellvue, CO

Dressing:

1	cup vegetable oil
4	tablespoons sugar
6	tablespoons rice or white wine vinegar
2	teaspoons salt (or less if desired)
	Pepper to taste

Salad:

1	head red cabbage, thinly sliced
4	or more green onions with tender green tops, sliced
4	tablespoons almonds, toasted*
4	tablespoons sesame seeds, toasted*
2	packages Ramen noodle soup mix (discard soup mix packet)

Combine ingredients for dressing in small bowl; whisk until thoroughly blended; reserve. Just before serving, combine cabbage, onions, almonds, and seeds. Crush noodles into small pieces and add to cabbage mixture. Add dressing and toss to coat. (10 to 15 servings.)

*To toast almonds and sesame seeds: Spread in single layer on baking sheet or toaster oven pan; bake at 375°F, stirring twice, until light brown, about 5 minutes. Watch carefully as they can burn easily. Do not toast almonds and sesame seeds together.

From a small club cookbook from one of my women's groups. I have yet to find anyone who does not like this salad!

Colorful Cole Slaw

Dean Lewis
Ghost Ranch staff

2	cups shredded green cabbage
2	cups shredded red cabbage
1 1/2	cups celery, diced
1	small onion, minced (optional)
1/3	cup chopped green pepper
1/3	cup chopped red pepper
1/3	cup chopped yellow pepper

Dressing:
1/4	cup chili sauce
12	sliced green olives with pimiento
3/4	cup mayonnaise

Combine vegetables. Combine dressing ingredients and pour over vegetables. Toss to coat vegetables with dressing. (6-8 servings.)

Mandarin Orange & Avocado Salad

Ghost Ranch

Poppy Seed Dressing:
1 1/2	cups sugar
2	teaspoons salt
2	teaspoons dry mustard
1/2	small red onion
2	cups vegetable oil (not olive oil)
1/4	cup poppy seeds

Romaine lettuce, torn into bite-size pieces
Fresh spinach, washed, dried, torn into bite-size pieces
Mandarin orange slices
Sweet red onion, sliced
Avocado, sliced

To make dressing, place sugar, salt, mustard and onion in food processor or blender. Cover and process until smooth. With machine running, slowly add oil until thick. Stir in poppy seeds. Cover and refrigerate in non-metallic container. (Makes 4 cups.)

To make salad, place romaine and spinach in large salad bowl. Toss with remaining ingredients. Serve with poppy seed dressing.

Avocado Rings

Nancy Noyes
Santa Fe, NM

2	tablespoons Knox gelatin
1/2	cup cold water
1 1/4	cups hot water
6	tablespoons lemon juice
1 1/2	teaspoons (or more) grated onion
2	teaspoons salt
	Dash of Tabasco
6-8	avocados, mashed
3/4	cup mayonnaise

Filling:
1	can mandarin oranges, drained (10 oz.)
1/4	cup vegetable oil
1/4	cup vinegar

Soften gelatin in cold water, dissolve in hot water. Season with lemon juice, onion, salt, and Tabasco. Stir in avocado and mayonnaise. Blend well. Pour mixture into a 6 cup ring mold. Cover with plastic wrap and refrigerate overnight. To unmold, fill a large bowl with very hot water, dip mold in it for 8 seconds. Shake loose or run a knife around the edges, and invert over a plate. Shake hard to unmold. (8-10 servings.)

Marinate mandarin oranges in oil and vinegar, use as center filling.

This recipe comes to me by way of my mother-in-law, Winifred Noyes. It is a nice dish for a buffet supper. You can make more of a "guacamole" flavor by increasing the amount of Tabasco and onion. To make a slightly stiffer molded salad, increase the amount of gelatin. The lemon juice prevents discoloration.

Leaf Lover's Salad

Toni M. Kash
Austin, TX

Honey and Lemon Dressing:
1/4	cup honey
1/4	cup lemon juice (or vinegar)
1	tablespoon prepared yellow mustard
1/8	teaspoon salt
1	cup canola, sunflower or other vegetable oil

Salad:

8	romaine leaves, torn into bite-size pieces
1	tomato, cut into 8 wedges
1	banana, sliced
30	green or red seedless grapes
4	slices cotto salami (or turkey), cut into 1/2" triangles
1	Bermuda onion, cut lengthwise into thin slices

To make dressing, combine honey, lemon juice, mustard and salt in medium bowl. Beat in oil until thick. Add more salt to taste. Cover and refrigerate in non-metallic container. (Makes more than is needed for salad ingredients listed.)

To make salad, combine romaine, tomato, banana, grapes, salami and the onion in medium salad bowl. Toss with 3/4 cup dressing just before serving. Pass remaining dressing. (4 servings.)

This salad comes from a superb restaurant in Puerto Rico. It was served as a first course with hot French bread. The bread was supposed to be used to sop up the dressing.

Cherry Salad

Dorothy Fowler
Rimrock, AZ

1	can cherry pie filling (21 oz.)
1	can pineapple chunks, drained (20 oz.)
1	can mandarin oranges, drained (8 oz.)
2-3	bananas, sliced
1	cup miniature marshmallows (optional)

Combine cherry pie filling, pineapple and mandarin oranges in 2-quart salad bowl. Stir in bananas and marshmallows. (6 to 8 servings.)

Quick and easy!

Strawberry-Banana Salad

Miriam Wilcox
Porterville, CA

1	package strawberry jello (6 oz.)
1	cup boiling water
1	cup cold water
3	bananas
1	box frozen strawberries, thawed (10 oz.)
3/4	cup mayonnaise
3/4	cup sour cream

In large bowl dissolve jello in boiling water. Add cold water. Crush 1 1/2 bananas on a plate until smooth and stir into jello (it will be lumpy). Add strawberries, stir. Pour 1/2 mixture into 9" square pan, refrigerate until set. Mix mayonnaise and sour cream together and spread 1/2 of mixture over set jello. Slice remaining 1 1/2 bananas over mixture and spoon remaining jello over all, refrigerate to set. When firm, spread remaining mayonnaise mixture over last layer of jello. You may add some grated Cheddar cheese for eye appeal if desired.

India Salad

John and Barbara Decker
Hutchinson, KS

1/2	cup whole blanched almonds
1/4	cup sugar
1 to 2	tablespoons water
1	carton vanilla yogurt (8 oz.)
1/2	cup whipping cream or sour cream
	Honey to taste
1/8 to 1/4 teaspoon ground cardamon	
2	bananas, sliced
	Lettuce, torn into pieces

Place almonds in medium non-stick pan over medium heat. Add sugar. When sugar begins to melt, add water; stir. Cook and stir until water evaporates and sugar crystallizes, coating the almonds. Pour almonds onto waxed paper and let cool.

Combine yogurt and whipping or sour cream in small bowl; add honey to taste. Stir in cardamon, adding more as desired. Gently fold in bananas. Spoon onto lettuce-lined plates; top with sugared almonds. (4 servings.)

Strawberry Pretzel Salad

Dottie Hill
San Pedro, CA

2	cups crushed pretzels (not too finely crushed)
3	tablespoons granulated sugar
3/4	cup melted butter or margarine
1	package cream cheese, at room temperature (8 oz.)
1/2	cup sifted confectioners' sugar
1	container non-dairy whipped topping (9 oz.)
2	cups miniature marshmallows
1	large package strawberry-flavored gelatin (6 oz.)
4	cups water, divided
1	package frozen strawberries (16 oz.)

Combine pretzels, granulated sugar and margarine. Press into a 9 x 12" pan. Bake at 350°F for 15 minutes; cool. Beat cream cheese and confectioner's sugar in medium bowl until light and fluffy. Fold in whipped topping and marshmallows. Spread over cooled pretzel crust. Dissolve gelatin in 2 cups of the boiling water. Add 2 cups cool water, add strawberries; stir until strawberries are thawed and gelatin starts to set. Pour over cream cheese mixture in pretzel crust. Cover and refrigerate until firm. (12 servings.)

Cranberry Harvest Salad

Marion Sweet
Verona, WI

1	package raspberry-flavored gelatin (3 oz.)
1 1/2	cups hot water
1	can jellied cranberry sauce (16 oz.)
1	orange
1/2	cup chopped nuts

Dissolve gelatin in hot water; refrigerate until it begins to set. Add cranberry sauce. Grind unpeeled orange by hand or with food processor or blender. Add to cranberry mixture with the nuts. Serve mounded in a dish (it does not mold well) or on lettuce-lined salad plates with a dollop of mayonnaise or whipped cream. (8 servings.)

Cran-Apple Relish

Ghost Ranch

1	pound fresh cranberries, rinsed and drained
2	cooking apples, cored and quartered
2	unpeeled oranges, quartered, seeds removed
1	unpeeled lemon, quartered, seeds removed
2 1/2	cups sugar

Put first 4 ingredients in food processor. Process until chunky. Add sugar, blend. Refrigerate for several hours to several days. (Makes 3 pints.)

Cranberry-Pear Relish

Anne Hunt
Hawthorn Woods, IL

1	pound fresh cranberries, washed, sorted
2	teaspoons Kirsch or brandy (optional)
1/2	cup sugar
2	large pears, peeled, cored, quartered
1	Granny Smith or Golden Delicious apple, peeled, cored, quartered
2	teaspoons lemon juice

Place cranberries in bowl of food processor. Chop with 5 or 6 on/off turns, then process until minced, about 3 seconds. Remove to a large bowl and add Kirsch and sugar. Coarsely chop pears and apple, in 2 batches, in food processor. Add to cranberry mixture; add lemon juice. Cover and refrigerate at least 4 hours. Keeps up to 1 week. (Makes 4 cups.)

A wonderful fresh-tasting accompaniment to poultry or pork! From a 1983 cookbook published by Francis W. Parker School in Chicago.

Brook's Cranberry Sauce

Deborah J. Hunter
Ghost Ranch staff

1 1/2   pounds fresh whole cranberries, washed and sorted
2   large Valencia oranges, peeled, seeded
1/2   cup honey
1/2   cup water

Coarsely chop cranberries and orange in food processor. Place chopped cranberry mixture in a medium saucepan; add honey and water. Heat to boiling; cover and simmer over medium-low heat, stirring occasionally, for 1 hour. Uncover and continue cooking for 10 minutes. Store covered in the refrigerator. (8 servings.)

The orange peel can be placed on a "fired-up" wood stove-top (if you have one) to release the subtle aroma of the essential oil of orange. If you don't have a wood stove, squeeze the orange peels at a candle flame for a nice surprise.

Cranberry-Pineapple Relish

Alice Miller
La Luz, NM

1   can regular or whole-berry cranberry sauce (16 oz.)
1   can crushed pineapple or pineapple tidbits, drained (8 oz.)

Crush cranberry sauce in medium bowl; stir in the pineapple. Cover and refrigerate.

Note: Select whichever ingredients give the texture you prefer.

Frozen Cranberry Salad

Shirley Snow
San Pedro, CA

1	can crushed pineapple, drained (20 oz.)
1	can whole cranberry sauce (16 oz.)
1	can sweetened condensed milk (14 oz.)
1/2	cup chopped walnuts
1/4	cup lemon juice
1	container non-dairy whipped topping (9 oz.)

Combine pineapple, cranberry sauce, sweetened condensed milk, walnuts and lemon juice in large bowl. Fold in whipped topping. Freeze in a 13 x 9" pan. Remove from freezer 10 minutes before servings. Leftovers can be refrozen. (12 servings.)

Frozen Fruit Salad

Ruth Teutsch
Oceanside, CA

1	package cream cheese, at room temperature (8 oz.)
1/2	cup mayonnaise
1	can fruit cocktail, drained (16 oz.)
1	can mandarin oranges, drained (8 oz.)
1/2	cup maraschino cherries, cut in half
1/2	cup chopped pecans or walnuts
1	cup miniature marshmallows
1/2	teaspoon ground allspice
	Red food coloring
1	cup whipping cream, whipped
	Salad greens

Topping:

1	can crushed pineapple, drained (8 oz.)
1	cup whipping cream, whipped
	Fresh strawberries

Beat cream cheese and mayonnaise until smooth. Add fruits, nuts, marshmallows, allspice and enough red food color to turn a delicate shade of pink. Fold in whipping cream. Spoon into 1 1/2 quart mold. Freeze until solid. Slice and serve on salad greens. For topping, fold crushed pineapple into whipped cream in small bowl. Spoon a small amount over the salad and garnish with strawberries. (8 to 10 servings.)

Buffet Salad Tropicale

Barloe Bareis
Rapid City, SD

1	large package lime-flavored gelatin (6 oz.)
2	cups hot water
1	cup fat-free whipped salad dressing
1	cup low-fat cottage cheese
1	can crushed pineapple, not drained (16 oz.)
1/2	cup chopped walnuts

Dissolve gelatin in hot water in large bowl. Chill until thickened but not set. Fold in remaining ingredients. Pour into 7 1/2 x 11 1/2" glass dish or 1 1/2 quart mold. Chill until firm. (8 to 10 servings.)

Molded Lime-Pear Salad

Nadine Walker
Jamestown, ND

1	can pear halves (2 1/2 lbs.), drained, juice reserved
2	packages lime-flavored gelatin (3 oz. each)
2	packages cream cheese, at room temperature (3 oz. each)
2	cups non-dairy whipped topping

Add enough water to juice to measure 2 cups. Heat juice to boiling in small pan; add gelatin. Cool until gelatin begins to thicken. Dice or mash pears; reserve. Beat cream cheese in large mixer bowl with electric mixer until smooth; gradually add gelatin, beating after each addition until smooth. Fold in reserved pears and whipped topping. Spoon into large ring mold or 9 x 13" pan. Cover and refrigerate until firm. (12 to 15 large servings.)

For the last 25 years, this is the only salad requested at Thanksgiving, Christmas, or special dinners by our 4 sons and now by their families.

Under the Sea Salad

Sallie Smith
Socorro, NM

1	package lime-flavored gelatin (3 oz.)
1 1/2	cups boiling water
1	can pears, with juice (17 oz.)
1	teaspoon vinegar
1/4	teaspoon salt
1	package light cream cheese, at room temperature (8 oz.)
6	pieces candied ginger, diced

Dissolve gelatin in boiling water in medium bowl. Add 1/2 cup of the pear juice (add water, if necessary to make 1/2 cup); reserve the pears. Add the vinegar and salt. Pour a 2"-deep layer in a large mold or a 1/2" layer in each of 7 individual molds. (There will be some gelatin mixture remaining.) Refrigerate the molded gelatin. Pour the remaining gelatin into blender; add cream cheese and blend on high speed. Cut up reserved pears and fold into the cream cheese mixture with the candied ginger. Pour evenly over clear molded layer. Refrigerate until firm. Unmold to serve. (7 servings.)

Pinto Bean Patio Salad

Criselda Dominguez
Ghost Ranch staff
Abiquiu, NM

2 1/2	cups pinto beans, cooked
4	hard boiled eggs, chopped
1	cup American cheese, 1/4" cubes
1/2	onion, chopped
2	teaspoons salad dressing, such as Miracle Whip
1	teaspoon chili sauce
1	teaspoon mustard
1/4	teaspoon salt
1/4	teaspoon pepper
	Bacon, cooked crisp
	Parsley, minced

Combine beans, eggs, cheese, and onion. Mix salad dressing, chili sauce, mustard, salt, and pepper. Add to bean mixture. Chill. Sprinkle with crumbled bacon and minced parsley. (4-6 servings.).

Tabbuleh

Ghost Ranch

2	cups bulgur or cracked wheat
1	can chick peas (garbanzos), drained (15 oz.)
2	medium onions, chopped (about 1 cup)
2	cups chopped fresh tomatoes
2	cups peeled, chopped cucumber
1/2	cup chopped fresh mint leaves (1/4 cup dried)
1	cup olive oil
1/2	cup lemon juice
1	teaspoon salt
1	teaspoon fresh ground pepper

Soak bulgur in boiling water to cover for about 45 minutes. Drain and squeeze out excess water. Combine bulgur and remaining ingredients in large bowl. Serve as a salad or as a main dish. (6-8 servings.)

Best of the Brunch Rice Salad

Anne Hunt
Hawthorn Woods, IL

2/3	cup olive or vegetable oil
1/2	cup rice (or white wine) vinegar
1/2	teaspoon fresh ground pepper
1	cup wild rice or mix of wild and brown and white (do not use seasoning packet that may come with rice)
1	pound lean ham, cut into strips, 1/4 x 1"
1 1/2	cups golden raisins, plumped in hot water, drained
1	cup thinly sliced green onions with tender green tops
1	cup pecan halves, toasted*

Whisk together oil, vinegar and pepper in large bowl. Prepare rice according to package directions; add to oil and vinegar mixture and mix well. Stir in ham, raisins and onions. Cover and refrigerate. At serving time, toss lightly and top with toasted pecans. (8 to 10 servings.)

* To toast pecans: Spread in single layer on baking sheet or toaster oven pan. Bake at 375°F, stirring twice, until toasted, 5 to 10 minutes. Watch carefully as they burn easily.

This recipe brought me a prize in a church cook-off. I was awarded a plaque that hangs in my kitchen. It reads, "Best of the Brunch. Presented to Anne Hunt by a group of hungry Presbyterians. Lincoln Park Presbyterian Church."

Basic French Dressing

Ghost Ranch

1	cup sugar
1	cup vinegar
1	cup catsup
1	cup vegetable oil
1	medium onion, minced
1	teaspoon black pepper

Mix ingredients and shake well.

Onion & Mint Dressing

Rebecca Martinez
Ghost Ranch

1	bunch green mint
4	tablespoons onion, chopped finely
1/2	green pepper, sliced
1	cup basic French dressing, see above

Chop mint leaves finely. Add onions, green peppers, dressing. Chill. (Makes 1 cup.)

Celery Seed Dressing

Rose Marie Christison
Aurora, CO

1	can tomato soup (10 3/4 ounces)
1	soup can vegetable oil
1	cup sugar
3/4	cup vinegar
1	tablespoon celery seed
1	tablespoon garlic salt

Place all ingredients in blender. Blend until smooth. Store, covered, in refrigerator in non-metallic container. (Makes about 4 cups.)

Ghost Ranch Celery Seed Dressing

Ghost Ranch

2 1/2   cups powdered sugar
1   tablespoon dry mustard
1   tablespoon salt
1/2   cup vinegar
3   cups vegetable oil
1   tablespoon paprika
1   tablespoon celery seed

At least 3 hours before serving, mix sugar, mustard, salt and vinegar. Mix well. Just before serving, add oil, paprika, and celery seed. Blend well. This is especially good on fruit salad. (Makes 1 quart.)

Fruit Salad Dressing

Mildred E. Koper
Jenkintown, PA

2   cups sugar
1   cup vinegar
1/2   teaspoon salt
1/2   teaspoon dry mustard
1   cup vegetable oil
3   tablespoons grated onion
1   teaspoon celery seed

Combine sugar, vinegar, salt and mustard in small saucepan. Heat to boiling; boil 1 minutes. Remove from heat; cool. Add remaining ingredients. Store, covered in refrigerator in non-metallic container. Shake well before using. (Makes about 1 1/2 cups dressing.)

Honey Salad Dressing

Barbara A. Miller
Folsom, PA

1	cup vegetable oil
1	cup cider vinegar
1	cup mild-flavored honey
1	teaspoon salt
1	tablespoon prepared mustard
1 to 2	teaspoons Worcestershire or tamari sauce
1	tablespoon dehydrated onion flakes

Measure ingredients into a quart jar in the order listed. Shake until well blended. Store covered in refrigerator in non-metallic container. (Makes about 3 cups.)

My mother, Marjorie Miller, who along with my father Ernest spent several summers at the Ranch in the 1970s, made this dressing in bulk to sell. She donated the money to the hunger fund at the First Presbyterian Church of Lansdowne, PA.

Favorite Salad Dressing

Nola Scott
Ghost Ranch staff

3	tablespoons sugar
1/2	cup corn oil
	Catsup
	Salt and pepper
1/4	cup vinegar

Mix in shaker and pour over lettuce salad.

Poppy Seed Dressing

Judy Shibley
Ghost Ranch staff

1/2	cup sugar
2	tablespoons poppy seeds
1 1/2	teaspoons dry mustard
1 1/2	cups vegetable oil
1/2	cup vinegar

Place sugar, poppy seeds and mustard in blender; process at high speed until blended. With motor running, add oil in small quantities until it is emulsified. Add vinegar in the same way. (Makes about 1 pint.)

Sweet and Sour Salad Dressing

Paulette Roades
Sebring, OH

1	cup vegetable oil
2/3	cup sugar
1/3	cup vinegar
1	medium onion, cut up
1	teaspoon prepared mustard
1	teaspoon celery salt

Place all ingredients in blender container; process at high speed until blended. Store covered in refrigerator in non-metallic container. (Makes 2 cups.)

Spicy French Dressing

Ghost Ranch

2	teaspoons salt
1	teaspoon cracked pepper
1	teaspoon paprika
1	teaspoon sugar
1	teaspoon dry mustard
1/4	teaspoon cayenne
1/4	cup vinegar (wine vinegar is good)
1	cup olive oil

In a blender, mix dry ingredients with vinegar. While blending, slowly add olive oil. Shake before using. May drop in a clove of garlic for flavor. (Makes about 1 1/2 cups.)

Cucumber Dressing

Ghost Ranch

1	cucumber, peeled and chunked
1/2	onion
1/2	cup vinegar
	Juice of 1/2 lemon
1	clove garlic
1	cup light mayonnaise
1	cup skim milk
	Salt to taste
2	tablespoons poppy seeds

In blender, combine cucumber, onion, vinegar and lemon juice. Blend until smooth. Add garlic, mayonnaise and milk. Blend about 2 minutes, adding poppy seed last few seconds of blending. Salt to taste. (Makes about 3 1/2 cups.)

Lowfat Ranch-style Dressing

Ghost Ranch

1/4	cup low calorie mayonnaise
3/4	cup plain lowfat yogurt
1	cup buttermilk
1	tablespoon onion, minced
1/4	teaspoon basil
1/4	teaspoon sage
1/4	teaspoon thyme
1/4	teaspoon garlic powder
1	tablespoon parsley, minced

Combine mayonnaise, yogurt, buttermilk, and seasonings. Mix well. Cover and refrigerate.

This dressing can be used as a dip for vegetables, bagel chips and crackers, or as a topping for baked potatoes.

Ria's Salad Dressing

'Becca May
Ghost Ranch staff

1/2	cup sugar
1	teaspoon salt
1	shake paprika
1	teaspoon celery seed
1/2	teaspoon dry mustard
1/4	cup green onion slices
1/2	cup vinegar
1	cup salad oil

In blender, combine sugar, salt, spices, and onion. Add vinegar. Blend. Slowly add oil while blending. (Makes about 2 cups.)

This recipe is from my Dutch friend, Ria Spier.

Meats

Meats 108

Fajita Stir-Fry

Gene Huff
Cleveland Heights, OH

8	flour tortillas
4	teaspoons vegetable oil
1	pound lean beef, cut in 1/8"thick strips
1	large onion, sliced into rings
3	fresh jalapeño peppers, seeds and stems removed, minced*
1	red or yellow bell pepper, cut in thin strips
2	cloves garlic, minced
2	teaspoons ground cumin
1	teaspoon cornstarch
3	tablespoons lime juice
	Salt and pepper
2	medium tomatoes, diced (about 1 cup)
1	avocado, diced
	Sour cream
	Lime wedges

Wrap tortillas in foil; heat in 350°F oven until soft, about 15 minutes. Meanwhile, heat 1 teaspoon of the oil in wok or large skillet over high heat. Add half the beef; cook and stir until brown, 2 to 3 minutes. Place browned meat in large bowl; repeat with remaining beef, adding 2 teaspoons oil, if necessary. Remove and reserve meat. Add remaining 1 teaspoon oil to pan. Add onion, jalapeño peppers, bell peppers and garlic. Cook and stir until onion is crisp, about 2 minutes. Mix cumin, cornstarch and lime juice in small bowl; stir into onion mixture. Add reserved beef and tomatoes. Heat to boiling, stirring constantly. Season to taste with salt and pepper. To make fajita, spoon beef mixture onto warm tortilla; top with avocado, sour cream. Squeeze lime juice on top. (4 servings.)

* Caution: Take care when handling jalapeño peppers. Use rubber gloves; avoid contact with eyes.

Beef Burgundy

3	tablespoons vegetable oil
2	pounds lean beef, cubed
2	tablespoons flour
1	teaspoon salt
1/4	teaspoon pepper
1/4	teaspoon thyme
1	cup undiluted beef broth
1	cup burgundy
1	small can white onions (optional)
1	can mushrooms (3 oz.)

Heat oil, brown meat. Stir in flour, salt, pepper, and thyme. Mix well.
Mix broth and wine, pour over meat. Place in a covered casserole and
bake at 325°F at least 2 1/2 hours. Add drained onions and mushrooms.
Stir and cover. Bake 35 minutes. This freezes very well. Serve with
noodles—may add butter and caraway seeds to noodles. (8 servings.)

Festive Beef Cantonese

3	tablespoons oil
1/2	cup almonds, blanched
2	pounds round steak, 1/2" thick
1	can water chestnuts, sliced
1	can button mushrooms (7 oz.)
3	cups bouillon
1	tablespoon cornstarch (or flour to thicken)
1	teaspoon salt
1	teaspoon seasoning salt
1	teaspoon soy sauce
1/8	teaspoon pepper
1	medium green pepper, cut into thin rings
2	medium tomatoes, peeled and cut into wedges

Heat skillet to 350°F. Add oil and brown almonds. Drain on paper and use these later as a garnish. Cut beef into small strips about 2" long and 1/4" wide, brown in oil, add water chestnuts and mushrooms. Cover and simmer about 30 minutes until tender. Combine bouillon with cornstarch and other seasonings, add this to meat mixture and cook until thickened, then add green pepper rings and tomatoes, and cook about 3 minutes. Do not overcook. Garnish with almonds and serve with rice. (6-8 servings.)

Boolkagi (Korean Broiled Beef)

Carolyn Jones
Exeter, CA

2	tablespoons soy sauce
1	teaspoon sugar
1	teaspoon sesame oil (available in oriental section of food store)
1	teaspoon dry sherry
1/4	teaspoon pepper
4	green onions with tender green tops, chopped (about 1/4 cup)
1	clove garlic, minced, crushed
1	pound beef flank steak, thinly sliced

Combine all ingredients except beef in small bowl; whisk or stir with a fork until combined. Pour over steak in non-metallic bowl. Cover and marinate for 30 minutes. Drain and broil or stir-fry beef just before serving. (4 servings.)

This is a version of a recipe in Cooking Delights, a cookbook published in 1961 by the Woman's Society of Scarsdale Community Baptist Church, Scarsdale, NY. I use the marinade on top round, blade steaks and other tender beef cuts that can be broiled.

Cocktail Sirloin Strips

Ghost Ranch

1 1/2   pound meat (sirloin or round), cut in strips

Teriyaki Sauce:
2   cloves garlic
1/2   cup soy sauce
2   teaspoons ginger
1/4   cup brown sugar
2   tablespoons vegetable oil (not olive oil)

Combine sauce ingredients. Marinate uncooked meat strips in this sauce
for 24 hours. Remove meat from sauce and cook in pressure cooker
about 15 minutes, or broil over charcoal. (6-8 servings.)

Braised Star Anise Beef

Carolyn Jones
Exeter, CA

2   pounds boneless chuck beef
3 to 4   cups cold water
2   tablespoons sugar
5   tablespoons soy sauce
2   tablespoons dry sherry
4   slices peeled fresh ginger root
1   whole star anise (available in oriental section of food store)
1   tablespoon sesame oil (available in oriental section of food store)

Place beef in large heavy pot (3 to 4-quart); add water to cover. Bring to
a boil over high heat; skim. Stir in sugar, soy sauce, sherry, ginger root
and anise. Reduce heat and simmer, partially covered, until beef is
tender, 2 1/2 to 3 hours. There should be about 1 cup liquid left in the
pan. Add oil and simmer 10 minutes. Remove beef; let cool slightly.
Slice into very thin slices. Discard ginger and anise; pour sauce over
beef. If serving cold, let beef cool in the sauce. (6 servings.)

Beef Jerky

Evelyn King
Chattanooga, OK

Round steak, uncooked, 1/2" thick, trimmed, tenderized, cut in
strips 1/2" wide
Seasoning salt
Coarse black pepper
Liquid smoke

Put half of meat in shallow non-metallic container that seals tightly.
Sprinkle with each of the remaining ingredients. Add second layer of
meat and repeat seasoning. Cover tightly and marinate in refrigerator 8
hours, turning several times. Lay strips across wire racks in oven and
bake for 8 hours at 125°F. Line oven with foil to catch drips.

Stay-a-Bed Stew

Ghost Ranch

3	pounds stew meat
1/2	cup beef bouillon
3	large carrots, cut in 1" pieces
3	potatoes, cut in chunks
3	onions, quartered
2	bay leaves
3/4	cup croutons
1/2	cup dry red wine
3	stalks celery
1	can tomatoes (#2 1/2)
1	tablespoon brown sugar
4	tablespoons minute tapioca
2	teaspoons salt
1/2	teaspoon pepper

Combine ingredients in large casserole. Cover tightly with lid or foil and
bake at 250°F for 7 hours. (10-12 servings.)

*No, don't brown the meat or anything. Just mix it all together and go back to
bed!*

Beef-Noodle Delight

Miriam Wilcox
Porterville, CA

4	tablespoons flour, divided
1	teaspoon salt
1	teaspoon garlic salt
1/2	teaspoon black pepper
1 1/2	pounds lean tender beef steak, cut into thin bite-size strips
1	tablespoon vegetable oil
8 to 10	mushrooms, sliced
1	medium red or yellow onion, sliced
3	tablespoons margarine or butter
2	cans beef broth (10 1/2 oz. each)
1/2	cup cooking sherry
1	cup sour cream (8 oz.)
8 to 10	ounces egg noodles, cooked, drained

Combine 2 tablespoons of the flour and the seasonings. Dredge beef in flour mixture. Heat oil in large skillet. Brown beef in hot oil; remove and reserve. Add mushrooms and onions to skillet; cook and stir until onions are transparent, about 2 minutes. Remove and reserve. Melt margarine in the skillet; add remaining 2 tablespoons flour. Cook and stir 2 minutes; gradually add beef broth. Cook, stirring constantly, over medium heat until thickened. Add reserved meat and mushroom mixture to sauce; stir in sherry. Reduce heat, cover and simmer over low heat 15 or 20 minutes. Just before serving, gently stir in sour cream. Serve over individual portions of cooked noodles. (6 servings.)

Brisket Seasoning

Ghost Ranch

4-5	pounds brisket
1 1/2	teaspoons salt
1 1/2	teaspoons pepper
2	tablespoons chili powder
1/2	teaspoon garlic
1	teaspoon crushed bay leaf

Mix spices, spread on meat. Wrap meat in heavy foil or cook in tightly covered dish. Bake 275°F for 3-1/2 to 4 hours or until tender. Scrape off sauce. Chill. Slice. Use sauce for BBQ. Reheat meat in sauce. (10-12 servings.)

Easy Tamale Casserole

Peg Pack McKinley
Santa Fe, NM

1	pound lean ground beef
1	medium onion, chopped (1/2 cup)
1	can tomato sauce (8 oz.)
1	can chopped green chilies, drained (4 oz.)
1	can sliced ripe olives, drained (4 1/2 oz.)
	Salt and pepper to taste
2	cans tamales, husks removed (about 16 oz. each)
1 1/2	cups shredded Cheddar or Monterey Jack cheese (6 oz.)

Brown ground beef in large skillet over medium heat until it loses its red color. Add onion, tomato sauce, chilies, ripe olives and salt and pepper to taste. Place tamales in shallow greased baking pan, about 10" long. Spoon beef mixture over tamales. Bake at 350°F for 20 minutes; add cheese. Bake 10 minutes longer. Note: This casserole freezes well without the cheese. (6 servings.)

I got this recipe from rancher friends. I have used it many times to feed friends that help us on our ranch during brandings, shipping calves and changing pastures. Everyone loves it!

editor's note: Peg is the daughter of Arthur Pack. Thanks to her for sending the "Ghost Ranch Cookbook," printed in the 1930's.

Tamale Pie

Criselda Dominguez
Ghost Ranch staff
Abiquiu, NM

2	cups cornmeal
1	teaspoon salt
1	quart boiling water
1	pound round steak, ground
1	tablespoon olive oil
1	can crushed tomatoes (16 oz.)
1	buffet-size can ripe olives, chopped
2	onions, minced
2	teaspoons chili powder
1/2	teaspoon dried basil
	Salt and pepper to taste

Stir the cornmeal and salt into one quart of boiling water. Boil for about 20 minutes, stirring constantly to keep from lumping. Saute the meat and onion in olive oil in large skillet. Add tomatoes, olives, and seasonings; cook for a while. Add water if it starts to get dry. When the cornmeal has become mushy, put 1/2 on the bottom of a low buttered casserole, then add the meat mixture and top with the other 1/2 of the cornmeal. Bake in a medium oven (350°F) for 30 minutes. (8-10 servings.)

Aunt Olive's Empanadas

Julie Thompson
San Diego, CA

Filling:

1	pound lean ground beef
2	large onions, chopped (1 1/2 to 2 cups)
1	clove garlic, chopped
1	can tomatoes, undrained, broken up (28 oz.)
2	cans tomato paste (6 oz. each)
2	cans tomato sauce (15 oz. each)
1/2	teaspoon salt
1/2	teaspoon ground cumin
1/4	teaspoon each: dried oregano, marjoram, pepper
2	cans sliced ripe olives, drained (4 1/2 oz. each)
1	cup raisins (about 1/2 box)

Dough:
2   cups all-purpose flour
1   teaspoon salt
1/3   cup vegetable shortening
2/3   cup milk
           Oil for frying

To make filling: Brown beef, onions and garlic in large heavy pot. Add tomatoes, tomato sauce, tomato paste and seasonings. Heat to boiling; reduce heat and simmer over medium heat until thick, about 1 hour. Mixture should be thick enough to hold its shape. Add olives and raisins. Cook until raisins are plump, 2 to 3 minutes. Set aside.

To make dough: Mix flour and salt in medium bowl. Cut in shortening with pastry blender or 2 knives. Stir in milk. Turn onto floured surface. Knead until smooth. Form into 12 balls the size of large walnuts; let rest 20 minutes. Roll each ball into an 8 to 9" oval.

To assemble: Brush edges of dough with water. Spoon some of the filling in center of each oval; fold over and crimp edges of dough to seal. Fry in hot oil in large skillet, crimped-side down. Drain on paper toweling. (Makes 12 empanadas.)

This recipe was given to me by my great aunt Olive. She was the eccentric "black sheep" of the family who went off to live in Puerto Piñasco in a trailer and make jewelry out of shells.

Enchilada Casserole

Betty Sterrett
Escondido, CA

Meat Sauce:
2	pounds ground beef (chuck preferred)
1	large onion, chopped (3/4 cup)
1	can tomatoes, cut up, undrained (16 oz.)
1	package frozen chopped spinach (10 oz.)
	Salt and pepper to taste

Cream Sauce:
1/2	cup butter or margarine (1 stick)
1	can cream of mushroom soup (10 3/4 oz.)
1	can golden mushroom soup (10 3/4 oz.)
1	cup sour cream (8 oz.)
1/2	cup milk
1/2	teaspoon minced garlic

12 to 16 flour tortillas, divided
1	can chopped green chilies, drained (4 oz.)
2	cups shredded mild cheese (8 oz.)

To make meat sauce: Brown beef and onion in large skillet; drain fat. Add tomatoes and spinach; cook until spinach is thawed. Season to taste with salt and pepper. Reserve.

To make cream sauce: Melt butter in a large saucepan. Add soups, sour cream, milk and garlic.

To assemble: Dip both sides of 1/3 of the tortillas in cream sauce. Place in bottom and up sides of a large casserole dish. Spoon 1/2 of the meat sauce and 1/2 of the green chilies into the tortilla-lined dish. Sprinkle with 1/3 of the cheese; repeat layers. Top with remaining 1/3 of the tortillas, coated in cream sauce, and the remaining cheese. Cover and refrigerate 8 hours. Bake at 350° for 35 to 45 minutes. (10 to 12 servings.)

Meat Burritos

Criselda Dominguez
Ghost Ranch staff
Abiquiu, NM

1	pound ground beef
1	medium onion, chopped
2	stalks celery, chopped
1	teaspoon salt
2	heaping tablespoons chili sauce
1	tablespoon chili powder
1	cup pinto beans, cooked
1/4	cup bean liquid
1	small can tomato soup
1/2	cup sharp cheese, grated
1	dozen flour tortillas

Crumble ground beef into medium-sized bits; brown lightly. Drain most of the fat, leaving small quantity. Add onion. Cook over low heat until tender and add celery, soup, beans, and bean liquid. Add remaining ingredients, cover, and allow to simmer until liquid cooks down (about 10 minutes). Place one heaping tablespoon mixture in center of warmed tortilla. Sprinkle mixture with cheese if desired. Fold over one end about an inch and roll up. Lay flat in pan and keep warm until ready to serve. Cover with foil or lid or they will get too crisp. (12 burritos.)

Mexicali Pie

Suzi Plooster
Boulder, CO

1 1/2	pounds ground beef
1/2	pound hot sausage
1	teaspoon chili powder
1/2	teaspoon ground cumin
1/4	teaspoon salt
1/4	teaspoon pepper
1	can tomatoes, drained, broken up (16 oz.)
1	can whole kernel corn, drained (11 oz.)
1	can green chile (8 oz.)
1	can sliced ripe olives, drained (4 1/2 oz.)
1	small onion, diced (about 1/4 cup)
1/2	cup shredded Cheddar or Monterey Jack cheese (2 oz.)
1	box corn muffin mix, Jiffy brand preferred (8 1/2 oz.)

Cook ground beef, sausage and seasonings in large skillet until beef loses its red color. Drain fat. Spray 9 x 13" pan with non-stick vegetable oil spray. Spoon meat mixture evenly in bottom of pan. Combine tomatoes, corn, green chile and olives in medium bowl; pour over meat mixture. Sprinkle with onion and cheese. Prepare corn muffin mix according to directions; spread evenly over mixture in pan. Bake at 400°F until golden brown, about 25 minutes. (If top gets too brown, lower heat to 375°F after 15 minutes.) Let cool slightly, then cut into squares. (10 to 15 servings.)

I cooked the Lenten dinners for a number of years for the First Presbyterian Church in Boulder. I developed this dish for our 'Mexican Fiesta Night.' Everyone always enjoys it, even the kids.

Tagiarinni

Barbara Martin
Santa Fe, NM

2	tablespoons olive oil
1	green bell pepper, chopped (about 1/2 cup)
1	small onion, chopped (about 1/4 cup)
3	cloves garlic, minced
1	can tomatoes, broken up (29 oz.)
2	pounds ground beef
	Chili powder to taste
	Salt and pepper to taste
1	can cream-style corn (17 oz.)
1	can pitted ripe olives, chopped, 1/2 liquid reserved (16 oz.)
3	cups shredded longhorn cheese (12 oz.)
1	package fettuccine noodles, cooked, drained (16 oz.)

Heat oil in large skillet. Cook green pepper, onion and garlic in hot oil until tender; add tomatoes. Reduce heat and simmer, uncovered, 10 minutes. Remove and reserve mixture. Brown beef in the skillet. Add chili powder; season to taste with salt and pepper. Add green pepper mixture, corn, olives and olive liquid. Alternate layers of cooked fettuccine, meat mixture and cheese in 1 large or 3 medium greased casseroles. Cover and bake at 350°F until heated through, about 15 minutes (longer for larger casserole.) (12 to 14 servings.)

Delicio

Ruth Hall
Ghost Ranch

1	onion, finely chopped
1	cup celery, finely chopped
1	pound ground beef
1/4	pound ground pork, optional
1	package spaghetti, cooked (8 oz.)
1	tablespoon vegetable oil
1	can tomato soup
1	small can mushrooms
1	can green chilies (4 oz.)
1	can cream style corn (16 oz.)
1	tablespoon Worcestershire sauce
	Salt and pepper
1	pound cheese, grated

Saute onions and celery in oil: add meat and brown. Mix remaining ingredients with half the cheese. Top with remaining cheese and bake 30-40 minutes in a covered 2 qt. casserole at 350°F. (6-8 servings.)

editor's note: Ruth Hall got this recipe from her mother. It was a favorite with Jim and their boys as they were growing up.

Hamburger Beef Stroganoff

Marloe Bareis
Rapid City, SD

1 1/2	pounds lean ground beef
2	teaspoons salt
1/8	teaspoon garlic powder (optional)
2	cans chopped mushrooms, undrained (4 oz. each)
2	tablespoons all-purpose flour
1	can onion soup (10 1/2 oz.)
1	can cream of chicken soup (10 3/4 oz.)
1	cup light sour cream (8 oz.)
	Cooked rice, noodles or Chinese noodles

Brown ground beef with salt and garlic powder in large skillet over medium heat. Drain fat. Stir in flour. Add mushrooms and soups. Simmer over medium heat, 10 to 20 minutes. Stir in sour cream; heat but do not boil. Serve over rice, noodles or Chinese noodles. (8 servings.)

This has been a long time favorite of our four children, now grown.

Beef Porcupines

Ghost Ranch

1	pound ground beef
1/2	cup raw rice
1/4	cup onion, chopped
1	teaspoon salt
1/4	teaspoon pepper
2	tablespoons vegetable oil
2	cans tomato sauce (8 oz. each)
1	cup water

Mix beef, rice, onions, and seasonings. Form into small balls and fry in oil, turning frequently until not too brown. Add tomato sauce and water. Mix well, cover, and simmer about 45 minutes. If you wish, add a handful or so of raw rice and a little more water to the "sauce" and allow it to simmer along with the rest. (4-6 servings.)

Barbequed Meat Balls

Ghost Ranch

1	cup soft bread crumbs
1/2	cup milk
1	pound ground beef
1	teaspoon salt
	Pepper to taste
1 1/2	tablespoons Worcestershire sauce
3	tablespoons sugar
1/4	cup vinegar
1/2	cup ketchup
1/2	cup water
1/2	cup onion, chopped
1/2	cup green pepper, chopped

Moisten bread crumbs in milk; mix with beef. Shape into balls and put in baking dish. Combine rest of ingredients and pour over meat. Bake at 350°F for 45 minutes to an hour. (6-8 servings.)

Korean Beef Patties

Cassandra Gaines
Houston, TX

1/2	pound lean ground beef
1	block bean curd
2	tablespoons soy sauce
2	tablespoons green onion, minced
1	teaspoon garlic, minced
	Pinch black pepper
2	teaspoons sesame seeds, toasted
1 1/2	tablespoons sesame oil

Sauce:

1/4	cup soy sauce
1	tablespoon rice vinegar (or to taste)

Mash bean curd with fork. Mix in ground beef. Add seasonings and oil, mix again. Shape into patties. Broil on grill or in oven broiler on both sides. Serve with sauce. (4 servings.)

My husband Sandy and I met at Ghost Ranch in 1967 when we spent 3 months training to serve in the Peace Corps in Korea. We thought a Korean recipe might be an appropriate offering.

Campsite Stew

Pat Morgan
Midland, TX

1	pound ground beef
1/2	cup chopped onion (1 medium onion)
1	can beef broth (10 1/2 oz.)
1	can cream-style corn (16 oz.)
3	large potatoes, peeled, diced (about 3 cups)
1	teaspoon salt
1/8	teaspoon pepper
	Tabasco sauce (optional)
	Flour tortillas (optional)

Brown beef and onion in large heavy pot. Stir in remaining ingredients. Cover and cook over low heat, 20 to 25 minutes, stirring often. Serve with Tabasco sauce and flour tortillas. (4 servings.)

During our summer stays in the Ghost Ranch Campground, this recipe was a family favorite for campout meals. We never served it at home, so it remained "special."

Western Meal-in-One

Betty Sterrett
Escondido, CA

1	tablespoon vegetable oil
1	pound ground beef
1	large onion, chopped (about 1 cup)
1	green bell pepper, chopped (about 1 cup)
1	clove garlic, minced
1	teaspoon salt
1	teaspoon chili powder
1	can tomatoes, undrained, broken up (16 oz.)
1	can kidney beans, drained, rinsed (15 oz.)
3/4	cup uncooked rice
3/4	cup shredded cheese (6 oz.)

Heat oil in large skillet or dutch oven. Cook beef until it loses its red color. Add onion, green pepper, garlic, salt and chili powder. Cook, stirring occasionally, over medium heat, 5 minutes. Mix in tomatoes, kidney beans and rice. Pour into greased 2-quart casserole. Cook at 350°F for 45 minutes. Add a little water, if it becomes dry. Sprinkle cheese on top and continue baking 15 minutes. (8 servings.)

Macaroni Beef Casserole

Margaret W. Shibley
Estacada, OR

4	pounds ground beef
1	pound ground pork
1	cup chopped onions (about 1 large onion)
2	quarts (8 cups) cooked tomatoes (or 2 cans, 29 oz. each)
1	quart canned or frozen peas (32 oz.)
2	teaspoons salt
1	cup shredded Cheddar cheese (4 oz.)
8	cups uncooked elbow macaroni, cooked, drained

Cook beef, pork and onions in large pan or dutch oven. Drain excess fat. Add broken up tomatoes with juice. Stir in peas and salt. Combine meat mixture with cooked macaroni. Pour into large baking or roasting pan. Top with cheese. Bake at 350°F for 45 minutes. (50 servings.)

A good, simple casserole that is well-liked by Grangers in central Oregon. editor's note: Margaret is the mother of Ghost Ranch's ranchland superintendent, Jim Shibley.

Chow

Norma S. Raby
Tempe, AZ

1	pound ground beef (not cooked)
1	quart tomatoes, broken up (4 cups)
3 or 4	carrots, sliced
3 or 4	stalks celery, sliced
4	ounces shredded cheese (1 cup)
8	ounces uncooked spaghetti (1/2 package)
	Salt and pepper to taste

Place all ingredients except spaghetti in crock pot. Cook on low setting 7 to 8 hours or overnight. An hour before serving, add spaghetti; stir. Continue cooking until noodles are tender. (6 servings.)

This was invented during the Depression and has long been a family favorite.

Phred's Meat Loaf

Fred Mansfield
Santa Fe, NM

2	eggs, beaten
1	cup milk
3	cups soft bread crumbs
1	teaspoon salt
1	teaspoon dry mustard
2 to 3	teaspoons medium salsa
1	teaspoon Worcestershire sauce
1	teaspoon A-1 sauce (optional)
1 1/2	pounds ground beef
1/2	pound medium-spicy sausage

Combine all ingredients except ground beef and sausage in large bowl. Crumble in the meat. Stir gently to combine. Place in loaf pan, cover with aluminum foil and bake at 350°F for 1 hour or cook, covered with plastic wrap or waxed paper, in microwave on high, 20 minutes. Let cool slightly; drain excess drippings. (Makes 1 meat loaf.)

In an episode of "Laverne and Shirley," the women and their boyfriends are at a French restaurant and are obviously confused by the menu. One of the men asks, "How do you say meat loaf in French?" The waiter, with his most friendly smile, answers, "You don't." The addition of salsa and spicy sausage adds a touch of excitement to this version of an old favorite. Add more hot spices, if you want.

Meatloaf

Annabelle Salazar
Ghost Ranch staff
Abiquiu, NM

2	pounds lean ground beef
1	cup celery, diced
1	cup onion, diced
1	cup bell pepper, diced
1	tablespoon pepper
1	teaspoon salt
1	cup tomato sauce
4	eggs
2	cups quick oatmeal
1/4	cup soy sauce

Mix all ingredients in large bowl. Mix well. Form into loaf, place in greased baking dish. Pat well to hold consistency. Bake at 375°F for 40 minutes. (8 servings.)

Roma Meat Loaf

John and Barbara Decker
Hutchinson, KS

1 1/2	pounds lean ground beef
1	egg, beaten
3/4	cup cracker crumbs
1/2	cup chopped onion (1 medium onion)
1	teaspoon salt
1/2	teaspoon dried oregano
1/8	teaspoon pepper
2	cans tomato sauce, divided (8 oz. each)
2	cups mozzarella cheese, divided (8 oz.)

Combine all ingredients except 1 can tomato sauce and the cheese in a large bowl. Shape into a rectangle, 10 x 12" on waxed paper. Sprinkle 1 cup of the cheese evenly over the meat mixture. Roll up like a jelly roll, beginning on the long side; press ends of roll to seal. Place in 13 x 9" baking dish, seam-side down. Bake at 350°F for 1 hour. Drain off fat. Pour the remaining can of tomato sauce on top of the meat loaf; sprinkle with remaining 1 cup cheese. Bake until cheese melts, about 15 minutes. (Makes 1 meat loaf.)

Ham Loaf

John and Barbara Decker
Hutchinson, KS

Meat loaf mixture:
8	pounds cured ham, ground
4	pounds fresh ham, ground
1	pound ground beef
12	eggs, beaten
1	quart milk
1	pound crushed unsweetened cereal flakes
	Salt and pepper

Topping:
3	cups packed brown sugar
1 1/2	teaspoons dry mustard
1 1/2	cups vinegar
1 1/2	cups water
1	cup sweet pickle juice

To make meat loaf mixture: Combine all ingredients in large container. Form into individual loaves, using 2/3 to 3/4 cup of the mixture for each. Place in large baking pans. To make Topping: Combine ingredients in large pot in order listed. Heat to boiling. Pour topping over loaves and bake at 325°F, for 1 1/4 hours, basting every 15 minutes. If desired, meat loaves can be baked without topping for 20 to 30 minutes, drain fat and add topping. Meat mixture freezes well; thaw before baking. (65 servings.)

Freezer Meat Sauce

Betty Farrell
Arlington, TX

1/3	cup vegetable oil
3	large onions, chopped (about 3 cups)
3	green bell peppers, chopped (about 3 cups)
3	cloves garlic, minced
3	pounds ground beef
2	cups boiling water
4	cans tomato sauce (8 oz. each)
3	cans tomato paste (6 oz. each)
1	tablespoon salt
1	tablespoon paprika
1	teaspoon each: celery salt, garlic salt, chili powder
3	tablespoons A-1 sauce
3	tablespoons bottled chili sauce
2	tablespoons Worcestershire sauce

Heat oil in large pot. Cook onions, green peppers and garlic in hot oil 5 minutes. Add ground beef and cook, stirring frequently, until it loses its red color. Add all other ingredients, stirring well after each addition. Reduce heat; simmer uncovered 2 hours. Cool quickly in shallow containers in refrigerator. Freeze in 1-pint containers. Can be used for spaghetti, lasagna, omelets, stuffed peppers, etc. (Makes 7 pints.)

In today's busy world it is so helpful to have this in the freezer "on the ready" for surprise guests or quick-fix meals. If you're going to mess up the kitchen to cook, why not cook up a big batch for those days when time is limited?

Spaghetti Meat Sauce

Ghost Ranch

1	pound lean ground beef
1	can tomatoes (16 oz.)
1	can tomato sauce (8 oz.)
1/2	tablespoon garlic salt
1/2	cup onions, chopped
1	tablespoon oregano
6	bay leaves

Brown beef and onions. Drain off excess fat; crush tomatoes by hand and add to meat. Add tomato sauce, garlic, oregano, and bay leaves. Cover and simmer 20 minutes or more. Before serving, remove bay leaves. (6 servings.)

Pizza

Ghost Ranch

Dough ingredients:

1	package yeast
1	cup water
2	tablespoons salad oil
1	teaspoon sugar
1	teaspoon salt
2 1/2	cups flour

Sauce ingredients:

1/4	teaspoon salt
1	clove garlic, minced
1/8	teaspoon pepper
1/2	cup onions, chopped
1	cup tomato sauce (8 oz.)

Topping ingredients:

1/4	cup grated Parmesan cheese
2	cups mozerella, shredded (8 oz.)
2	teaspoons oregano
1	cup sliced pepperoni (can substitute other toppings for pepperoni)

Dissolve yeast in warm water. Stir in remaining dough ingredients. Beat vigorously about twenty strokes. Allow dough to rest about 5 minutes while preparing sauce. Mix sauce ingredients and set aside. Heat oven to 425°F. Divide dough in half. On lightly greased baking sheets pat dough into 10" circles with floured fingers. Spread sauce on each circle. Sprinkle with Parmesan cheese and oregano. Arrange pepperoni on top. Sprinkle with mozarella. Bake 20-25 minutes or until crust is hot and brown. (Makes 2 pizzas.)

If you don't need both pizzas for this meal, freeze one and use it later!

Golabki (Cabbage Rolls)

Catherine H. Harper
Española, NM

1	whole cabbage
1/2	cup uncooked rice
2	tablespoons butter
1	onion, finely chopped (about 1/2 cup)
1	egg, beaten
1	pound ground beef
1/2	pound ground pork or veal
	Salt and pepper
5	slices bacon
	Sour cream, ketchup or mushroom sauce

Core cabbage with sharp knife. Place cabbage in colander; pour boiling water into cored center. Remove leaves, a few at a time, as they wilt; reserve. Cook rice as package directs, but for only half the time; drain. Place rice in large bowl. Melt butter in skillet. Saute onion in butter until transparent; add to rice with egg, meat and seasonings. Mix well. Spoon a heaping tablespoonful of meat mixture in center of each leaf (vein-side down). Fold over stem end, then the sides. Roll towards the thin edge of the leaf. Fasten with a toothpick and place in large greased baking pan, at least 11 x 14". Cover with bacon. Bake at 300°F for 2 hours, basting occasionally with pan drippings. Serve with sour cream, ketchup or mushroom sauce. (Makes many!)

My maternal grandfather came to America from Germany in 1884. He always claimed to be from Pomerania, which was once Polish. When my mother found Treasured Polish Recipes for Americans *(published by the Polanie Club in 1948), she said, 'This is how we used to cook!' I have used her well-worn copy for many years, and "Golabki" has long been my favorite recipe.*

Orange Pork Chops

Ghost Ranch

6	thick pork chops
4	tablespoons brown sugar
1/2	teaspoon cinnamon
3	whole cloves
1	teaspoon salt
1	teaspoon prepared mustard
1/4	cup catsup
1	tablespoon vinegar
1	can Mandarin oranges (11 oz.)

Brown pork chops on both sides. Drain oranges, saving juice. Combine 1/2 cup juice with the remaining ingredients and pour over the pork chops. Cover and simmer gently for 45 minutes. Serve with rice. (6 servings.)

Smothered Pork Chops

Watson S. Custer
Tampa, FL

8	lean pork chops, trimmed
1/2	cup olive oil and/or margarine
3	cups sliced onions
1	cup chopped celery
1/2	cup chopped green pepper
1	can tomatoes, drained, broken up (16 oz.)
2	cups tomato juice or vegetable juice cocktail (16 oz.)
2	tablespoons chopped fresh parsley
1	tablespoon ground or crushed garlic
6	medium potatoes, not peeled, boiled, drained

Brown pork chops in heavy skillet (cast iron preferred) without oil or margarine. Remove. Add the oil or margarine to the skillet. Cook onions in hot oil/margarine until light brown. Add celery, peppers, tomatoes, juice, parsley, garlic and pork chops. Heat to boiling; reduce heat, cover and simmer until pork chops are tender, about 1 hour. Serve pork chops with "smashed" potatoes, covered with cooking mixture. (6 to 8 servings.)

When I was a youngster in Pittsburgh, my mother prepared pork chops that were cooked in a liquid. The liquid was used to cover mashed potatoes. I don't know what the ingredients were or what cooking procedure was used, so I developed this recipe on my own.

Posole

Ghost Ranch

1 1/2	pounds pork, cubed*
2	pounds frozen posole, rinsed, drained
8	cups water
2	cloves garlic
2	teaspoons dried oregano
	Salt to taste

Cook meat in large heavy pot over medium heat, stirring frequently, until brown, about 30 minutes. Add posole and water. Heat to boiling; reduce heat, cover and cook until meat is tender, 3 to 4 hours. Add water if necessary. When nearly done, add garlic, oregano and salt to taste. Serve in soup bowls. (8 servings.)

* Chicken can be substituted for pork. If using chicken, cook posole in water until nearly done, then add chicken and seasoning.

Shepherd's Pie

Tricia Bowen
Kansas City, KS

3	cans pork (29 oz. each)
3	package mixed frozen vegetables (16 oz. each)
3	small packs brown gravy mix (18 oz.)
7 1/2	cups water, divided
3	teaspoons salt
1	cup magarine or butter
4	cups milk
8	cups instant mashed potato flakes

Carefully spoon off as much fat as possible from pork. Cook vegetables in broth from meat. Mix gravy packs in 1/2 cup water. Add to vegetables. Cook 1-2 minutes to thicken. Add pork chunks. Pour into 12 x 20 x 2" pan. Reconstitute mashed potatoes with the remaining water, salt and milk. Using ice cream scoop or tablespoon, spoon potatoes over vegetables. Make even rows of mounds to use as a guide when serving. Bake until lightly browned and bubbly, 50-60 minutes, at 350°F. May be refrigerated and baked the next day. (Serves 28-32.)

Viking Mariner's of Southridge Presbyterian Church in Roeland Park, Kansas cooks for and serves 120-150 meals once a month at the Argentine food kitchen in Kansas City, KS. This is one of the most popular main dishes. We usually make 5 pans, served with a combination vegetable salad, hot French bread, fruit "dump cake," juice, milk, and coffee.

Saged Pork Chops

Betty Currin
Midland, MI

6	pork chops, 3/4" thick
1/2	teaspoon each: powdered sage, garlic powder, dried thyme and (optional) salt
1/4	teaspoon black pepper
1	small onion, finely chopped (about 1/4 cup)
1	stalk celery, finely chopped
1/2	cup croutons
1	can creamed-style corn (17 oz.)

Place chops close together in greased baking pan. Sprinkle with seasonings. Combine onion, celery, croutons and corn in small bowl. Spread mixture evenly over the chops. Bake, covered, at 325°F until chops are done, 1 to 1 1/4 hours, depending on thickness of chops. (6 servings.)

Rice & Sausage Casserole

Ghost Ranch

1/2	pound link sausage, cut up
2	tablespoons vegetable oil
1	onion, chopped
1	green pepper, chopped
1/2	cup celery, chopped
1	cup uncooked wild rice, washed (soak several hours or precook a short time)
1	can mushrooms, undrained (2 oz.)
1	can pimentoes, drained (2 oz.)
1	cup cheese, grated
1	can cream of chicken soup, undiluted (10 3/4 oz.)
1	can cream of mushroom soup, undiluted (10 3/4 oz.)

In oil, fry sausage until lightly browned. Remove sausage from oil, drain. In remaining oil, saute onion, pepper, and celery 3-5 minutes. Vegetables should still be fairly crisp. Combine all ingredients in 1 1/2 quart covered casserole. Bake 1 1/2 hours at 300°F. (8 servings.)

International Incidents

Cal Graham
Sacramento, CA

1	pound sausage meat*
3	green bell peppers, chopped
6	green onions with tender green tops, chopped
4	hard-cooked eggs, chopped
1	can or jar ripe or stuffed Spanish olives, chopped (about 4 oz.)
1	can Mexican-style hot tomato sauce or salsa (8 oz.)
1	can regular tomato sauce (8 oz.)
1	pound shredded or chopped Cheddar cheese (4 cups)
15	hard French rolls, split

Cook sausage, green peppers and onions in large skillet until sausage is brown. Pour off drippings. Add remaining ingredients except the rolls. Spoon onto split rolls; wrap in foil and heat at 350°F for 5 minutes. Serve hot. (15 servings.)

* To make without sausage, brown peppers and onions in 1/3 cup olive oil.

Wrap in newspaper and take on a winter picnic.

Sausage & Potato Stir

Ghost Ranch

1 1/2	pound red potatoes, diced
1 1/2	pound sausage, diced
1/4	cup chopped bell pepper
1/2	cup chopped green onion
	Salt and pepper to taste
1	teaspoon parsley

Saute potatoes and sausage in skillet about 5 minutes. Add other ingredients, cover, and simmer for 15 minutes. Add 15 minutes to cooking time if using coarse-ground sausage. (8-10 servings.)

Hot Sausages with Fettuccine

Kathy Swearingen
Berkeley, CA

8	hot Italian sausages, cut in 1" pieces
6	cloves garlic, minced
1/2 to 3/4 cup finely chopped fresh basil
5	tomatoes, peeled, seeded, quartered
1/2	cup Marsala or red wine
1	pound fresh or dry-packaged fettuccine, cooked, drained
5	ounces crumbled chevre (goat) cheese (about 1 cup)
	Freshly grated Parmesan cheese

Brown sausages in large skillet over medium high heat. Add garlic, basil, tomatoes and wine. Reduce heat; simmer until thickened, 8 to 10 minutes. (If sauce is thin, thicken with a little flour mixed with water into a thin paste.) Place hot, drained pasta on large serving platter. Crumble chevre cheese over pasta, add sauce, and toss lightly. Pass freshly grated Parmesan cheese. (4 to 6 servings.)

Sausage and Pepper Stir-Fry

Nancy Petersen
Rancho Palos Verdes, CA

1	pound Italian sausage, cut in 2" pieces
	Non-stick vegetable oil spray
2	green bell peppers, sliced
1/2	medium red onion, sliced in rings
2	tomatoes, cut in wedges
1/2	cup red wine
1	clove garlic or 1/2 teaspoon garlic powder
1/2	teaspoon dried oregano
1/2	teaspoon dried basil

Saute sausage in large skillet sprayed with vegetable oil spray. Remove sausages. Cook vegetables in drippings from sausages. Drain off excess fat. Add wine, spices and sausages. Simmer, covered, over medium heat for 20 minutes. (4 servings.)

Navarin D'Agneau (Lamb Stew)

Per Curtiss
Santa Monica, CA

4	tablespoons (or less depending on how lean meat is) butter or margarine
6	pounds lamb (shoulder, neck, breast)
1	cup chopped onion (about 1 large onion)
3	tablespoons all-purpose flour
4	cups chicken broth (or water)
	Bouquet garni (parsley, bay leaf and herbs such as thyme or rosemary, tied together or wrapped in cheesecloth)
1	tablespoon chopped garlic
1	tablespoon tomato paste
1	tablespoon salt
1/2	teaspoon freshly ground pepper
3	cups diced carrots
4	cups diced red potatoes
1	pound frozen peas (16 oz.)
1/8	teaspoon dried thyme
2	tablespoons Madeira wine

Optional: In addition to, or in place of, other vegetables: turnips, green beans, zucchini

Melt butter in large heavy skillet over high heat. Brown lamb, stirring frequently. Add chopped onion and flour. Reduce heat; cook and stir until onion is brown. Add broth, bouquet garni, garlic, tomato paste, salt and pepper. Heat to boiling; reduce heat, cover and simmer over low heat, 10 minutes. Add vegetables except the peas and continue to cook, covered, until potatoes and carrots are tender. Add peas and cook 5 minutes. Remove bouquet garni; stir in the thyme and Madeira. Taste and adjust seasoning. (8 servings.)

I first came across this recipe in 1978 at a men's cooking class in Los Angeles.

New Zealand Stuffed Lamb Chops

Ruth Livingood Auld
Claremont, CA

1	cup trimmed, cubed bread
2	tablespoons milk
1	tablespoon butter or margarine, melted
1/4	cup minced onion
1	teaspoon mixed herbs
6	lamb chops, trimmed
6	slices bacon

Combine bread, milk and butter in small bowl. Stir in onion and herbs; mix well. Place 1 heaping tablespoon bread mixture on top of each lamb chop. Wrap bacon around chop and secure with toothpick. Place in greased 9 x 13" pan. Bake at 350°F for 45 minutes. (6 servings.)

My husband, Bill, and I served a Presbyterian Church in New Zealand in 1987-1989. They eat a lot of lamb there. When we were in California, serving several churches there, we came to Ghost Ranch with our children and our high school youth groups to work at the ranch during Spring Break. We have many fond memories of those days.

Poultry

Wild Rice & Piñon Stuffing and Turkey

Yuvonnia K. Owen
Abiquiu Elementary

1	15-18 pound turkey
	Soy sauce (may use Tamari)
1 1/2	cups long grain white rice
1/2	cup wild rice
4	cups water
2-4	tablespoons vegetable oil
1/2	cup shelled piñon
1	cup celery, finely chopped (optional)
2	cups bread, cubed and toasted
	Favorite spices such as basil, tarragon, thyme, savory, oregano
	Do not add sage or salt!

Wash turkey well. Pat dry inside and out. Rub soy sauce lavishly inside and out. Set aside. Bring water to a boil, add rices, stir. Cover tightly and cook on low heat for 30 minutes. Cover bottom of large skillet with oil. Heat; add piñon, watching carefully. As it starts to brown, turn off heat, remove piñon. Add more oil and brown celery until clear. On low heat, add cooked rice, bread, piñon, and spices to taste. Sprinkle whole mixture liberally with soy sauce and stir well. Gently stuff both body cavities. Again rub soy sauce all over outside. Put turkey upside down in a cooking bag. Cook upside down on low heat, 20 minutes per pound, 275°F-300°F. (15 servings.)

This is the all-time Owen family favorite. I read about using soy sauce and rice for stuffing in a newspaper in Boulder in the early seventies. Through the years I kept adding other ingredients. The kids talk about Mom's wild rice stuffing and it's so easy and elegant. Delicious any time of year!

Bay Colony Chicken

Jean Childress
West Barnstable, MA

2	large carrots, sliced
1/2	cup water
1/2	cup butter or margarine, divided
1/4	cup all-purpose flour
1 1/2	cups chicken broth
8	ounces Cheddar cheese, shredded (about 2 cups)
4	cups diced, cooked chicken
1/2	cup peas, cooked
1	cup herbed bread crumbs

Cook carrots in 1/2 cup water in small sauce pan until crisp-tender, about 5 minutes; drain and reserve. Melt 1/4 cup of the butter in the saucepan; stir in flour. Add broth slowly; cook, stirring constantly, until thickened. Stir in cheese. Remove from heat; stir in chicken, peas and reserved carrots. Turn into shallow 2-quart baking dish. Melt remaining 1/4 cup butter; toss with bread crumbs. Spread buttered crumbs over chicken mixture. Bake at 350°F for 30 minutes. (6 servings.)

Russian Chicken

Fran Lother
Chagrin Falls, OH

1	bottle Russian dressing (8 oz.)
1	package dry onion soup mix
1	cup apricot preserves
4 or 5	whole chicken breasts, skinned, boned, split
	Seasoned all-purpose flour (with or without salt)

Mix Russian dressing, soup mix and preserves in medium saucepan. Cook and stir over medium heat until preserves melt, about 2 minutes; reserve. Coat chicken with seasoned flour; place in 9 x 13" baking pan. Pour sauce over chicken. Cover and bake at 350°F for 40 minutes; uncover and continue cooking 15 minutes. (6 to 8 servings.)

Good served with rice pilaf.

Zesty Yucatan Chicken

Don Sanderson
Ames, IA

1/2	teaspoon cornmeal
1/2	teaspoon paprika
1/4	teaspoon salt
1/4	teaspoon garlic powder
1/4	teaspoon ground cumin
1/4	teaspoon dried crushed oregano
1/4	teaspoon ground cayenne pepper
2	whole medium chicken breasts, skinned, boned, split
2	tablespoons lime juice
1	can stewed tomatoes, undrained (16 oz.)
1	can chopped green chilies, drained (4 oz.)
1	clove garlic, minced (or 1/4 tsp. garlic powder)
	Corn tortillas, warmed (optional)
	Fresh lime slices, halved (optional)

Combine cornmeal, paprika, salt, garlic powder, cumin, oregano and cayenne in small bowl or plastic bag; reserve. Arrange chicken in 8 x 8 x 2" microwave-safe baking dish. Sprinkle with lime juice and reserved seasoning mix. Cover with vented microwave-safe plastic wrap. Micro-cook on High (100%) 8 to 10 minutes, until chicken is tender and no longer pink, rearranging once. Combine tomatoes, chilies and garlic in a 4-cup glass measure; microwave on High until hot, 4 to 5 minutes. Serve chicken with tomato sauce, tortillas and lime slices in shallow bowls. (4 servings.)

A Yucatan Peninsula trip inspired Janet Kruse Black of Kailua, Hawaii to mix chicken, lime and local spices which won her a $50 Better Homes and Gardens Test Kitchen prize. Those with sensitive palates may want to cut back on the garlic and/or cayenne pepper.

Chicken Dijon

Paul Stang
San Rafael, CA

5	chicken breast halves, skinned, boned
	Seasoned all-purpose flour (with or without salt)
1	tablespoon margarine or butter
1	tablespoon olive oil
1/2	cup white wine
1	clove garlic, crushed
1/4	teaspoon crushed basil
1	tablespoon half-and-half cream
2	teaspoons Dijon-style mustard

Coat chicken with seasoned flour. Heat margarine and olive oil in large skillet; brown chicken in hot oil over medium-high heat. Add wine, garlic and basil. Heat to boiling; reduce heat; cover and cook until chicken is tender, 5 to 10 minutes. Remove chicken; keep warm. Add cream to skillet. Heat to boiling; cook until liquid is reduced and slightly thickened. Remove from heat; stir in mustard. Serve chicken with mustard cream. (5 servings.)

On a business trip to Akin, SC, I had dinner in a restaurant that served Chicken Dijon. I asked the waiter how this dish was prepared. He told me what was in it and I worked up the proportions.

Chicken Burgundy

Elizabeth Vaught
Hesperus, CO

3	tablespoons butter or margarine
2	medium onions, chopped (about 1 cup)
4	slices bacon, chopped
8	ounces mushrooms, sliced
1	bay leaf
1/8	teaspoon dried thyme
1/8	teaspoon dried oregano
2	cups red wine
1	large whole frying chicken

Heat butter in deep ovenproof skillet or Dutch oven. Cook onions in butter until tender. Stir in bacon, mushrooms, seasonings and wine. Place chicken in center of pan; cover with foil. Bake at 350°F for 1 hour. Remove foil and continue baking until chicken is brown and tender, about 15 minutes. Remove and discard bay leaf; carve chicken and serve with pan juices. (4 to 5 servings.)

Chicken Elegant

Yvonne B. Fairchild
Santa Fe, NM

4	ounces chipped beef
4	whole chicken breasts, boned, split
8	slices bacon
1	can cream of mushroom soup (10 3/4 oz.)
1	cup sour cream (8 oz.)
	Paprika

Line the bottom of a greased 8 x 12" baking dish with the chipped beef. Wrap each chicken half in a slice of bacon; arrange chicken on top of chipped beef. Combine soup and sour cream in small bowl; pour over chicken. Sprinkle with paprika. Bake uncovered at 275°F for 3 hours. (4 servings.)

Orange Chicken

Jean Lovejoy
Lake Havasu City, AZ

1/4	cup all-purpose flour
1/2	teaspoon salt
1/8	teaspoon pepper
1	frying chicken, cut up or 6 breasts or thighs
3	tablespoons vegetable oil
1/3	cup packed dark brown sugar
1/2	teaspoon dried oregano
1/2	teaspoon dried nutmeg
3	ounces frozen orange juice concentrate, thawed (about 1/3 cup)
3	ounces sherry or water (about 1/3 cup)
1/2	medium onion, thinly sliced

Combine flour, salt and pepper. Season chicken with flour mixture. Heat oil in large skillet; brown chicken. Pour off excess fat. Combine remaining ingredients in small bowl; add to chicken. Heat to boiling; reduce heat and simmer, turning chicken often. Cook until tender, about 20 minutes. (4 to 6 servings.)

When my daughter, Helen, worked for Volunteers in Serving America (VISA) in Cushman, Arkansas, she and her colleagues had a very limited budget. Helen made this with locally-raised chicken, offered as gifts to the volunteers. I added the sherry for flavor.

King's Ranch Chicken

Judy Shibley
Ghost Ranch staff

1	package tortilla chips, crushed, divided (8 oz.)
1	chicken, cooked and boned
3/4	cup chopped onion (1 large onion)
1/2	cup chopped green pepper (about 1/2 green pepper)
1	can cream of chicken soup (10 3/4 oz.)
1	can cream of mushroom soup (10 3/4 oz.)
1	can Rotel tomatoes with chilies, chopped, not drained (10 oz.)
1	can green chilies, drained, minced (10 oz.)
1	cup milk
1	teaspoon chili powder
8	ounces Cheddar cheese, shredded (about 2 cups)
	Chopped lettuce
	Diced tomatoes

Place half the chips in a greased 9 x 13" baking dish. Top with half the chicken, most of the remaining chips and then the rest of the chicken. Combine onion, green pepper, soups, tomatoes, chilies, milk and chili powder in a medium bowl. Pour over chicken. Top with the remaining chips. Bake at 350°F for 40 minutes. Remove from oven and sprinkle with cheese. May top with lettuce and tomatoes at serving. (10 to 15 servings.)

editor's note: This recipe, with only slight variations, was also submitted by Carol Mackey, Pampa, TX; Rose Marie Christison, Aurora, CO; Mary Armstrong, Corrales, NM; and Emily Brudos, Albuquerque, NM.

Chicken Enchilada Casserole

Ghost Ranch

2	tablespoons vegetable oil
1/2	cup red chili powder
1	tablespoon flour
3	cups water or chicken stock
	Salt to taste
	Garlic to taste
1	can cream of chicken soup (10 1/2 oz.)
12	corn tortillas
1	cup vegetable oil for frying
1 1/2	cups chicken, diced
1/2	cup onion, diced
1	cup Cheddar cheese, grated

Put vegetable oil in saucepan. Add red chili and water or stock to make your sauce. Add salt, garlic, and soup. Blend well. In separate skillet soften tortillas in vegetable oil. After that is done, place everything in layers, beginning with chili sauce, tortillas, chicken, onion, and cheese, then chili again, until all ingredients are used. Cover with foil and bake in 350°F oven 45 minutes. (8-10 servings.)

Green Chili Chicken Enchilada

Lori Salazar
Ghost Ranch staff
Coyote, NM

1	can cream of chicken soup
1	cup onions, diced (optional)
1	tablespoon garlic, chopped fine (optional)
1	pound green chile
1	dozen corn tortillas
2	cups cheese, grated

Combine soup, onion, and garlic. Bring soup mixture to a boil for about 4 minutes. Fry corn tortillas in oil, turning once on each side. Make sure they are soft. Place 6 tortillas on bottom of pan. Add 1/2 of the soup mixture, sprinkle with cheese, then remaining tortillas, rest of soup, cheese. Bake at 350°F until cheese melts. (4-6 servings.)

Cream of mushroom soup may easily be substituted for chicken soup to make this a vegetarian entree.

Sour Cream Enchiladas

Mary Ashley
Palo Alto, CA

Sauce:

2	cans cream of chicken soup (10 3/4 oz.)
1	cup sour cream
1	cup diced canned green chilies

Filling:

2	cups shredded longhorn or Cheddar cheese (about 8 oz.)
1/2	cup chopped green onions with tender green tops
2 to 3	cups diced cooked chicken or turkey
12	corn tortillas
	Oil to soften tortillas

To make sauce: Combine soup, sour cream and chilies in medium bowl; reserve. To make filling: Combine cheese, onions and chicken or turkey in medium bowl. Soften tortillas in hot oil in small skillet; drain. Spoon sauce and filling on each tortilla; roll up. Place tortillas, seam-side down, in greased 9 x 13" baking dish. Pour remaining sauce on top. Bake at 350°F until bubbly, 20 to 30 minutes. (6 servings.)

My geologist husband brought this recipe home after a field season in Tucson, AZ. It is the #1 leftover Thanksgiving turkey recipe. Not exactly low fat or low calorie, but you can substitute sour half-and-half or imitation sour cream and soften the tortillas in the microwave without oil.

Pastel de Montezuma

Freda Elliott
Santa Fe, NM

Green Sauce:

1	pound tomatillos, skins and stems removed*
1	small onion
5	cloves garlic
1	can green chilies (4 oz.)
1	small bunch fresh cilantro, stems removed
1	teaspoon salt

Casserole:

6	cups boned, cooked turkey, cut in bite-size pieces (1/2 x 1")
2	cups plain yogurt (low-fat or non-fat)
12	corn tortillas, cut in 1/2" pieces (blue corn tortillas preferred)
3 to 4	cups shredded Monterey Jack cheese (12 to 16 oz.)

Place ingredients for green sauce in blender; cover and blend until smooth. Arrange half the turkey in a greased 9 x 13" baking dish. Pour half the green sauce over the turkey. Spoon half the yogurt over the green sauce; top with half the corn tortillas and half the cheese. Repeat layers, ending with cheese. Bake covered at 375°F for 40 minutes; uncover and bake until bubbly, about 8 minutes. (10 to 14 servings.)

* Tomatillos are available fresh in the produce department of some supermarkets or in Mexican specialty stores.

Deep Fried Chicken Tacos

Marcela Coronado
Medanales, NM

1	whole chicken

Sopapillas:

1	package active dry yeast
1/4	cup warm water (105-115°F)
1 1/2	cups milk
3	tablespoons lard or vegetable shortening
2	tablespoons sugar
1	teaspoon salt
1	cup whole wheat flour
4	cups all-purpose flour
	Vegetable shortening for frying (Butter-flavored Crisco preferred), heated
1	head lettuce, chopped
3	tomatoes, diced
1/2	cup minced fresh cilantro
1/2	onion, minced (about 1/4 cup)
	Salsa, Sour Cream, Honey

Boil chicken until very tender. Drain and shred; reserve.

To make sopapillas: Mix yeast and water in small bowl; let stand until bubbly. Combine milk, lard, sugar and salt in large pot; heat just to lukewarm; stir in yeast mixture. Stir in whole wheat and all-purpose flour, one cup at a time. Turn onto floured surface. Knead until smooth; let stand 5 minutes. Roll out dough on lightly-floured board into 6 to 7" circles. Fill with shredded chicken. Pinch closed as for a fruit turnover. Heat shortening to 365°F. Deep fry sopapillas until light golden brown. Remove to paper toweling. Open and fill with lettuce, tomatoes and cheese. Serve with salsa, sour cream and honey. Best served warm. (14 servings.)

Chicken Broccoli Casserole

Mary E. King
Great Bend, KS

1	bunch or 1 package frozen broccoli, cut, cooked, drained (10 oz.)
1/2	chicken, baked or boiled, cut in bite-size pieces (about 2 cups)
1	can cream of chicken soup (10 3/4 oz.)
1/2	cup sour cream
1/2	cup mayonnaise
1	tablespoon lemon juice
1	cup shredded Cheddar cheese
1/2	cup buttered bread crumbs

Place broccoli in 8 x 8" baking pan. Top with chicken. Combine soup, sour cream, mayonnaise and lemon juice in small bowl; pour over chicken and broccoli. Sprinkle with cheese; top with bread crumbs. Bake at 350°F until bubbly, 35 to 40 minutes. (4 servings.)

Chicken Macaroni

Dee Cameron
El Paso, TX

1	cup uncooked macaroni, cooked, drained (about 2 1/4 cups cooked)
5	tablespoons margarine or butter, divided
2	slices bread, trimmed, torn into crumbs
3	tablespoons all-purpose flour
1	can chicken broth (10 1/2 oz.)
1/2	cup milk (low-fat milk preferred)
1	cup (or more) cooked chicken, cut in bite-size pieces

Prepare macaroni; reserve. Melt 2 tablespoons of the margarine in a medium pan or large skillet. Toss with bread crumbs; remove and reserve. Melt remaining 3 tablespoons margarine in the pan. Stir in the flour; cook and stir 2 minutes (do not brown). Slowly add chicken broth and milk. Cook, stirring constantly, until thickened. Stir in chicken and drained macaroni. Pour into greased casserole. Top with reserved crumb mixture. Bake at 350°F for 45 minutes. (3 to 4 servings.)

This recipe was adapted from From Amish and Mennonite Kitchens by Phyllis Pellman Good and Rachel Thomas Pellman. When I asked my family to suggest a favorite recipe for the Ghost Ranch Cookbook, this was the answer!

Chicken Seville

Pat Waltermire
Plaza Resolana

2	tablespoons olive oil
1	frying chicken, cut up
2	cloves garlic, chopped
1	cup uncooked rice
1	cup dry white wine
1	tablespoon butter or margarine
8	ounces uncooked mushrooms, sliced
1	cup small white onions (fresh or frozen)
1	cup stuffed green olives
2	cups chicken broth
1/2	teaspoon salt
1/4	teaspoon dried oregano
1/2	cup sliced almonds

Heat olive oil in large skillet. Brown chicken in hot oil; remove and reserve. Add garlic and rice to drippings. Stir wine into rice. Spoon rice mixture into a large, flat baking dish. Add butter to skillet. Heat butter; add mushrooms and cook until brown. Scatter mushrooms, onions and olives over rice in the baking dish. Place chicken on top. Mix salt and chicken broth; pour over chicken. Sprinkle with oregano. Bake at 375°F until chicken is tender, 1 to 1 1/2 hours. Remove from oven and sprinkle with sliced almonds. (8 to 10 servings.)

This recipe was a regular for work parties building the preschool at the Church of the Mountains Presbyterian Church on the Hupa Indian Reservation along the Trinity River in Northern California.

Oven-Baked Dijon Chicken

Anne Hunt
Hawthorn Woods, IL

	Non-stick vegetable oil spray
1/2	cup dry bread crumbs
1/4	cup grated Parmesan cheese
1/4	cup sesame seeds
3	whole chicken breasts, boned, skinned, split
1/2	cup Dijon-style mustard
	Lemon wedges

Spray baking sheet with vegetable oil spray. Combine bread crumbs, cheese and sesame seeds in broad shallow dish. Coat chicken with mustard; roll in crumb mixture. Place chicken on baking sheet. Bake at 475°F on bottom rack of oven 5 minutes; turn and continue baking until light brown, 5 to 6 minutes. Serve with lemon wedges. (6 servings.)

Chicken Paella

Jan and Wil Hufton
Saginaw, MI

1/4	cup olive oil
1	chicken, cut in small serving pieces (3 lbs.)
1	large onion, chopped (about 3/4 cup)
1	green bell pepper, seeded, cut into strips
1	clove garlic, minced
2	tomatoes, chopped
2	tablespoons tomato paste
1	bay leaf
1	teaspoon dried thyme
1	teaspoon paprika
2	cups uncooked rice
3 1/2	cups chicken broth
1/2	cup dry white wine
	Salt and fresh ground pepper

Heat olive oil in 3-quart paella pan or ovenproof casserole. Cook chicken in hot oil over medium-high heat until golden; remove and reserve. Cook onion, green bell pepper and garlic in drippings until onion is transparent. Add tomatoes, tomato paste, bay leaf, thyme and paprika. Cook over medium heat 10 minutes, stirring frequently. Stir in rice. Heat broth and wine to boiling in medium saucepan; add to rice. Cook over moderate heat, stirring occasionally, 5 to 6 minutes. Season with salt and pepper. Arrange chicken pieces over rice. Cover and bake at 325°F until liquid is absorbed and chicken is done, 20 to 25 minutes. Remove and discard bay leaf before serving. (4 to 6 servings.)

Mexican Chicken, Country Style

Flossie H. Moorhead
Lincoln, NE

1	whole chicken, cut up
1/3	cup all-purpose flour, seasoned with salt, pepper, paprika
	Oil for frying
4	strips bacon, cut in small pieces
2 or 3	cups sliced carrots
1	can diced green chilies, drained (4 oz.)
1	tablespoon chopped fresh parsley (2 tsp. dried parsley flakes)
1	small bay leaf
1	small sprig fresh thyme (1/8 tsp. dried thyme)
1	lemon (or lime), sliced
2	cups tomato juice
	Cooked rice

Coat chicken with seasoned flour. Heat oil in large skillet; cook chicken in hot oil until golden brown. Remove chicken to a 2 to 3-quart casserole or baking dish. Layer bacon, carrots, chilies, parsley, bay leaf and thyme over chicken. Sprinkle with any remaining seasoned flour. Place lemon slices on top of chicken; cover with tomato juice. Cover and bake at 350°F until chicken is tender, about 1 hour. Remove and discard bay leaf before serving. Serve with rice. (6 to 8 servings.)

After living in Oklahoma, we moved East. We missed the Mexican food. I found this recipe in a magazine and it has been a family favorite since. While it is not like the Mexican food we had eaten in Oklahoma, it has become our Mexican company dish.

Oven-Barbecued Chicken

Jean Vieten
Redlands, CA

2	broiler-fryer chickens, cut in pieces (or 6 breasts)
1	onion, sliced
2/3	cup ketchup
1/3	cup vinegar
1	clove garlic, minced
1	teaspoon crushed dried rosemary
1	teaspoon salt
1/4	teaspoon dry mustard
4	tablespoons butter or margarine

Place chicken, skin-side down, in greased baking pan, 9 x 13" or larger. Top with onion slices. Combine remaining ingredients in small sauce-pan; heat to boiling. Pour over chicken. Bake at 400°F for 30 minutes; turn, baste and continue baking until done, 20 to 30 minutes more. (4 to 6 servings.)

Wonderful Chicken Salad

Helen Thoming
Sun City, AZ

1	quart cooked chicken, cut in bite-size pieces (4 cups)
1	can water chestnuts, drained, halved (8 oz.)
1	pound seedless green grapes, halved
1/2	cup diced celery
1/3	cup slivered almonds, slivered, divided
1 1/2	cups mayonnaise
1	tablespoon curry powder
1	tablespoon soy sauce
1	tablespoon lemon juice
	Crisp lettuce leaves

Combine chicken with water chestnuts, grapes and celery and half the almonds in large bowl. Combine mayonnaise, curry powder, soy sauce and lemon juice in small bowl; stir into chicken mixture. Cover and refrigerate several hours. Serve on lettuce leaves, topped with remaining almonds. (8 servings.)

This recipe was also submitted by Jane Higby of Indianapolis, IN. Jane garnishes hers with fresh pineapple spears.

Chicken Salad

Ruth G. Calhoun
Austin, TX

1	chicken, cooked and boned
1	head lettuce, chopped
4	green onions with tender green tops, chopped
1	teaspoon butter
1/4	cup sliced almonds
2	tablespoons sesame seeds
1/4	cup vinegar
1/4	cup oil
1	tablespoon sugar
2	teaspoons salt
1/4	teaspoon black pepper
1/8	teaspoon cayenne pepper

Combine chicken, lettuce and green onions in large bowl. Heat butter in small skillet. Cook almonds and sesame seeds in skillet over medium heat, stirring frequently and watching closely, until light brown; add to chicken mixture. Combine remaining ingredients in small bowl; pour over chicken mixture. (10 to 12 servings.)

Green Chile Stew

Felipe Ortega and Jason Leidy
La Madera, NM

1/2	pound chicken breasts or other lean meat
1/4	cup hot or mild green chile
1	quart water
	Garlic
	Fresh parsley
	Basil
	Fresh sliced garden vegetables such as onion, carrots, squash, corn, tomatoes (according to season)
	Salt to taste

Boil chicken and chile in water, then turn down to a simmer. Add garlic, parsley, and basil. Simmer four hours; add fresh vegetables and simmer for another half-hour. (4 servings.)

editor's note: Felipe Ortega teaches a Jicarilla Apache micaceous pottery seminar at Ghost Ranch during the summer. Using these next few recipes, he prepares lunch for his students in a mica pot.

Red Chile Stew

Felipe Ortega and Jason Leidy
La Madera, NM

1	pound deboned chicken breast or other lean meat
1	onion, diced
	Garlic to taste
	Oregano to taste
2	tablespoons powdered red chili (hot or mild)
1	quart water or chicken broth
	Tomatoes, diced
	Green beans
	Corn
	Mushrooms

Brown meat, add onion and continue to saute. Add garlic, oregano, and red chili powder. Add water, simmer for 2 hours. Add tomatoes, green beans, corn, and mushrooms. Simmer for another half hour. (4 servings.)

Red Chile, Indian Style

Felipe Ortega and Jason Leidy
La Madera, NM

2	pounds deboned chicken breast
1	onion, chopped
3	cloves garlic, chopped
3	tablespoons red chili (hot or mild)
1 1/2	quarts water or chicken broth
3	tablespoons blue corn atole mix (or some whole wheat flour)
	Cold water

Brown chicken, saute onion and garlic. Add red chili and water. Bring to a boil, reduce heat and simmer for 2 hours. 15 minutes before serving, mix atole or flour with enough cold water to make a paste. Add paste to the chicken mixture for the world's best-tasting chili.

Atole mix is blue cornmeal available in the Southwest and in gourmet shops elsewhere.

Garbanzo Stew

Felipe Ortega and Jason Leidy
La Madera, NM

1	cup dried garbanzo beans
1/2	chicken, cut up
	Mushrooms to taste
	Onion, diced, to taste
	Garlic
	Basil (not too much)
1 1/2	quarts water
	Cayenne pepper

Soak garbanzo beans in water overnight. Drain. Mix garbanzos, mushrooms, onion, garlic, basil, water, and chicken. Bring to boil, then reduce heat and simmer for 4 hours or until garbanzos are tender. Add pepper for flavor. (4 servings.)

Atole and Chicken or Rabbit

Felipe Ortega and Jason Leidy
La Madera, NM

1/2	chicken or rabbit
2	quarts water
1	tablespoon red chili (or 1/4 teaspoon cayenne pepper)
1/2	cup atole, thoroughly mixed with 1 cup cold water

Place meat in stewpot, add water, red chile or pepper. Boil, then reduce to simmer for 4 hours. Add atole/water mixture, continue to simmer for 30 minutes more. (4 servings.)

Blue Corn Posole

Felipe Ortega and Jason Leidy
La Madera, NM

12	ounces blue corn posole, dried
1	onion, diced
5	cloves garlic, sliced
2	quarts chicken broth
	Enough mushrooms
3	chicken breasts or lean meat

Mix posole, onion, garlic, chicken broth, and mushrooms. Bring to a boil; reduce heat to simmer 4 hours. During the fourth hour add meat; simmer for 2 more hours. (4 servings.)

Seafood

Almond-Stuffed Fish Fillets with Tarragon Sauce

Frances Trujillo
Plaza Resolana staff

1/4	cup shredded Swiss cheese (1 oz.)
2	tablespoons chopped almonds
1	tablespoon chopped chives
1	tablespoon margarine or butter, at room temperature
2	fillets flounder or sole (8 oz. total)
	Paprika
3	tablespoons dry white wine
3	ounces uncooked fettuccine or linguine, cooked, drained

Creamy Tarragon Sauce:

1	tablespoon margarine or butter
1/4	cup shredded carrot
2	tablespoons all-purpose flour
1/4	teaspoon salt
1/8	teaspoon white pepper
1/8	teaspoon dried, crushed tarragon
1/2	cup milk
1/4	cup shredded Swiss cheese (1 oz.)
1	tablespoon dry white wine

Combine Swiss cheese, almonds, chives and margarine in small bowl. Spoon half of the mixture onto one end of each piece of fish. Roll fish around stuffing. Place fish, seam-side down in small baking dish. Sprinkle with paprika. Pour 3 tablespoons wine into dish. Bake, uncovered at 375°F until fish flakes with fork, about 15 minutes. Place rolls on warm pasta on plate. Serve with creamy tarragon sauce. (2 servings.)

To make tarragon sauce: Melt margarine in small saucepan or skillet; add carrot. Cook 3 to 4 minutes. Stir in flour, salt, pepper and tarragon. Add milk; cook and stir until thickened and bubbly. Stir in 1/4 cup shredded Swiss cheese and 1 tablespoon dry white wine.

Mexican Snapper

Ghost Ranch

1 1/2-2 pounds red snapper
1   can tomato sauce (12 oz.)
1   can green chile (4 oz.)
1   onion, chopped
1   can stewed tomatoes (16 oz.)
1   clove garlic

Combine onion with tomato sauce, green chile and tomatoes. Heat.
Poach red snapper in sauce until done, about 20 minutes at 350°.

Sole Dijon

Benton Rhoades
Claremont, CA

1   pound fish fillet (sole, turbot, walleye), rinsed and dried
3   tablespoons mayonnaise
3   tablespoons Dijon-style mustard (Grey Poupon preferred)
3   tablespoons grated Swiss cheese

Arrange fish in shallow greased baking dish. Mix mayonnaise, mustard
and cheese in small bowl; spread on fish. Bake, uncovered at 350°F until
fish flakes with fork, 12 to 15 minutes. Brown under broiler, 1 to 2
minutes. (2-4 servings.)

A restaurant owner in Illinois refused to give me this recipe, saying this was a
"house secret." Later, after being my house guest in New York, he sent it to me
in a thank-you note. editor's note: Benton and his wife, Doris, are two of the
people who helped the Farm to Market project become a reality at Ghost Ranch.
Thanks Benton and Doris!

Baked Fish Mediterranean

Catherine Bremer
Sausalito, CA

2	cups coarsely chopped tomatoes (cherry tomatoes or 2 to 3 medium tomatoes)
2	green onions with tender green tops, cut up
2	cloves garlic
2	tablespoons soybean oil
2	teaspoons tamari sauce
1	teaspoon dried basil
2	pounds fish fillets (cod, flounder, haddock)

Place tomatoes, green onions, garlic, oil, tamari and basil in blender. Cover and process on low, then on medium speed until smooth. Place fish fillets in a thick layer on the bottom of an 8 x 8" casserole dish. Pour tomato mixture over fish. Bake, uncovered, at 375°F until fish flakes with fork, about 30 minutes. (4 servings.)

Grilled Tuna with Mango Salsa

Kimberly Sweet
Plaza Resolana staff

6	tuna or marlin steaks (6 oz. each)

Marinade:

1	cup olive oil
2	tablespoons chili caribe (or minced hot peppers or hot salsa)
1	lemon, sliced
1	lime, sliced
10	sprigs fresh thyme
3	cloves garlic, slivered
1/8	teaspoon salt

Black Beans:

1	cup black beans, washed, sorted
3	cups water
2	chicken bouillon cubes
1	tablespoon chili caribe

Orange Vinaigrette:
1   tablespoon Dijon-style mustard
1/2   teaspoon seeded, finely chopped serrano chilies
         Zest of 2 oranges, finely chopped
1/3   cup balsamic vinegar
1 1/2   cups olive oil
         Salt and pepper

Rajas:
2   red bell peppers
2   green bell peppers

Salad:
1/2   head red leaf lettuce
1/2   head radicchio
1   bunch arugula
1/2   head endive
1   bunch cilantro
1   bunch watercress

Mango Salsa:
3   large ripe mangoes, peeled, seeded, diced
6   tablespoons diced red and yellow bell peppers
1 1/2   tablespoons seeded, minced serrano chilies
4   tablespoons chopped cilantro (1/4 cup)
         Juice of 3 limes (about 1/2 cup)
         Sugar and/or salt, if needed

Combine all ingredients for marinade in small bowl. Pour over fish in a large, non-metallic container; cover and refrigerate at least 4 hours or overnight.

Cook black beans with 3 cups water, bouillon cubes and 1 tablespoon chili caribe in large heavy pot over medium heat until beans are tender, about 1 1/2 hours; drain. To make vinaigrette, combine mustard, 1/2 teaspoon chopped serrano chilies, orange zest and vinegar in small bowl; slowly whisk in oil. Season with salt and pepper. Mix 1 cup of the vinaigrette with drained beans; cover and refrigerate overnight. Cover and refrigerate remaining vinaigrette.

Sear peppers for Rajas over medium heat until blistered and black; remove from heat, place in a bowl and cover with plastic. Let stand 20 minutes; remove skins. Reserve. To make Mango Salsa, combine mangoes, red and yellow peppers, 1 1/2 tablespoons serrano chilies, the cilantro and lime juice. Taste and correct seasoning with sugar and/or salt, if necessary. Let stand at least 1 hour.

To serve, combine salad greens, torn in bite-size pieces; toss with reserved orange vinaigrette. Arrange dressed salad greens and marinated black beans to cover 6 serving plates. Remove fish from marinade; grill over medium heat, 1 1/2 to 2 minutes on each side, depending on thickness of fish. Place fish, either whole or cut into pieces in the center of the prepared plates. Top with Mango Salsa. Cut Rajas into strips and arrange decoratively around the perimeter of the plate. (6 servings.)

Chipolte Shrimp with Corn Cakes and Black Bean Salsa

Kimberly Sweet
Plaza Resolana staff

Black Bean Salsa:

1 1/2	cups black beans
1	quart water
3	chicken bouillon cubes
2	cloves garlic, mashed
1	tablespoon chili caribe (or minced hot peppers or hot salsa)
2	tomatoes, chopped
1/2	cup chopped cilantro
1/4	cup finely chopped red onion
1/2	cup finely chopped, seeded serrano chilies
1/4	cup olive oil
	Juice of 3 to 4 limes (about 1/2 cup)
	Salt and pepper

Corn Cakes:

1	cup all-purpose flour
3/4	cup polenta (Italian-style yellow corn grits; can substitute yellow corn meal)
2	teaspoons sugar
1	teaspoon salt
1/2	teaspoon baking powder
1/2	teaspoon baking soda
1 1/2	cups buttermilk
3	tablespoons butter, melted
2	eggs, beaten
1 1/2	cups corn, fresh or frozen
3	green onions with tender green tops, chopped

Chipolte Butter and Shrimp:
2   cups butter, at room temperature (1 lb.)
1 to 2   tablespoons chipotle (to taste)*
3   green onions with tender green tops, chopped
           Salt and/or sugar, if necessary
1 1/2- 2 pounds large shrimp, peeled, deveined
           Cilantro
           Lime wedges

Cook beans with water, bouillon, garlic and chili caribe in large pot until beans are tender, 1 1/2 to 2 hours. Drain and rinse with cold water; combine with remaining ingredients. Reserve.

To make corn cakes: Combine dry ingredients in large bowl; whisk in buttermilk, butter and eggs. Puree half the corn in blender or food processor; add to batter with remaining corn and green onions. Cook on hot greased skillet or griddle over medium heat until done, turning once. Reserve. (Makes 18 to 20 corn cakes, 2 1/2" in diameter.)

To make chipolte butter, combine butter with chipotle; add sugar and/or salt, if necessary to balance flavor. Grill shrimp over medium heat with a little chipotle butter. To serve, place 3 corn cakes on plate; top with shrimp and a dollup of Chipotle Butter and chopped green onions. Place a serving of black beans on plate. Garnish with cilantro and lime wedges. (6 servings.)

*Note: The chipotle pepper is a large, dried, smoked jalapeño, made from fresh huachinango. Chipotle chilies are available canned in a red adobo sauce. They are moderately hot.

I used to be a chef in one of Santa Fe's restaurants and have adapted these recipes for my own use.

Seafood Lasagna

Jean and Bill Jones
Dallas, TX

1	tablespoon butter or margarine
8	ounces mushrooms, sliced (about 2 cups)
1/2	cup chopped onion (about 1 medium onion)
1/2	pound scallops
1	pound shrimp, cooked, shelled, deveined
2	cans cream of mushroom soup, divided (10 3/4 oz. each)
1	cup cottage cheese (8 oz.)
1	package cream cheese, at room temperature (8 oz.)
1	package lasagna, cooked, drained (9 to 12 noodles)
1	cup sour cream (8 oz.)
3/4	cup shredded Cheddar or mozzarella cheese (about 3 oz.)

Heat butter in large skillet. Saute mushrooms and onion in hot skillet until tender; add scallops. Cook and stir 2 minutes. Remove skillet from heat. Stir in shrimp and 1 can of the mushroom soup. Reserve. Combine cottage cheese and cream cheese in small bowl. Layer 3 or 4 noodles in bottom of greased 9 x 12" baking dish. Spread some of the seafood mixture on the noodles, then some of the cheese mixture. Repeat until all mixtures and noodles have been used. Combine remaining mushroom soup and the sour cream in small bowl; spread on top of seafood and noodle layers; sprinkle with Cheddar or mozzarella cheese. Bake at 350°F for 30 to 40 minutes. Let stand 10 minutes before serving. (8 servings.)

Protest Halibut Loaf

Bruce and Anne Hunt
Hawthorn Woods, IL

Fish Loaf:

1	pound boned, uncooked halibut
1	teaspoon salt
1/2	teaspoon celery salt
2	cups soft white bread crumbs
1	cup evaporated skim milk
4	egg whites, stiffly beaten

Shrimp Sauce:

3	tablespoons butter or margarine
3	tablespoons all-purpose flour
1/2	teaspoon salt
1/4	teaspoon pepper
1	cup whole or reduced-fat milk
1/2	cup evaporated skim milk
1	cup small frozen cooked shrimp, thawed
1/8	teaspoon cayenne pepper or few drops Tabasco

To make fish loaf: Grind fish in food processor (or chop finely with a knife); add salt and celery salt. Put fish mixture in large bowl. Puree bread crumbs and 1 cup evaporated skim milk in processor (or mix to make a smooth paste). Combine bread mixture with fish mixture. Fold in beaten egg whites. Spoon into a 9 x 5" loaf pan, lined with greased waxed paper. Bake in a water bath (shallow pan of water) in 350°F oven until firm, about 45 minutes. Turn onto a platter and remove waxed paper. Serve with shrimp sauce. (8 servings.)

To make shrimp sauce: Melt butter, add flour and seasonings; cook and stir 3 minutes. Slowly add whole milk and 1/2 cup evaporated milk. Cook over low heat, stirring constantly until thickened. Add shrimp; heat but do not boil. (May be doubled.)

Eating lobster was always a high point of our yearly treks to visit family in New England. (Until last year, Bruce was the only member of his family ever to move more than 30 miles from Boston since they landed there in 1640.) One summer, we arrived and his mother announced, "No lobster! They want $5.00 a pound, and I'm not paying it." It was clearly a matter of principle. Instead, we were served this delicious, thrifty Halibut loaf.

Chili Shrimp

Pomona Hallenbeck
Abiquiu, NM

2	packages Oriental-flavored ramen noodles, divided
2	tablespoons olive oil
1/4	medium onion, chopped (about 2 tablespoons)
1	clove garlic, minced
2	tablespoons chili powder
1	teaspoon white pepper
1/4	teaspoon salt
1	pound shrimp, boiled, shelled, deveined

Set aside seasoning packet from noodles; cook noodles as directed. Reserve noodles. Heat olive oil in large skillet. Saute onion and garlic 2 to 3 minutes in hot oil. Add seasoning packet from ramen noodles, chili powder, pepper and salt. Stir in shrimp and cooked noodles; heat through. (4 servings.)

Clam Spaghetti

Pomona Hallenbeck
Abiquiu, NM

3	tablespoons butter or margarine
1/2	medium onion, chopped (about 1/4 cup)
1	clove garlic, chopped
2	cans chopped clams, undrained
2	cans cream of mushroom soup (10 3/4 oz. each)
1	soup can water
1	tablespoon salt substitute such as Spike or Mrs. Dash
1	package spaghetti, cooked, drained (16 oz.)

Heat butter in large skillet or saucepan. Cook onion and garlic in butter until tender. Add remaining ingredients except the spaghetti. Heat to boiling; reduce heat. Simmer uncovered over low heat 20 minutes. Serve sauce over hot, cooked spaghetti. (4 servings.)

Shrimp Egg Rolls

Nancy Evans
Columbia, MO

1/2	pound ground pork
1	small onion, chopped (about 1/4 cup)
1	clove garlic, minced
1	cup finely chopped mushrooms
1	can water chestnuts, drained, finely chopped (8 oz.)
1	cup fresh bean sprouts
1	cup chopped celery
1	cup finely shredded cabbage
1	can shrimp, drained (8 oz.)
3	tablespoons soy sauce
1/2	teaspoon hoisin sauce (available in Oriental section of food store)
2	packages egg roll wrappers
1	egg, beaten
	Vegetable oil for frying

Sweet and Sour Sauce:

1/2	cup sugar
2	tablespoons cornstarch
1/2	cup pineapple juice
1/4	cup rice vinegar (or white vinegar)
3	tablespoons ketchup
2	tablespoons soy sauce
2	tablespoons sherry

Saute pork, onion and garlic until pork is done. Add vegetables; cook and stir 2 minutes. Stir in shrimp, soy sauce and hoisin sauce. Place 1/4 cup mixture on each egg roll wrapper. Fold wrapper like envelope, using beaten egg to hold together. Fry in deep oil (1 1/2 to 2" deep), heated to 375°F until light brown. Drain on newspaper covered with paper toweling. Serve with rice and sweet and sour sauce. (6 servings.)

Sweet and Sour Sauce: Mix sugar and cornstarch in small saucepan. Add remaining ingredients. Heat to boiling over medium heat, stirring constantly, until thick and smooth.

Crab Casserole

Rodney T. Martin
Louisville, KY

1	package herb-seasoned stuffing mix, Pepperidge Farm preferred (14 oz.)
1/2	cup margarine or butter, melted (1 stick)
2	pounds yellow squash, sliced, cooked, drained, mashed
1	can cream of chicken soup (10 3/4 oz.)
1	jar pimiento (2 oz.)
3	large carrots, grated
1	medium onion, grated or finely chopped
1	cup sour cream (8 oz.)
2	cups crab meat
1	cup sharp Cheddar cheese, shredded (4 oz.)

Combine stuffing mix and margarine in large bowl. Stir in squash, soup, pimiento, carrots, onion and sour cream. Add crab meat; spoon into greased 2-quart casserole. Top with cheese. Bake at 350°F for 30 minutes. Carrots will be a little crunchy — like nuts. (6 servings.)

Vegetarian Entrees

Brown Rice and Tofu

Anne Hunt
Hawthorn Woods, IL

4 1/2	cups water
2	cups brown rice, uncooked
2	tablespoons margarine or butter
1	pound firm tofu, drained, cubed
1/2	pound fresh mushrooms, sliced (about 2 cups)
1	cup shredded carrots
1	bunch green onions with tender green tops, sliced
1/2	cup reduced salt soy sauce
1/4	cup chopped fresh parsley

Heat water to boiling in large pan. Meanwhile, cook rice in large non-stick skillet over medium heat, stirring constantly, until rice is lightly toasted. Stir rice into boiling water; heat to boiling. Reduce heat, cover and cook over low heat until liquid is absorbed, 45 to 50 minutes. Turn off heat and let rice stand, covered, 15 minutes. Heat margarine in the skillet. Add tofu, mushrooms, carrots and onions. Saute until tofu is hot and onions are soft, about 5 minutes. Stir soy sauce and then tofu mixture into rice. Garnish with chopped parsley. (8 to 10 servings.)

Tofu Manicotti

Paul Ryer
Ghost Ranch volunteer

2	pounds tofu
1/2	cup olive oil
2	tablespoons lemon juice
1	tablespoon honey or sugar
2	teaspoons salt
3/4	teaspoon garlic powder
1	cup onion, chopped
1	package frozen chopped spinach, thawed and drained
6	cups spaghetti sauce
1	package manicotti noodles, cooked, drained (18 oz.)

For manicotti filling, mash tofu, mix in 1/4 cup oil, lemon, honey, salt, and garlic. Set aside. Saute onions in remaining oil, add spinach. Pour 2 cups spaghetti sauce over 9 x 13 "pan. Carefully fill noodles with 1/3 to 1/2cup filling, place in pan in rows. Cover with remaining sauce. Bake 30 minutes at 350°F. (8-10 servings.)

Tofu Stroganoff

Doreen Baca
Ghost Ranch staff
Ojo Caliente

1 1/2	pounds firm tofu, drained
1/4	cup butter, melted
2	medium onions, chopped
1/2	pound mushrooms, sliced
1	teaspoon salt
1/2	teaspoon pepper
4	tablespoons chives
2	teaspoons garlic powder
1	cup sour cream or sour cream substitute
1/2	cup soy sauce

Slice tofu in small squares, fry in butter until golden-brown. Add more butter if needed. Add mushrooms and onions on low flame, saute until tender. Add salt, pepper, chives, and garlic powder. Drain excess water. Add sour cream and soy sauce to tofu mix. Simmer, covered, for 5 minutes. Serve over noodles or rice. (10-12 servings.)

Hominy Casserole

Ghost Ranch

1	can hominy , drained (29 oz.)
1	bell pepper, chopped
1	onion, chopped
1/4	cup margarine
3	tablespoons flour
1 1/2	cups milk
1	can green chilies, chopped (4 oz.)
1/2	cup pimento, chopped
	Garlic salt
1/2	pound longhorn cheese, cubed

Saute green peppers and onions in margarine. Remove vegetables, set aside. Add flour and milk to melted margarine, cook over medium heat until thickened. Add green chilies, pimento, and garlic salt. Pour mixture over hominy in a greased 9 x 13" casserole. Sprinkle cheese over all. Bake about 30 minutes at 350°F. (Serves 6-8.)

Donna's Monterey Sunday Supper

Betty Jean G. Young
San Rafael, CA

8	ounces Monterey Jack cheese, divided
3 to 4	cups cooked rice (1 cup uncooked)
1	can chopped green chilies, drained (4 oz.)
3	medium zucchini, sliced, steamed or parboiled, but still firm
1	large tomato, sliced
1	cup sour cream (8 oz.)
2	tablespoons chopped green bell pepper
2	tablespoons chopped onion
1	teaspoon garlic powder
1	teaspoon dried oregano
1	tablespoon chopped fresh parsley

Cut 6 ounces of the cheese into strips; shred the remaining cheese and reserve it for topping. Layer rice, cheese strips, green chilies, zucchini and tomato in a 9 x 12" greased baking dish. Mix sour cream, green pepper, onion, garlic powder and oregano in small bowl; pour over rice and vegetable layers. Sprinkle reserved cheese and parsley on top. Bake at 350°F for 30 minutes. (6 servings.)

Note: A variation of this recipe was submitted by Kay Kipp of Sacramento, CA. Kay adds another cup of sour cream.

In the '70s, I helped start a food co-op. We got together enough simple meatless recipes for a small cookbook, typed in one of the member's homes. This was our family's favorite of those recipes.

Zucchini Casserole

Carolyn Jones
Exeter, CA

4 or 5	cups thinly sliced zucchini, parboiled
4	ounces shredded Cheddar cheese (about 1 cup)
1	can chopped green chilies, drained (4 oz.)
2	eggs
3/4	cup buttermilk baking mix (Bisquick)
1 1/2	cups milk

Layer half of the zucchini in bottom of greased 1 1/2-quart casserole. Sprinkle with half the peppers and half of the cheese; repeat layers. Beat eggs in small bowl; add baking mix and milk. Pour batter over layered vegetables and cheese. Bake covered at 350°F for 30 minutes. Uncover and continue baking until crusty and brown on top, about 30 more minutes. (6 servings.)

From the Wilson Jr. High School Cook Book, published by the classes of 1978-1979.

Zucchini Lasagna

Ghost Ranch

4	cups meatless spaghetti sauce
1	teaspoon each: salt, dried basil, dried oregano, dried rosemary
3	cups small-curd cottage cheese (1 lb. 8 oz.)
1	cup sour cream (8 oz.)
12	lasagna noodles, cooked, drained
2 1/2	pounds zucchini, thinly sliced
2	cups shredded longhorn cheese (8 oz.)

Combine spaghetti sauce, salt and herbs in medium bowl; reserve. Combine cottage cheese and sour cream in medium bowl; reserve. Spray a 9 x 12" baking pan with non-stick vegetable oil spray. Spoon a layer of spaghetti sauce over the bottom of the pan. Layer noodles, cottage cheese mixture, cheese, and zucchini. Repeat layers, setting aside 1/2 cup cheese. Bake at 350°F for 45 minutes; add reserved cheese, and bake for 15 minutes more. Let cool slightly before serving. (8-10 servings.)

Vegetarian Lasagna

Patsy Ornales
Plaza Resolana staff

2	tablespoons olive oil
2	cups sliced zucchini or broccoli
1/2	cup chopped onion (1 medium onion)
1	jar or 3 1/4 cups homemade meatless spaghetti sauce (26 oz.)
2	teaspoons dried oregano
16	ounces low-fat ricotta cheese, drained (4 cups)
2	eggs, beaten
1/4	cup grated Parmesan cheese
8	ounces lasagna noodles, cooked, drained
3	cups shredded mozzarella cheese (12 oz.)

Heat oil in large skillet. Add zucchini or broccoli and onion; cook over medium heat, stirring frequently, until vegetables are tender. Stir in spaghetti sauce and oregano; continue cooking 10 minutes. Combine ricotta cheese, eggs and Parmesan cheese in medium bowl; reserve. Pour half the zucchini mixture into a 9 x 13" greased baking pan; top with half the noodles and all the ricotta mixture. Sprinkle with half the mozzarella. Repeat layers of noodles, zucchini mixture and mozzarella, in that order. Bake at 350°F for 45 minutes. Let stand a few minutes before serving. (12 servings.)

Kathy's Vegetarian Lasagna

Kathy Morrison
Ghost Ranch

1	can crushed tomatoes (28 oz.)
1	can tomato paste (6 oz.)
1	cup water
1	tablespoon olive oil
1	onion, chopped
1	clove garlic, minced
1	tablespoon Italian seasoning
1	teaspoon anise, crushed
	Salt to taste
1	carton low fat cottage cheese (16 oz.)
1	package part skim mozzarella cheese, grated (8 oz.)
1/2	pound tofu, sliced and drained
10	lasagna noodles, cooked

To prepare sauce, sautee onion and garlic in olive oil. Add tomatoes, paste, and water. Stir until smooth. Add seasonings and let simmer for 1/2 hour, adding more water if needed. Spread a little sauce on the bottom of a large shallow pan, begin layering noodles, cottage cheese, tofu, and mozzarella , then cover with sauce. Repeat layers, ending with sauce on top. Bake at 350°F 45-60 minutes, until it bubbles in the center. Remove from oven, let set up for 10 minutes. (10-12 servings.)

Lasagna Roll Ups

Ghost Ranch

1/2	cup onion, chopped
1	garlic clove, crushed
1 1/3	cups tomato paste (two 6 oz. cans)
1 2/3	cups water
1	teaspoon oregano
1/2	teaspoon basil
1	package frozen chopped spinach, cooked and drained
2	cups ricotta cheese
1	cup Parmesan cheese, grated
1 1/2	cups shredded mozzarella
1	egg, slightly beaten
1/2	teaspoon salt
1/4	teaspoon pepper
10-12	lasagna noodles, cooked and drained

Vegetarian Entrees 184

Place onion, garlic, tomato paste, water, and spices in a pan. Cover, boil gently for 20 minutes. Combine spinach, cheeses (reserve 1/2 cup mozzerella), egg, salt and pepper in medium bowl. Mix well. Spread about 1/2 cup cheese mix on each noodle. Roll up, place seam side down in 9 x13" greased pan. Pour sauce over rolls. Top with remaining cheese. Bake 30-40 minutes at 350°F. If from refrigerator, bake covered 30 minutes, uncovered 30 minutes. (6-8 servings.)

Sun-Dried Tomatoes with Pasta

Pomona Hallenbeck
Abiquiu, NM

1	tablespoon olive or other vegetable oil or butter
1	onion, chopped (1/2 cup)
1 1/2	tablespoons minced garlic
3/4	cup piñon nuts
1	can vegetable stock or chicken broth (10 1/2 oz.)
4	cups water, divided
2	cups sun-dried tomatoes, chopped or torn up (hard to cut)
1	tablespoon fresh or 1 teaspoon dried basil
	Salt to taste
1	pound pasta, cooked, drained

Heat oil in large saucepan. Saute onion, garlic and pinons in oil over medium heat, stirring frequently, until light brown. Add chicken broth and 2 cups of the water to onion mixture. Stir in dried tomatoes and basil. Cook uncovered over medium heat for 20 minutes. Add 2 more cups water; continue cooking uncovered to desired consistency, about 20 minutes. Serve over hot pasta. (4 servings.)

Originally from Roswell, NM, Pomona has led watercolor seminars at the ranch for many years, and did the artwork for this cookbook.

Stuffed Spinach Shells

Marlea Gruver
Jobstown, NJ

1	package frozen chopped spinach (10 oz.)
1/4	cup chopped green onions with tender green tops
1 1/2	cups low-fat cottage cheese (12 oz.)
1	egg (or comparable egg substitute)
1/4	cup skim milk (optional)
1/4	cup chopped fresh parsley
1/4	teaspoon garlic powder
1/4	teaspoon pepper
	Salt to taste
20	large pasta shells, parboiled 9 minutes, drained
4	cups meatless spaghetti sauce

Cook spinach with green onions as directed on spinach package. Drain and press out all water; reserve. Mix cottage cheese, egg, milk and parsley in medium bowl. Stir in spinach mixture, garlic powder, pepper, and salt to taste. Stuff pasta shells with spinach mixture. Spread 1 cup spaghetti sauce on bottom of 9 x 12" baking dish. Arrange stuffed shells on sauce. Cover with remaining sauce. Bake at 350°F for 30 minutes. (Makes 4 servings, 5 shells each.)

Note: 1 cup shredded part-skim mozzarella may be added to stuffing, if desired.

Vegetable Quiche

Ghost Ranch

3	egg whites
2	cups canned evaporated skim milk
1	cup chopped onion
1	cup chopped, cooked broccoli
1	cup chopped green bell peppers
1	cup diced fresh tomatoes
1	teaspoon dried basil
1	teaspoon dried oregano
1/4	teaspoon salt
1/8	teaspoon pepper
2	baked 8" pie shells
1	cup shredded cheese

Beat eggs and milk in large bowl; stir in remaining ingredients. Pour mixture into 2 pie shells. Sprinkle 1/2 cup cheese over each. Bake at 350°F for 35 minutes. (8 servings.)

Green Chile Quiche

Kathleen Jimenez
Plaza Resolana staff

1	pie shell (9")
3	tablespoons green onions with tender green tops, chopped
2	tablespoons margarine
1 1/2	cups milk
3	eggs, beaten
1/2	cup green chile, chopped (more or less)
1	cup Monterey Jack cheese, grated
	Salt
	Black olive garnish

Pre-bake shell 10 minutes. Saute onion in margarine. Mix milk, eggs, chile, and onions. Spread cheese evenly in warm (not hot) pie crust. Pour milk and egg mixture over cheese. Bake at 375°F for 30 minutes. Garnish with black olive sliced in half and bake 10 minutes more. (Serves 4-6.)

California Quiche

Nancy Noyes
Santa Fe, NM

1	pound zucchini or yellow squash, sliced or mixed
1/2	onion, sliced thinly
4	eggs, beaten (or 1 carton egg beaters)
1 1/2	cups swiss cheese, grated
	Salt and pepper to taste
1/4	teaspoon dried oregano
1/4	teaspoon dried basil

Steam squash and onion until limp (but not too soft). Beat eggs and add cheese. Mash squash and onion mixture; add. Add seasonings. Pour into a greased 8x8" dish and bake in a 325°F oven for 40 minutes. (4-6 servings.)

Swiss Chard Pie

Gordon Schlegel
Ghost Ranch staff
Tierra Amarilla, NM

1/2	pound Swiss chard, cleaned and cut into small pieces
2	tablespoons olive oil
2	cloves garlic, minced
1/4	teaspoon salt
6	eggs

In pressure cooker, cook chard for 5 minutes in a small amount of water. Allow pressure to go down slowly. Remove chard, drain and set aside. In cooker, saute garlic in olive oil 3 minutes, add chard, toss to coat with garliced oil. Place chard in oiled 9 x 13" pan , spread evenly in pan. Make 6 "nests" in hot chard mixture, break an egg in each "nest", being careful to not break yolks. Bake at 350°F for about 10 minutes or until eggs are cooked to "sunny side up" stage. Let cool 10 minutes before slicing. (6 servings.)

Easy Garden Vegetable Pie

Erika Erskine Lauffer
Middletown, PA

2	cups chopped broccoli, cooked until almost tender, drained
1/2	cup chopped onion (1 medium onion)
1/2	cup chopped green bell pepper (1/2 green pepper)
1	cup shredded Cheddar cheese (4 ounces)
1 1/2	cups milk
3/4	cup buttermilk baking mix (Bisquick)
3	eggs
1	teaspoon salt
1/4	teaspoon pepper

Combine broccoli, onion, green pepper and cheese in a lightly greased 10" pie plate. Place remaining ingredients in blender; cover and blend until smooth. Pour over vegetable mixture. Bake at 400°F until golden brown, 35 to 40 minutes. Let stand 5 minutes before cutting. (6 to 8 servings.)

I found this easy, delicious recipe at Strites Orchards near Middletown — a wonderful place to buy produce in the summertime.

Spinach Pie

Christina Amburgey
Puyallup, WA

1	package frozen chopped spinach, thawed, drained (10 oz.)
2	cups cottage cheese
3	eggs, beaten
2	cups shredded Cheddar or Swiss cheese (8 oz.)
1	teaspoon ground nutmeg
1	unbaked pie crust

Press water out of spinach. Combine spinach and remaining ingredients except pie crust in large bowl. Pour into pie crust. Bake at 400°F for 1 hour. (4 to 5 servings.)

The easiest, healthiest recipe I have. My 18 year-old high school football player will eat it for breakfast, lunch, and dinner—hot or cold.

June's Vegetable Casserole

June Sommer
Houston, TX

2	cans asparagus, chopped or whole, drained (15 oz.)
1	can peas, drained (15 oz.)
1	can cream of mushroom soup (10 3/4 oz.)
	Salt and pepper to taste
1	can sliced water chestnuts, drained (8 oz.)
8	ounces American or Cheddar cheese, shredded (about 2 cups)
4 to 5	slices bread, trimmed, each cut into 4 strips
1/2	cup butter or margarine, melted (1 stick)

Place asparagus on bottom of 9 x 13" glass baking dish. Combine peas and mushroom soup in small bowl; season to taste. Spread over asparagus. Arrange water chestnuts over soup mixture; sprinkle with cheese. Dip bread in melted butter and arrange on top. Bake at 350°F until light brown, 20 to 25 minutes. (12 servings.)

Corn Ole!

Elizabeth Ackerman
Zellwood, FL

1	can whole kernel corn, drained, liquid reserved (15 oz.)
1	can cream-style corn (15 oz.)
1/2	cup margarine or butter, melted (1 stick)
1	cup sour cream (8 oz.)
1	can (4 oz.) chopped green chilies, drained
2	eggs, beaten
1	small box corn muffin mix (8 1/2 oz.)
2	cups shredded Cheddar cheese (8 oz.)

Measure and reserve 1/3 of the corn liquid. Combine whole kernel corn, cream-style corn, melted margarine, sour cream, green chilies, eggs, muffin mix and reserved corn liquid in large bowl. Pour into greased 9 x 13" baking pan. Sprinkle cheese on top. Bake at 350°F for 30 to 45 minutes. (Makes 10 servings.)

Tamale Ring

Phoebe and Arthur Pack
former owners of Ghost Ranch

2	eggs, separated
1	can tomatoes, pressed through a sieve (15 oz.)
1	clove garlic, minced
1 1/2	tablespoons chili powder
1	cup corn meal
2	cups pitted, sliced ripe olives
1	can whole kernel corn, drained (15 oz.)
	Salt to taste
	Worcestershire sauce to taste

Beat egg yolks; add to tomatoes in large bowl. Stir in garlic, chili powder, corn meal, olives and corn; season to taste with salt and Worcestershire sauce. Beat egg whites until stiff in small bowl. Gently fold egg whites into tomato mixture. Spoon into greased ring mold. Bake at 350°F in a pan of hot water until firm, about an hour.

This recipe is adapted from the section "Hot Dishes from the Summer Porch," in Recipes from Ghost Ranch, published in the 1930s. The Tamale Ring was sometimes served with meatballs in the center of the ring.

El Prado Cacerola

Vivian Pearson
Los Alamos, NM

1 to 2	tablespoons vegetable oil
1	small onion, chopped (about 1/4 cup)
2	eggs or 3 egg whites
2	cups low-fat milk
1 1/2	cups shredded Cheddar or Monterey Jack cheese (6 oz.), divided
1	cup whole kernel corn, fresh, frozen or canned (8 oz.)
3/4	cup chick peas (garbanzos)
1/4	cup seeded, chopped green chilies
1/2	teaspoon garlic powder (or more to taste)
5	corn tortillas, 6" in diameter, cut in quarters
1	cup chopped tomatoes
1/4	cup chopped fresh parsley
1/4	teaspoon dried basil

Heat oil in small skillet. Cook onions in oil until translucent; reserve. Beat eggs in large bowl. Add milk, 1 cup of the cheese, corn, chick peas, chilies, garlic powder and the reserved onion. Line bottom and sides of 10" pie plate with tortilla pieces. Spoon egg mixture into tortilla-lined dish. Sprinkle with tomatoes, parsley, basil and the remaining 1/2 cup cheese. Bake at 350°F until firm in center and brown on top, 40 to 45 minutes. (4 servings.)

I got the basic recipe in 1972 while living in El Prado, NM and have altered it to my taste. It is a family favorite. We usually eat it once a week with salad, and rolls or bread. It is a complete protein (beans + corn + milk + milk product) and is low in fat and calories. Light cheese can be used.

Shirl's Pinto Beans

Shirley B. Watkins
Yuma, AZ

2	cups pinto beans (organic beans preferred), washed, sorted
1	cup chopped onion (2 medium onions)
2	cloves garlic, minced
1	bay leaf
4	tablespoons safflower or other vegetable oil
4	tablespoons tamari (soy) sauce
1	teaspoon salt (sea salt preferred)
	Freshly ground pepper to taste
	Cooked rice
	Diced fresh tomato, green bell pepper, celery
	Salsa

Cover beans with cold water in medium bowl; refrigerate overnight. Pour off water; add water to cover in large pot. Add garlic, bay leaf, oil, tamari, salt and pepper. Heat to boiling; reduce heat and cook, covered, stirring occasionally, until beans are tender, 2 to 2 1/2 hours. Add hot water if necessary. Remove bay leaf. Serve over cooked rice, topped with diced tomato, green pepper and celery; pass the salsa. (8 or more servings.)

editor's note: If you'll boil the dry beans in water about 5 minutes before soaking, the beans will be easier to digest.

Chilies Rellenos Jose

Ghost Ranch

1	can whole green chilies (1 lb., 10 oz.) or 18 whole chilies
1	pound Monterey Jack cheese, cut in 1 x 3 x 1/2" strips.
5	large eggs
1/4	cup flour
1 1/4	cups milk
1/2	teaspoon salt
	Black pepper to taste
	Tabasco to taste
1/2	pound Cheddar cheese, grated
1/8	teaspoon paprika

Carefully rinse seeds from chilies with cold water. Spread chilies on a single layer of paper towel. Carefully pat chilies dry. Slip a strip of Monterey Jack cheese into each chile. Beat eggs. Gradually add flour, beating until smooth. Add milk, salt, black pepper and Tabasco. Beat thoroughly. Arrange half of the stuffed chilies in a well-greased casserole. Sprinkle half of the Cheddar cheese and paprika over it. Repeat layers, ending with cheese. Carefully pour egg mixture over all. Bake, uncovered, at 350°F about 45 minutes or until knife comes out clean. (Makes 6-8 generous servings.)

Red Cheese Enchiladas

Mary Leyba
Ghost Ranch staff
Canjilon, NM

12	corn tortillas
1/3	cup vegetable oil
3-4	cups red chile sauce
3	cups longhorn cheese, grated
1/2	cup onions, chopped

Red Chile Sauce:

3	tablespoons oil
2	tablespoons flour
1/2	cup ground red chili
2	cups water
1	teaspoon garlic salt
	Salt to taste

Fry tortillas in oil just until soft, drain on paper towels. Layer tortillas on 13 x 9 " pan, topping with grated cheese, chopped onions and chili sauce. (2 layers). Heat in 350°F oven for about 25 minutes. (6-8 servings.)

For sauce: Heat oil. Blend in flour. Add chili powder. Blend in water and cook to desired consistency. Add garlic salt and salt to taste.

Ghost Ranch Bean Burritos

Ghost Ranch

2	cups refried beans
1	cup chopped onions
1	cup shredded Cheddar cheese
1	cup green chile, chopped
1	tablespoon oregano
1	teaspoon salt
10	flour tortillas
	Vegetable oil

In mixing bowl, blend together beans, onions, cheese, chile and spices. Carefully spread approximately 1/2 cup bean mixture on each tortilla. Roll tortillas and place in oiled baking dish, seam side down. Brush tops of burritos with a small amount of oil to prevent drying. Bake at 350°F for about 30 minutes. Serve with red chili sauce (see recipe above) if desired. (10 servings.)

editor's note: One day I asked Rebecca Martinez what was the funniest thing that had happened to her in the ranch kitchen. She started laughing and told me about the time the college staff was having a food fight in the dish room. (not recommended!) She opened the door to the dish room and was hit in the face with a plate of burritos. The offending staffer, expecting another college student rather than his boss, was as shocked as Rebecca and took off running around the circle, with Rebecca in close pursuit. Lucky for him she didn't catch him! Ten years later, that young man still visits Ghost Ranch every couple of years and he and Rebecca always sit down together and laugh about the day she wore her burritos instead of eating them.

Dean's Spicy Rice Salsa

Dean Lewis
Ghost Ranch staff

1/2	cup white onion, diced
1	large garlic clove, finely chopped
1	cup celery, finely chopped
1/2	cup green pepper, diced
1 1/2	tablespoons extra virgin olive oil
1	cup zucchini, diced
1	can tomatoes, diced, undrained (14 1/2 oz.)
1	cup hot water
1/2	teaspoon oregano
1/2	teaspoon dried cilantro
1/4	teaspoon ground cumin
1/4	teaspoon Española Valley ground red chili
1/2	teaspoon salt
	Basmati rice

Saute onion, garlic, green pepper, and celery in olive oil in a deep skillet until onion is translucent. Add hot water, tomatoes, zucchini, and spices. Cover and simmer for 45 minutes or until vegetables are done to the desired crunch. For a less spicy dish, cut back on all spices except chili. Makes about 4 cups. (4-6 servings.)

I serve it over brown Basmati because the aromas of salsa and rice meld so wonderfully as they are cooking. I invented this a few years ago to help control weight and cholesterol and because it was perfect for a commuter. Cook it up on Sunday night, put it in the refrigerator and heat it up with the rice and a bowl of pinto beans, a glass of skim milk and a chunk of cornbread at night after getting home.

Frito Pie Spanish Plate

Frances Maestas
Abiquiu Elementary School

Fritos
2	cups pinto beans, cooked and drained
1/2	pound Cheddar cheese, grated
1/2	head lettuce, shredded
1	tomato, chopped
	Chili sauce (see recipe above)
	Onion, chopped

Heat pinto beans. On a plate, put cheese on bottom, then fritos, beans, chili, more cheese, lettuce, and tomatoes on top and it is ready to eat. This is an individual plate. Onion, if you like it, on top. (4 plates.)

My boys favorite dish!

Three-Bean Casserole

Marion Sweet
Verona, WI

2	tablespoons vegetable oil
1	large onion, finely chopped (about 1 cup)
1	clove garlic, minced (or 1/4 teaspoon garlic powder)
2	packages frozen baby lima beans (10 oz. each)
1	can tomato-style baked beans (15 oz.)
1	can red kidney beans, drained (15 oz.)
1/2	cup ketchup
1	tablespoon brown sugar
3	tablespoons vinegar
2	tablespoons water
1	teaspoon dry mustard
1	teaspoon salt
1/4	teaspoon pepper

Heat oil in large skillet or pot. Saute onion and garlic in hot oil until golden brown; reserve. Cook lima beans as directed on package, for 10 minutes, but using only 2/3rd of water; do not overcook. Drain and add to onion mixture with remaining ingredients. Heat to boiling. Pour into 2-quart casserole. Bake at 350°F for 30 minutes. (6 to 8 servings.)

Egg Foo Yoong

Ghost Ranch

8	eggs, beaten slightly
1/2	cup green onion, chopped
2	tablespoons soy sauce
1	cup zucchini, finely grated
1/4	cup whole wheat flour
1	teaspoon honey
1/2	cup rice, cooked
	Salt to taste
	Oil for frying

Combine all ingredients except oil. Fry in oil using mixture as you would a pancake batter. Turn once when lower side is golden brown. (6-8 servings.)

Spinach Souffle

Ghost Ranch kitchen

2	pounds frozen spinach, thawed, drained
4	eggs, beaten slightly
2	cups cottage cheese
2	teaspoons basil
2	teaspoons oregano
1	teaspoon salt
1	teaspoon baking powder
1	cup Parmesan cheese, grated
1	cup Cheddar cheese, shredded

Combine all ingredients except Cheddar cheese, mix well. Put in well-greased 2 qt. casserole, top with cheese, bake at 350°F for 40 minutes. (Serves 8.)

Cheese Souffle

Ghost Ranch

5	slices bread, crust removed
2	tablespoons butter
1	teaspoon prepared mustard
1	cup sharp cheese, grated
3	eggs, well beaten
1	cup half & half
1/2	cup milk
1/2	teaspoon salt
1/4	teaspoon pepper

Spread bread with butter and trace of mustard. Cube and place in buttered 8" casserole. Sprinkle cheese over bread; mix eggs with half & half, milk, salt, and pepper. Pour over bread. Refrigerate overnight. Bake one hour at 350°F. Serve immediately. (4-5 servings.)

Sides & Grains

Oriental Asparagus

Ghost Ranch

2	tablespoons butter or margarine
2	tablespoons almonds, slivered
1	package fresh frozen cut asparagus (10 oz.)
1	stalk celery, sliced
1	can water chestnuts, sliced (5 oz.)
1	tablespoon soy sauce
	Salt and pepper if desired

In small saucepan, melt butter over medium heat. Add almonds and toast over low heat; remove almonds and set aside. Add remaining ingredients to butter. Cover and simmer over medium-high heat about 10 minutes or until asparagus is tender, stirring occasionally. If necessary remove lid during last few minutes to allow liquid to evaporate. There should be just a thin glaze on vegetables. Add toasted almonds. (4 servings.)

Broc Au Gratin

Ghost Ranch

1	box frozen chopped broccoli (10 oz.)
1	cup cottage cheese
2	eggs
1/4	teaspoon salt
1	teaspoon seasoning salt
1/4	teaspoon pepper
1	teaspoon onion, minced
2	tablespoons butter, melted
1/4	cup soft bread crumbs

Cook and drain broccoli according to directions on box, mix with all ingredients except butter and bread. Sprinkle with buttered breadcrumbs. Bake for 30 minutes at 350°F. (4-6 servings.)

Jade Green Gingered Broccoli

Anne Hunt
Hawthorn Woods, IL

6	cups sliced trimmed broccoli pieces
1/3	cup chicken broth
2	cloves garlic, minced
1	teaspoon grated fresh ginger
3	tablespoons reduced-sodium soy sauce
1	tablespoon brown sugar
1	teaspoon sesame oil (available in oriental section of food store)
1	tablespoon cornstarch
2	tablespoons cold water

Place broccoli in large pot of boiling water. Return to boil and cook 2 minutes; drain and reserve. Heat chicken broth in wok or large skillet over medium heat. Add garlic and ginger; stir 1 minute. Add soy sauce, brown sugar and sesame oil. Combine cornstarch and cold water; add to skillet. Cook and stir until sauce thickens. Stir in broccoli. (6 servings.)

My business partner, Mary Abbott Hess, is the kind of registered dietitian you want to know if you have to modify your diet! She knows how to make healthy food taste great! This recipe is from her best-selling book, The Art of Cooking for the Diabetic (Contemporary Books, 1988).

Broccoli Alla Pasta

Ruth and Mac Calhoun
Austin, TX

1	bunch broccoli florets and stems, cut in 1" pieces
1/4	cup olive oil
1	tablespoon butter or margarine
3	cloves garlic, chopped
1	teaspoon crushed dried red pepper flakes
2	fresh tomatoes, diced
8	ounces pasta (ziti or medium shells), cooked, drained
	Freshly grated Parmesan cheese

Blanche broccoli in rapidly boiling salted water until cooked but still crisp, 3 to 4 minutes; drain and reserve. Heat oil and butter in medium skillet; cook garlic and red pepper flakes in hot oil. Toss garlic mixture, broccoli and tomato into hot cooked pasta. Serve with freshly grated cheese. (8 to 10 servings.)

Broccoli Hot Dish

Marion Sweet
Verona, WI

2	tablespoons butter or margarine
1/2	cup chopped onion
1	can golden mushroom soup (10 3/4 oz.)
1/2	cup instant rice (Minute Rice preferred)
3/4	cup milk
1	package frozen chopped broccoli (10 oz.)
	Salt and pepper
	Grated Parmesan cheese

Melt butter in medium saucepan. Add soup, rice, milk and frozen broccoli. Cook over medium heat until broccoli thaws, stirring occasionally. Season to taste with salt and pepper. Spoon into greased casserole. Sprinkle with Parmesan cheese. Bake at 350°F for 30 minutes. (6 servings.)

Broccoli & Rice

Ghost Ranch

1	cup rice , uncooked
3 1/4	cups boiling water, divided
1	package frozen chopped broccoli
2	tablespoons margarine
1	cup celery, chopped
1/2	cup onion, chopped
1	can cream of chicken soup
1/2	cup half & half
1/2	pound Cheddar cheese, grated

In 2 1/4 cups water, cook rice, and salt; set aside. Pour 1 cup water over package frozen broccoli. Let stand to thaw then drain. Saute celery and onion in margarine; add, soup and half & half. Combine rice, broccoli and soup mixture in 2 quart greased baking dish. Sprinkle cheese on top. Bake at 350°F for 30 minutes or more. Good with variations—ham, chicken, etc. (Serves 6-8.)

Broccoli Rice Medley

Linda Stitt
Tucson, AZ

4	cups brown rice, cooked
1	bunch broccoli, trimmed and cut into bite-size pieces
1	bunch green onions with tender green tops, sliced
1	can cream of mushroom soup (10 3/4 oz.)
1/2	cup milk or water
1	cup shredded cheese (4 oz.)
1/2	cup coarsely chopped nuts

Spread cooked rice in bottom of 9 x 13" baking dish. Steam broccoli and onions until tender, about 8 minutes; spoon evenly over rice. Mix soup with milk and spoon evenly over broccoli mixture. Bake at 350°F for 30 minutes. Sprinkle with cheese and nuts; continue baking 5 minutes. (8 servings.)

Copper Penny Carrots

Ghost Ranch

2	pounds carrots, sliced
1	green pepper, sliced thinly
1	medium onion
1	can tomato soup
1/2	cup vegetable oil
1	cup sugar
3/4	cup vinegar
1	teaspoon prepared mustard
1	teaspoon Worcestershire
	Salt
	Pepper

Steam carrots until medium done, still slightly crisp. Arrange layers of carrots, green pepper, onions in bowl. Combine and blend remaining ingredients. Pour over vegetables. Serve warm. (8-10 servings.)

Carrot Ring With Peas

Criselda Dominguez
Ghost Ranch staff
Abiquiu, NM

2	eggs, beaten
2	cups milk
1	teaspoon salt
1/8	teaspoon pepper
2	cups carrots, diced and cooked
2	tablespoons onion, minced
2	cups peas, cooked
2	tablespoons butter
	Parsley sprigs (optional)

Blend eggs, milk, salt and pepper; stir in carrots and onion. Pour into oiled 5-cup ring mold. Bake at 350°F for 30 to 35 minutes or until inserted knife remains clean. Unmold; fill center with hot peas. Top with butter; garnish with parsley. (8 servings.)

Candied Ginger Carrots

Ghost Ranch

3/4	cup firmly packed brown sugar
1/2	cup orange juice
2	tablespoons margarine
1/2	teaspoon salt
1/4	teaspoon ground ginger
2	pounds medium-sized carrots, scraped and cut in 1/8" rounds.

Combine brown sugar, orange juice, margarine, salt and ginger in a large frying pan; heat slowly, stirring constantly until boiling. Stir in carrots, cover, simmer 25 minutes. Uncover and cook until tender. (8 servings.)

Celery en Casserole

Jan Wolverton
San Pedro, CA

4	cups diagonally-sliced celery
1	can water chestnuts, drained, thinly sliced (8 oz.)
1/4	cup diced pimiento
1/4	cup slivered blanched almonds
1	can cream of chicken soup (10 3/4 oz.)
1/2	cup soft bread crumbs
4	tablespoons butter or margarine, melted (1/2 stick)

Cook celery in 1/4 cup boiling water in medium saucepan until barely tender, about 4 minutes; drain. Stir in water chestnuts, pimiento, almonds and soup. Spoon into greased 1 1/2 quart casserole. Mix bread crumbs with melted butter; sprinkle over celery mixture. Bake at 350°F until crumbs brown, about 25 minutes. (8 servings.)

Dottie Hill insisted that I send this in. It came to me from my dear friend, Mary Jo Daily.

Company Cauliflower

Ghost Ranch

1	tablespoon sesame seeds
1	medium cauliflower, broken into flowerets
1/2	teaspoon seasoning salt
	Dash salt, pepper
1	cup sour cream
1	cup Cheddar cheese, grated

Toast sesame seeds. Cook cauliflower in 2 quarts of water for 8-10 minutes. Drain. Place half of the cauliflower in buttered casserole. Sprinkle with seasoning salt, salt, and pepper. Combine sour cream and cheese. Spread 1/2 cream mix on cauliflower, repeat layers. Bake 375°F for 15 minutes. (4-6 servings.)

Sweet 'n Sour Beets

Ghost Ranch

3	cups beets, cooked
1/2	cup sugar
1	tablespoon cornstarch
1/2	teaspoon salt
2	whole cloves
1/2	cup vinegar or dry white wine

Combine all ingredients except beets. Cook and stir these ingredients until clear. Add beets, toss and heat. Can add 2 tablespoons butter before serving. (6 servings.)

Squash-Apple Bake

Betty Currin
Midland, MI

1	medium butternut squash
2 or 3	apples, peeled, cored, quartered (if large cut into eighths)
1	tablespoon firmly packed brown sugar (optional)
1/2	teaspoon ground ginger
1/4	teaspoon ground mace
1	tablespoon margarine or butter

Bake squash in 350°F oven until almost tender, but still firm, about 30 minutes. Cool, peel, and cut it into cubes. In large bowl, combine squash, apples, brown sugar and spices. Spoon into greased 2 to 2 1/2-quart casserole; dot with margarine. Bake at 350°F until apples and squash are very tender, about 30 minutes. (6 to 8 servings.)

Zucchini Cheese Casserole

Ghost Ranch

3	medium zucchini squash, sliced
1/4	cup water
3	tablespoons vegetable oil
1	cup chopped celery
1/2	cup chopped onion (1 medium onion)
3	fresh tomatoes, sliced
3	cups low-fat cottage cheese, drained
1	teaspoon dried basil
1	teaspoon dried oregano
1/2	cup grated Parmesan cheese

Cover and steam squash in large skillet with 1/4 cup water. Drain; place in 2-quart casserole. Heat oil in skillet over medium heat. Saute celery and onion in oil until tender; add to zucchini. Add tomatoes, cottage cheese, basil and oregano to squash mixture; stir to combine. Sprinkle with cheese. Bake at 350°F for 45 minutes. (6 servings.)

Summer Squash Casserole

Ghost Ranch

3	pounds yellow summer squash, sliced
6	tablespoons chopped onion (1 small onion)
	Boiling salted water
2	cans cream of chicken soup (10 3/4 oz. each)
1 1/2	cups sour cream
1 1/2	cups shredded carrot
2	packages herb-seasoned stuffing mix
3/4	cup butter or margarine, melted (1 1/2 sticks)

Cook squash and onion in boiling salted water 3 minutes; drain. Combine soup, sour cream and carrots in large bowl. Add squash and onions; mix lightly but thoroughly; reserve. Combine stuffing mix and butter in medium bowl. Spread evenly in greased 10 x 13" baking pan. Spoon squash mixture over stuffing. Bake at 350°F for 30 minutes. (12 to 14 servings.)

Calavacitas

Annabelle Salazar
Ghost Ranch staff
Abiquiu, NM

3   pounds Mexican baby pumpkin, cubed
2   ears fresh yellow corn, shucked
1   cup onion or onion greens, chopped
1   teaspoon salt
3   tablespoons vegetable oil

Mix all ingredients and saute in skillet, stirring occasionally. Cook until
tender. (8 servings.)

_This is a traditional New Mexican dish that has been in my family for genera-
tions. I think that it should be or could be called Calavacitas only if these
ingredients—the Mexican baby pumpkins and corn—are used. It is a tradition
in our Spanish American familias to use only these fresh vegetables in this
recipe. The baby pumpkins can be used as early as the first week in July, when
they are at their peak, on until there is a frost. Pumpkins are picked for cooking
right before they begin seeding, when they are about as big as a softball.
Calavacitas can also be refrigerated up to 2 or 3 weeks. People from our communities look forward to the season of harvesting calavacitas so that they can cook
their first calavacitas of the summer. Because the yellow corn does not mature
by the time that the calavacitas are available, canned corn may be used. Or,
even better, use fresh corn from your local grocer._

Sides & Grains 209

Calavacita Casserole

Annabelle Salazar
Ghost Ranch staff
Abiquiu, NM

3	pounds baby Mexican pumpkin (may substitute zucchini or summer squash)
1	onion, chopped
2	cups fresh or canned corn
1	cup fresh or canned chopped green chile
1	teaspoon salt
1	teaspoon fresh chopped garlic
1	cup American or colby cheese, shredded
	Ground beef or ground turkey (optional)

Wash pumpkin or squash, chop small. Add onion, corn, chile, salt, and garlic. Bake at 350°F in greased baking dish until squash is tender (about 30 minutes). If desired, add cooked and drained beef or turkey. Top with cheese and bake an additional 10 minutes, until cheese melts. (8 servings.)

This recipe is a lot like the calavacitas, but can be prepared during the months when baby pumpkins are not available by substituting summer squash, zucchini, or canned corn.

Ratatouille

Nancy Hall
Alexandria, VA

2	tablespoons olive oil
1	clove garlic, chopped
2	pounds eggplant, unpeeled, cubed
2	pounds zucchini, cubed
1 or 2	green bell peppers, diced
1	onion, diced
1 1/2	pounds tomatoes, skinned, diced
1	teaspoon dried thyme
1	teaspoon dried basil
	Salt and pepper to taste

Heat oil in large saucepan. Brown garlic in oil. Add eggplant, zucchini, green peppers and onion. Cook over medium heat, stirring frequently, until browned. Stir in tomatoes and herbs. Add salt and pepper to taste. Reduce heat, cover and cook slowly, 30 minutes. (12 servings.)

This is a family recipe from Madame Lafont, the mother of a Huguenot family from Nîmes, in the south of France. The Lafont family befriended me during my Volunteer In Mission year in Nîmes. This is not the first time I bring France to Ghost Ranch. Those who know me from Service Corps will remember "storming the dining hall" (instead of the Bastille) on July 14! "Allons, enfants de la patrie... ."

Baked Spinach

Ghost Ranch

1	package chopped frozen spinach, cooked and drained
1	can cream of mushroom soup (10 3/4 oz.)
1	small clove garlic, crushed
1	teaspoon Worcestershire sauce
1	tablespoon butter
12	Ritz crackers, crushed

Topping:
6	Ritz crackers, crushed for topping
1	tablespoon butter, melted
1/4	cup Parmesan cheese
	Paprika

Mix together first six ingredients; pour into buttered casserole. Top with buttered cracker crumbs, cheese and paprika. Bake 25-30 minutes at 350°F. (4-6 servings.)

Spinach Casserole

Melinda Lewis
Albuquerque, NM

2	packages frozen, chopped spinach, thawed (10 oz. each)
1	package Neufchatel or cream cheese, at room temperature (8 oz.)
1	clove garlic, minced
2	eggs, beaten
1	teaspoon Worcestershire sauce (or more to taste)
10	ounces Cheddar cheese, shredded (about 2 1/2 cups), divided

Combine all ingredients except 1/2 cup of the cheese in a large bowl.
Spoon into 2 quart casserole; sprinkle with reserved cheese. Cover and
bake at 350°F for 45 minutes. Uncover and continue baking 15 minutes.
(6 to 8 servings.)

*I first had this in Philadelphia in 1975. The host was a Mickey Mouse fanatic.
We ate from Mickey Mouse plates with Mickey Mouse forks, drank from Minnie
Mouse glasses, wiped our mouths on Donald Duck napkins, talked on the
Mickey Mouse phone, and admired Mickey, Minnie, Donald and Pluto decora-
tions in the bathroom. As a result, I feel light-hearted and whimsical whenever I
eat this casserole.*

Green Chile Souffle

Sue Dallam
Iowa City, IA

2	cans whole green chilies (4 oz. each)
3/4	cup sharp cheese, grated (about 3 oz.)
2	eggs
3/4	cup milk
1/4	cup all-purpose flour
1/2	teaspoon salt

Split chilies; wash away seeds and membrane. Layer chilies and cheese
in a 2-quart casserole. Place remaining ingredients in blender. Cover
and blend at high speed; pour over chilies and cheese. Bake uncovered
at 350°F for 45 minutes. (4 to 6 servings.)

This recipe has been going to church suppers for 30 years!

Corn Pudding

Ann Lodge
Kayenta, AZ

2	eggs, slightly beaten
2	cups milk
1	can cream-style corn (17 oz.)
1	cup soft bread crumbs
1/3	cup minced onion
1	tablespoon butter or margarine, melted
1	teaspoon salt
	Pepper (optional)

Combine all ingredients in large bowl. Pour into 1 1/2 quart greased casserole or baking dish. Bake uncovered at 350°F for 1 hour. Can be doubled. (6 servings.)

After 2 years of taking food to potlucks on the Navajo Reservation, this was the first dish that actually got 'raves' from our friends there.

Grilled Potatoes and Onions

Linda Stitt
Tucson, AZ

4 to 5	red potatoes, baked or boiled, sliced
1	bunch green onions with tender green tops, sliced
4	cloves garlic, pressed or minced
	Salt and pepper to taste
3	tablespoons butter or margarine, cut into pieces

Place potatoes and onions on a large sheet of heavy-duty aluminum foil. Sprinkle with garlic, salt and pepper. Dot with butter. Seal foil on top and ends. Place on grill for 15 to 20 minutes or bake in oven at 350°F for 20 minutes. (4 servings.)

This is a convenient way to prepare a delicious potato dish while simultaneously barbequing or baking a main dish.

Potatoes Paprika

Jan and Wil Hufton
Saginaw, MI

4	tablespoons olive oil
1	onion, chopped (about 1/2 cup)
1	clove garlic, minced
1	tablespoon Hungarian paprika (mild or hot)
3	medium white potatoes, cut into French fry pieces, 2" long
1/2	teaspoon salt
2	cups water
1	green bell pepper, cut into strips
1	large tomato, chopped (about 1 1/2 cups)

Heat oil in large skillet or dutch oven. Saute onion and garlic over medium heat until onion is transparent. Stir in paprika. Add potatoes; sprinkle with salt. Cook and stir for 2 to 3 minutes. Stir in water; cover and simmer for 10 minutes. Add green pepper and tomatoes. Cover and simmer until potatoes are just tender, 10 to 15 minutes. Good with mild sausage. (4 servings.)

Scalloped Pineapple

Ghost Ranch

1	can crushed pineapple, 20 oz. (2 1/2 cups with juice)
10	slices dry bread, cubed (6 cups)
1/2	cup butter
3/4	cup sugar
	Pinch salt

Combine ingredients in buttered casserole. Refrigerate overnight. Stir before baking. Bake 1 hour at 325°F. Good served at Easter with ham. (6-8 servings.)

Sweet Potato Pecan Balls

Maurine McMillan
Belen, NM

1	can sweet potatoes, drained, mashed (16 oz.)
1/2	cup sugar
2	tablespoons butter or margarine, at room temperature
1/2	teaspoon salt
1/2	teaspoon cinnamon
1	teaspoon vanilla
3	cups finely chopped pecans
1/4	cup berry jelly (currant, strawberry)

Combine all ingredients except pecans and jelly in large bowl. Combine with a potato masher or pastry blender. Using a measuring tablespoon, shape mixture into 24 balls, 2" in diameter. Roll balls in chopped pecans. Place on large baking sheet, at least 2" apart. Indent top of ball with spoon and fill with 1/2 teaspoon jelly. (Can be made to this point a day ahead, covered and refrigerated, then baked just before serving.) Bake at 350°F until nuts are light brown, 15 to 20 minutes. Good hot, cold or at room temperature. (Makes 24 balls, 2 per serving.)

This recipe originated in Georgia, where yams (sweet potatoes) and pecans are native crops.

Sweet Potato Casserole

Annette Donald
Albuquerque, NM

3	cups sweet potatoes
1/2	cup butter
2	eggs
1	teaspoon vanilla
1/3	cup milk

Topping:
1/3	cup butter
1	cup brown sugar
1/2	cup flour
1	cup pecans

Boil and mash potatoes. Blend in butter, eggs, vanilla and milk. Pour into baking dish. For topping; melt butter, add sugar, flour, and pecans. Sprinkle on top and bake in 350°F oven for 25 minutes. (Serves 6-8.)

Sweet Potato Souffle

Ghost Ranch

1	can sweet potatoes (29 oz.) (Can add another 16 oz. can)
3/4	stick melted margarine
1/2	cups brown sugar
3/4	cup milk
2	eggs, beaten
1	teaspoon nutmeg
1	teaspoon cinnamon

Topping:
1/2	cup brown sugar
1/2	stick margarine, melted
1/2	cup walnuts or pecans, chopped
1	cup corn flakes, crushed

Cook potatoes in their juice for 15 minutes. Drain well and mash. Add remaining ingredients, mix. Bake 20 minutes at 400°F. Remove and add mixed topping ingredients. Bake 10-15 minutes, until top looks crunchy and brown. (6-8 servings.)

Sweet Potato Royale

Shirley Martz
Sun City, AZ

1	can (2 lbs., 14 oz.), drained or 3 large boiled, peeled, sweet potatoes or yams
4	eggs, beaten
3/4	cups sugar
1	cup milk
1/2	cup dry sherry
1/2	cup margarine or butter, melted
1	teaspoon baking powder
	Miniature marshmallows or chopped nuts (optional)

Mash sweet potatoes in large bowl. Add eggs, sugar, milk, sherry, butter and baking powder. Mix thoroughly. Pour into greased 2-quart casserole. Bake at 350°F for 30 minutes. Top with marshmallows and nuts, if desired. Continue baking until knife comes out clean when inserted in center, about 15 minutes more. (12 servings.)

This recipe comes from Hana, Maui. It is delicious with macadamia nuts on top. It has become a holiday tradition in our house and is 'royally' received anytime!

Baked Lima and Apple Casserole

Elizabeth Newell
Granville, OH

1/4	cup margarine or butter (1/2 stick)
1	cup chopped onion (2 medium onions)
3	cans (15 1/2 oz. each) lima beans, drained, 3/4 cup liquid reserved
3	large apples, peeled, cored, diced
1/2	cup packed brown sugar
1/4	cup prepared mustard
1/4	teaspoon cinnamon

Heat margarine in large pan. Add onion; cook over medium heat 5 minutes. Stir in beans, apples, sugar, mustard, cinnamon and the 3/4 cup drained liquid from beans. Spoon into heavy 3-quart casserole or bean pot. Cover and bake at 325°F for 3 hours. (6 to 8 servings.)

editor's note: In the South, lima beans are sometimes referred to as butter beans. Butter beans are actually larger than limas but have a similar flavor.

Fruity Baked Beans

Jan and Wil Hufton
Saginaw, MI

1/2	pound bacon, cut up
2	medium onions, chopped (about 1 cup)
1	pound ground beef
2	cans pork and beans (20 oz. each)
1	can crushed pineapple, undrained (9 oz.)
1/4	cup chili sauce
2	tablespoons brown sugar (or less, if desired)
1 1/2	teaspoons dry mustard
1/4	teaspoon salt

Saute bacon and onions over low heat in large pot until onions are soft. Remove and reserve; drain fat from pot. Add beef to pot. Cook until it loses its red color. Drain. Stir in reserved bacon and onions and remaining ingredients. Spoon into heavy 1 1/2-quart casserole or bean pot. Cover and bake at 250°F for 1 1/2 to 2 hours. (6 servings.)

Crock Pot Beans

Gertrude Anderson
Boulder, CO

1/2 to 1	pound ground beef
3/4	pound bacon, cut in small pieces
1	cup chopped onions (2 medium onions)
2	cans pork and beans (1 lb., 15 oz. each)
1	can kidney beans, drained (1 lb.)
1	can butter beans, drained (1 lb.)
1	cup ketchup
1/4	cup packed brown sugar
3	tablespoons white vinegar
1	tablespoon liquid smoke
1	teaspoon salt
1/8	teaspoon pepper

Brown ground beef in medium skillet over medium heat; drain and put beef into a large crock pot. Cook bacon and onions in skillet until onions are soft; drain and add to crock pot with remaining ingredients. Stir to combine. Cover and cook on low setting 4 to 6 hours. (If using a 2-quart crock pot, cut recipe in half.) (8 to 10 servings.)

Feijoada (Black Beans)

Lynett Gillette
Ghost Ranch staff

1/2	pound black beans, washed, sorted
1/2	pound mild Italian sausage
1	cup chopped onion (2 medium onions)
2	cloves garlic, minced
	Salt to taste

Cover beans with water and heat to boiling in large pot; reduce heat and simmer over medium heat until beans are almost tender, 2 to 4 hours. Brown sausage in small skillet; drain and add to beans. Saute onions and garlic in sausage drippings; drain and add to bean mixture. Cover and cook beans over low heat until thickened, about 2 hours.

From Peggy Orwell, Lynett's friend, who is now a botanist at the Missouri Botanical Gardens.

Latkes (Potato Pancakes)

Marian Schwartz
Ghost Ranch volunteer

6	potatoes, shredded
1	onion, finely chopped
2	eggs, beaten
1/4	cup matzah meal (or flour)
1/2	teaspoon baking powder
1	teaspoon salt
1/4	teaspoon pepper
	Oil for frying

Set aside shredded potatoes in a colander to drain. Mix onions, eggs, and rest of ingredients. Add drained potatoes to other ingredients and mix well. Heat oil in large frying pan. Drop potato mixture into hot oil by generous spoonfuls. Flatten in oil and fry until golden brown. Turn once and fry other side. Serve hot with applesauce or sour cream. Serves 6.

Latkes are traditionally eaten in Jewish households during the holiday of Hannukah. There are never enough!

Baked Rice

Ghost Ranch

2	cups rice
1/4	cup butter
4	cups boiling water
2	teaspoons salt

Combine ingredients in covered 2 quart casserole. Bake at 350°F for 30-40 minutes. (6-8 servings.)

Baked Rice Pilaf

Ghost Ranch

1	cup regular long grain rice
1	can onion soup (10 3/4 oz.)
1	soup can cold water
1	can water chestnuts, drained and sliced (4 oz.)
2	tablespoons butter

Combine rice, soup, water, water chestnuts and butter. Mix well. Bake, covered, in 325° oven for 1 hour and 15 minutes, or until rice is done. (Serves 6.)

Curried Rice

Lynett Gillette
Ghost Ranch staff

4	slices bacon
1	medium onion, chopped (about 1/2 cup)
1/2	green bell pepper, chopped (about 1/2 cup)
2	stalks celery, chopped (about 1 cup)
1	cup uncooked rice
1	teaspoon (scant) each: poultry seasoning, curry powder, paprika
1/4	teaspoon cayenne pepper
	Salt and pepper to taste
1	cup beef consomme
1	cup water

Cook bacon in large skillet until crisp. Remove bacon; drain, crumble and reserve. Saute vegetables in bacon drippings just until wilted; remove and reserve. Brown rice lightly in remaining bacon drippings. Add remaining ingredients, reserved vegetables and crumbled bacon to rice. Mix thoroughly. Spoon into greased 2-quart casserole. Bake covered at 350°F for 1 hour. Uncover and continue baking for 15 minutes. (6 to 8 servings.)

Cheese Grits

Anita Skeen
Okemos, MI

1/2	cup quick-cooking hominy grits
2	cups boiling water
1/3	pound Cheddar cheese, shredded (about 1 1/2 cups)
4	tablespoons butter or margarine (1/2 stick)
1	egg, well beaten
1/2	teaspoon salt
1/8	teaspoon hot pepper sauce or cayenne pepper (or more to taste)
	Paprika

Stir grits into rapidly boiling water in large pot. Reduce heat; cook, stirring frequently, until mixture is thick. Add cheese and butter to hot grits; stir until they melt. Mix egg, salt and red pepper sauce in small bowl; add to grits mixture. Spoon into greased casserole. Bake at 350°F for 40 to 50 minutes. Sprinkle with paprika 10 minutes before done. (6 to 8 servings.)

This recipe was given to me by the late P.J. Wyatt, folklorist, linguist and Native American scholar at Wichita State University. She served it with ham, red eye gravy, and fresh green beans. I consider it a "must" when friends gather for food and conversation.

Cheese Grits

Harold and Florence Hamel
Grand Junction, CO

1	cup hominy grits
3	cups boiling salted water
1	teaspoon salt
1/2	cup butter or margarine (1 stick)
1	package garlic cheese (4 oz.)
8	ounces sharp Cheddar cheese, shredded
2	tablespoons Worcestershire sauce
	Paprika

Stir grits into rapidly boiling salted water in large pot. Reduce heat; simmer, stirring occasionally until grits are thick. Add butter, garlic cheese, Cheddar cheese and Worcestershire sauce. Stir until butter and cheese melt. Spoon into large greased casserole; sprinkle with paprika. Bake at 350°F for 15 to 20 minutes. (8 to 10 servings.)

From a cookbook published for family and friends by our daughter-in-law, Denise, and her mother, Emma Lillian Plauche.

Baked Cheshire

Kathy Morrison
Ghost Ranch staff

3	cups water
1 1/2	teaspoons salt
1 1/2	cups cornmeal
4	eggs, beaten
4	cups cheese in 1/2"chunks
	Garlic powder to taste

Into boiling water, slowly stir salt and cornmeal so that it doesn't lump. Lower heat and simmer for 3-5 minutes, stirring constantly. Remove from heat, add eggs, cheese and garlic. Pour into oiled quiche pan, bake at 350°F for 45-60 minutes. (Serves 6.)

Hominy with Green Chilies

Janis Payne Simmons
Dallas, TX

2   cans white hominy (posole), drained (14 1/2 oz. each)
1   can chopped green chilies, drained (4 oz.)
1   cup sour cream (8 oz.)
2   cups shredded cheese (8 oz.)

Mix all ingredients except cheese in large bowl. Spoon into greased medium-size casserole dish. Cover with cheese. Bake at 350°F for 30 minutes. (6 to 8 servings.)

Gnocchi a la Romaine

Cirrelda Snider Bryan and Liz Snider Anderson
Albuquerque, NM

1   quart low-fat milk
2/3   cup butter or margarine, (1 stick plus 5 tbs.), divided
1   cup hominy grits (not quick-cooking)
1   teaspoon salt
1/2   teaspoon pepper
1   cup shredded Gruyere (Swiss) cheese (4 oz.)
1/3   cup grated Parmesan cheese

Bring milk to boiling in large saucepan over medium heat. Add 1 stick butter, cut into pieces; stir until melted. Gradually stir in grits. Heat to boiling; reduce heat and cook, stirring constantly until the mixture looks like cream of wheat. Remove from heat. Season with salt and pepper. Beat with electric mixer at high speed until grits are creamy, about 5 minutes. Pour into a greased 13 x 9 x 2" baking dish. Melt remaining 5 tablespoons butter; pour over grits. Sprinkle with cheeses. Bake at 400°F for 30 minutes. Place under broiler until the top is light brown and crusty, 2 to 3 minutes. This recipe can be double or tripled. (4 to 6 servings.)

Our mom would make these grits whenever she'd have company over. She'd usually serve it with ham, ham loaf or barbecued brisket.

Soups & Chili

Cold Berry Soup

Eleanor Shimeall
Stockton, CA

1	quart orange juice (4 cups)
1	quart any combination of plain yogurt, buttermilk, sour cream
2	tablespoons lemon or lime juice
1	tablespoon honey
1/8	teaspoon cinnamon
1/8	teaspoon nutmeg
1 1/2	pints fresh berries, washed and drained (blueberries, strawberries, raspberries)
	Fresh mint sprigs

Whisk together all ingredients except berries and mint in a large bowl. Cover and refrigerate. If strawberries are large, cut in half or slice. At serving time, ladle soup into bowls; add berries and garnish with mint sprigs. (4 to 6 servings.)

Gazpacho

Evelyn King
Chattanooga, OK

1	cup chopped, peeled tomato
1/2	cup chopped green bell pepper
1/2	cup chopped celery
1/2	cup chopped cucumber, peeled or unpeeled
1/4	cup chopped onion
2	tablespoons chopped parsley
1	teaspoon chopped chives
1	clove garlic, minced
2	tablespoons tarragon wine vinegar
2	tablespoons olive oil
1	teaspoon salt (optional)
1/2	teaspoon Worcestershire sauce
1/4	teaspoon black pepper
2	cups tomato juice

Combine everything except the tomato juice in a large bowl. Stir in tomato juice. Add more vinegar if desired. Can also add more tomato juice. Serve hot or cold. (6 to 8 servings.)

Blender Gazpacho

Peggy Welch
Blanco, TX

1	can tomatoes, undrained (28 oz.)
1	cup tomato juice
1	cup buttermilk
1	small onion, chopped
1	small cucumber, chopped
1	small green bell pepper, seeded and chopped
1	clove garlic
2	tablespoons olive oil
1/2 to 1	teaspoon chili powder
1/2	teaspoon salt
1/2	teaspoon ground cumin
	Hot sauce to taste

Combine all ingredients in a large bowl. Process in batches until smooth in a blender or food processor. Cover and refrigerate. (8 to 10 servings.)

Cold Curried Zucchini Soup

Jan and Wil Hufton
Saginaw, MI

6	tablespoons margarine
2	pounds (8 to 10 medium) zucchini, chopped
1	bunch chopped green onions with tender green tops (about 1 cup)
1	teaspoon curry powder
1	teaspoon ground cumin
2	cups chicken broth
1 1/2	cups plain yogurt
1 1/2	cups half-and-half cream
	Salt and pepper to taste

Melt margarine in large skillet over medium heat. Add zucchini and green onions. Cook until soft but not brown. Add curry powder and cumin. Cook 2 minutes, stirring constantly. Add broth. Puree in food processor or blender. Place in a large bowl and whisk in yogurt and half-and-half. Season to taste with salt and pepper. Cover and refrigerate before serving. (8 to 10 servings.)

Zucchini Soup

Jean Roath
Socorro, NM

3	tablespoons vegetable oil
1	onion, chopped (about 1/2 cup)
1	clove garlic, chopped
4	tablespoons all-purpose flour
2 1/2	cups grated zucchini (or chopped broccoli)
3	cups chicken broth (or milk)
1	teaspoon curry powder
1/4	teaspoon nutmeg
1	package cream cheese or Neufchatel (3 oz.)

Heat oil in large skillet. Cook onion and garlic in oil until soft but not brown. Add flour; cook and stir 1 minute. Add zucchini and chicken broth. Heat to boiling, stirring constantly. Reduce heat and continue cooking 3 to 6 minutes. Add curry powder and nutmeg. Place zucchini mixture in blender container; add cheese. Cover; hold top and process on high until smooth. Process in several batches if necessary. (4 to 6 servings.)

Low-Cholesterol Broccoli Soup

Lawrence D. Schmitz
Denair, CA

2	tablespoons safflower oil
1	cup chopped mushrooms
1/2	medium onion, minced (about 1/4 cup)
2	cloves garlic, minced
1	large can chicken broth, heated, divided (49 1/2 oz.)
3	stalks broccoli, cooked
16	ounces regular tofu, cubed
16	ounces Imo or other sour cream substitute
2	tablespoons cornstarch
1/4	cup water
	Salt to taste
	Paprika
2	tablespoons chopped parsley

Heat oil in a medium skillet. Saute onion, mushrooms and garlic in oil until tender. Add 1/2 cup of the chicken broth to the mushroom mixture. Puree broccoli stems and some florets in blender; mash remaining flowerets. Add broccoli to mushroom mixture. Place tofu, Imo and 1/2 cup of the chicken broth in blender and blend until smooth. Add to mushroom/broccoli mixture. Gradually stir in remaining chicken broth. Dissolve cornstarch in water and add to soup. Season to taste with salt. Heat just to boiling. Serve, garnished with paprika and chopped parsley. (8 to 10 servings.)

Corn Chowder

Peg Bohner Amann
Kerrville, TX

6	slices bacon, diced*
1	onion, chopped (about 1/2 cup)
1/2	green bell pepper, chopped (about 1/2 cup)
1	can cream of mushroom soup (10 3/4 oz.)
2	cans cream-style corn (17 oz. each)
1 1/2	cups milk
	Salt and pepper to taste

Cook bacon until crisp in a large saucepan. Remove and reserve bacon. Saute onion in bacon drippings. Add remaining ingredients; heat but do not boil. Add salt and pepper to taste. (8 servings.)
*May substitute turkey bacon or fat-free ham.

Goes well with a cold winter night, a roaring fire and good friends.

Tomato Soup

Criselda Dominguez
Ghost Ranch staff
Abiquiu, NM

1	cup water
1/2	cup celery, chopped
1/4	cup onion, chopped
1/4	cup green pepper, chopped
1	can tomatoes (#2 1/2)
1	teaspoon salt
	Dash pepper
3	pints milk

Cook celery, onion, and green pepper in water until tender. Add tomatoes; cook for 7 minutes. Season. Heat milk in double boiler; add tomato mixture all at once. (4-6 servings.)

Onion Soup

Ghost Ranch

4	large onions, sliced (1 1/2 lbs.)
4	tablespoons butter
2	cans beef broth or bouillon cubes & water to make 6 cups
2	teaspoons salt
1/4	teaspoon pepper
6-8	slices French bread
1/2	cup Parmesan cheese, grated
1/4	cup Swiss cheese, grated

Saute onion in butter in Dutch oven 15 minutes or until lightly browned. Stir in beef broth, salt and pepper. Bring to a boil, reduce heat, cover, simmer for 30 minutes.

Ladle soup into 6 oven-proof soup bowls or 12 oz. custard cups or 8 cup casserole. Lay bread slices on top. Sprinkle with cheeses. Heat in a very hot oven (425°) for 10 minutes, then place under pre-heated broiler until top is bubbly. (6-8 servings.)

Garden Fresh Vegetable Soup

Benny Chavez
Plaza Resolana staff

1	pound ground beef
8	slices bacon
1	large onion, chopped (about 3/4 cup)
4	quarts beef broth
2	cans kidney beans, rinsed, drained (16 oz. each)
1	can tomato sauce (16 oz.)
1	can stewed tomatoes (16 oz.)
1	cup uncooked elbow macaroni
8	cups diced or sliced vegetables (carrots, celery, peas, green beans, potatoes, zucchini)
1	teaspoon dried basil
1	teaspoon dried oregano
3	cups shredded cabbage, spinach or Swiss chard
	Grated Parmesan cheese

Brown ground beef, bacon and onion in 10 to 12-quart stock pot until beef is no longer pink. Drain excess fat. Add beef broth, kidney beans, tomato sauce, tomatoes, macaroni, 8 cups chopped vegetables and the herbs. Heat to boiling. Reduce heat and simmer for 1 hour or more. Twenty minutes before serving, add the cabbage. Serve with Parmesan cheese. (20 servings.)

Gratinee Lyonnaise (Alsace/Lorraine Onion Soup)

Per Curtiss
Santa Monica, CA

4	tablespoons butter
3	cups finely sliced onions (about 3 large onions)
1	teaspoon finely chopped garlic
1/4	cup all-purpose flour
10	cups water
3	teaspoons salt
1/4	teaspoon fresh ground pepper
1/2	pound French bread, sliced thin, toasted in the oven
2 1/2	cups grated imported Gruyére (Swiss) cheese (about 10 oz.)
2	egg yolks (optional)
1/2	cup sweet port or madeira wine (optional)

Heat butter in a large saucepan. Add onion; cook over medium heat, stirring occasionally, until onions are quite brown, about 15 minutes. Add garlic and flour. Cook, stirring constantly until light brown. Add water, salt and pepper. Bring to a boil; reduce heat and simmer for 25 minutes. Put the onion mixture through a food mill or puree in food processor. Place half the bread in a large oven-proof casserole; top with a third of the cheese (about 3/4 cup). Top with remaining bread and another third of the cheese. Pour the soup on top of the bread; cover with the remaining cheese. Bake at 425°F oven for 25 minutes. If desired, beat egg yolks with wine. Make hole in the top of the hot "gratinee" and pour in the egg mixture. Serve immediately. (8 first-course servings or 6 entree servings.)

Baked Potato Soup

Max and Suzanne Jones
Round Rock, TX

1/4	cup instant mashed potato flakes or granules
2	cups chicken broth
1/2	cup margarine
1/2	cup all-purpose flour
3	cups milk
3	large baked potatoes, with skin, diced
1/4	teaspoon sugar
1/4	teaspoon garlic powder
1/4	teaspoon black pepper
	Salt to taste
1/2	cup shredded Cheddar cheese
1/2	cup crisp-cooked bacon, crumbled
1/3	chopped chives

Combine potato flakes and chicken broth in small bowl; set aside. Heat margarine in medium saucepan over medium heat. Add flour. Cook, stirring constantly, until flour is lightly browned. Stir in potato flake mixture. Gradually stir in milk. Cook, stirring constantly, until mixture is thickened. Stir in diced baked potatoes. Add seasoning and salt to taste. Simmer until soup is hot and thickened. Serve topped with cheese, bacon and chives, or pass and let diners help themselves to toppings. (6 servings.)

Potato Soup

Ghost Ranch

1	medium onion, cut fine
3	stalks celery, diced
2	tablespoons butter
1	teaspoon salt
	Dash pepper
4	medium potatoes, diced
4	cups water
	Grate a little carrot for color, if desired
2	tablespoons flour
1	cup milk
2	tablespoons butter

In pressure cooker, saute onions and celery in butter. Add potatoes, carrots, and water. Cover and bring to boil. Cook 5 minutes and let pressure go down alone.

Mix flour and milk in small bowl; add to cooked potatoes. Add butter. Cook for a few minutes without lid to thicken a bit. If you're feeling fancy you may sprinkle parsley flakes on top before serving.

Old Fashioned Beef Potato Soup

Ghost Ranch

1 1/2	quarts boiling water
1	pound lean beef, browned and drained
1	quart raw potatoes, cubed
1/2	cup celery, chopped
1	cup frozen green chiles, diced
1/2	cup onion, chopped
2	tablespoons cilantro
1	teaspoon pepper
2	teaspoons salt

Boil water in a pot. Add beef, potatoes , celery, chilies, and onions. When all is tender add salt, cilantro and pepper. Boil a bit more and cover. Serve hot. Especially good with cornbread. (8-10 servings.)

Cream of Lima Bean Soup

Gertrude Anderson
Boulder, CO

1	can chicken broth (14 oz.)
1	box frozen lima beans (10 oz.)
1/3	cup sliced green onions, with tender green tops
2	tablespoons margarine

1/2 to 1 teaspoon curry powder

1/4	teaspoon dried tarragon, crushed
1/8	teaspoon pepper
1/2	cup half-and-half or milk
	Sliced green onions, with tender green tops for garnish (optional)

Combine first 7 ingredients in 2-quart saucepan. Heat to boiling; reduce heat, cover and simmer until vegetables are tender, 15 to 20 minutes. Cool slightly. Put into blender container; cover and blend until smooth. Return mixture to saucepan. Stir in cream or milk. Heat but do not boil. Sprinkle with additional sliced green onions, if desired. (4 to 6 servings.)

Senate Bean Soup

Benny Chavez
Plaza Resolana staff

3	pounds dried navy or great northern beans, washed, sorted
1	gallon water
	Smoked ham hocks or ham bone
8	potatoes, peeled, cooked, mashed
4	medium onions, chopped (about 2 cups)
2	cups diced celery
	Salt to taste

Cover beans with water in large stock pot; let stand overnight. In the morning, bring to a boil. Add ham hocks or ham bone. Do not add salt! Cover and simmer until beans are soft, 2 to 3 hours. Add mashed potatoes, onions and celery. Cover and simmer 1 hour more. Remove ham hocks or ham bone and take meat off the bone. Add meat to soup. Season to taste with salt. (20 servings.)

Fabia's Italian Bean Soup

Sara H. Goodnick
Corvallis, OR

1	onion, minced (about 1/2 cup)
1	tablespoon olive oil
1/2	tomato, finely chopped
3	cups hot water
3-4	thin rinds from outside piece of Parmesan or Peccorino Romano cheese (1 to 2" long x 1/4" thick)*
2	bouillon cubes (beef, chicken or vegetable)
2	cans canellini, chickpea, kidney, or navy beans, rinsed, drained (16 oz. each)
	Salt to taste
1/2	cup small pasta

Saute onion in olive oil in medium saucepan until golden. Add tomato and cook a few minutes more. Add hot water, cheese rind slices and bouillon cubes. Heat to boiling. Add beans and simmer 5 minutes. Mash some of the beans with a wooden spoon; add salt to taste. Add pasta 20 to 30 minutes before serving. Let stand 10 minutes before serving. (4 to 6 servings.)

*The cheese rinds are extremely important to the flavor, and are delicious to eat when cooked. Peccorino Romano, from sheep's milk, is much stronger in flavor than the Parmesan.

When I was a student at Colorado State University in Fort Collins in the early 1980s, Fabia, who had recently come to the US from the Perugia area of Italy, shared the house. She learned cooking from her grandmother. She used no recipes, and cooked by smell. I adapted this recipe from her.

Yucatan Black Bean Soup

Jan Knox
Austin, TX

2	tablespoons safflower or other vegetable oil
1	onion, chopped (about 1/2 cup)
2	cloves garlic, minced
2	cups black beans, washed, sorted
2	cups vegetable or chicken broth or water
	Salt to taste
	Black pepper to taste
1	tablespoon celery seeds
1/4	cup lemon juice

Heat oil in large heavy pot or dutch oven. Saute onion and garlic in oil until tender. Add beans and broth or water; heat to boiling. Add salt; cover and reduce heat. Simmer until beans are tender, about 2 hours. Puree pepper and celery seeds in blender. Add to beans. Add lemon juice. Taste and adjust seasonings. (8 servings.)

I first had this soup on a camping trip to the Yucatan Peninsula in Mexico. In the village of Playa del Carmen, we had this as part of a dinner we were served. The only changes I have made are to substitute safflower oil and celery seed.

Black Bean Soup

Margaret Colbert
Flagstaff, AZ

1	cup cooked black beans*
2	cups tomato juice cocktail (such as V-8)
1	teaspoon Beau Monde seasoning
	Lemon slices, if desired
	Parsley, if desired

Combine beans, tomato juice cocktail and seasoning in blender. Cover and process until pureed. Serve hot or cold with lemon and parsley garnish. (2 to 3 servings.)

*To cook beans: Wash, pick over and cover 1/2 cup black beans in water (about 1 1/2 cups). Soak overnight or simmer 5 minutes and then let stand for 1 hour. Cook in pressure cooker 15 minutes with 1 small onion and a little salad oil.

Bean Soup

Daniel M. O'Keefe
Mount Prospect, IL

4	cups water
1	package black beans, washed, sorted (12 oz.)
1	large onion, chopped (about 3/4 cup)
3	cloves garlic, minced
1	tomato, peeled, chopped
1	large stalk celery, chopped
1	ham bone
2	tablespoons cocoa powder
1/2	teaspoon dry mustard
1/2	teaspoon ground chili
	Ground black pepper to taste
3	tablespoons sherry
	Additional sherry, sour cream and sliced green onions for garnish, if desired

Bring water to a boil in a large pot; add beans. Heat to boiling; reduce heat and simmer 10 minutes. Remove from stove and let stand, covered, 1 hour. Add garlic, onion, celery, tomato and ham bone. Return to heat. Bring to boiling; reduce heat, cover and simmer until beans are tender, 2 to 3 hours. Add more water as it evaporates. Remove ham bone. Puree soup in blender container, covered, 2 cups at a time. Return to pot. Add cocoa, mustard, chili, pepper and 3 tablespoons sherry. Serve garnished with additional sherry, sour cream and sliced green onions. (3 to 4 servings).

Tex-Mex Lentil Soup

R. Kay and Suzanne Brown
Phoenix, AZ

2	tablespoons vegetable oil
1	large onion, chopped (about 3/4 cup)
2	garlic cloves, minced
1 1/4	cups lentils, washed, sorted
1	quart water
1	can chopped green chilies (4 oz.)
2	teaspoons dried oregano
1	teaspoon ground cumin
1	can tomatoes, crushed or chopped, undrained (16 oz.)
1	package frozen corn (10 oz.)
1	green bell pepper, chopped (about 1 cup)
	Salt to taste
1	cup shredded Monterey Jack cheese (about 4 oz.)

Heat oil in large pan over medium-high heat. Saute onion and garlic in oil until tender, about 5 minutes. Add lentils, water, chilies and herbs. Heat to boiling; reduce heat. Cover and simmer 30 minutes. Add tomatoes and tomato liquid, corn and green pepper. Cover and simmer until lentils are tender, 10 to 15 minutes. Add salt to taste. Serve topped with cheese. (4 to 6 servings.)

Lentil & Vegetable Soup

Ghost Ranch

6	cups water
1	cup dry lentils, rinsed
1/2	cup carrots, chopped
1/2	cup celery, chopped
1	tablespoon vegetable oil
2	tablespoons flour
1/2	cup onions, chopped
	Salt to taste
	Oregano leaves
	Fresh cilantro

Pour water in saucepan, add lentils and boil. While boiling add carrots and celery. Cook until tender, 1 1/2 to 2 hours. Brown flour in oiled skillet. Add onions, saute until slightly browned. Add onions and flour to soup. Add herbs to taste. (4-6 servings.)

Calico Bean Soup Mix

John and Barbara Decker
Hutchinson, KS

1	pound pearl barley
1	pound black beans
1	pound pinto beans
1	pound navy beans
1	pound great northern beans
1	pound lentils
1	pound split peas
1	pound black-eyed peas

Combine all dried beans in large container. Divide into ten 2-cup packages for gift-giving, and present with the following recipe for Calico Bean Soup:

Note: If you can't find the beans listed, substitute others.

Calico Bean Soup

2	cups Calico Bean Soup Mix, washed and sorted
4	or more quarts water, divided
1	ham bone
1	pound ham, diced
1	large onion, chopped (about 3/4 cup)
1	clove garlic, minced
1/2	teaspoon salt
1	can tomatoes, undrained, chopped (16 ounces)
1	can tomatoes with green chilies, (Rotel brand), undrained (10 ounces)

Cover beans with water, 2" above top, in large pot. Let stand overnight. Drain beans; add 2 quarts (8 cups) water and next 5 ingredients. Bring to a boil; reduce heat, cover and simmer until beans are tender, about 1 1/2 hours. Add remaining ingredients. Simmer 30 minutes, stirring occasionally. (8 to 10 servings).

Note: All ingredients may be combined and cooked in a crock pot, 4 to 6 hours on high or 8 to 10 hours on low. One pound ground beef, browned and drained or beef bouillon may be substituted for the ham bone.

Carol's Soup

Carol Mackey
Pampa, TX

1	pound lean ground meat
1	small onion, minced (about 1/3 cup)
1	large can tomato juice (46 oz.)
2	cans cream of celery soup (10 3/4 oz. each)
2	cups water, divided
2	cups shredded carrot
1/4 - 1/2 teaspoon garlic powder	
1	cup uncooked instant rice
	Salsa

Cook meat and onion over medium heat in large pot until meat is no longer pink; drain. Add juice, soup and 1 cup of the water. Heat to boiling; reduce heat. Add carrots and garlic powder. Cook over low heat until carrots are tender. Add rice and the remaining 1 cup of water; cover and cook until rice is done, 10 to 15 minutes. Add more water if necessary. Stir in salsa to taste, or pass at the table. (4 to 6 servings.)

My mother made this "Hamburger Soup" when I was a child. I loved it so much she began calling it by my name! I added the rice and salsa to suit my family's southwestern palate.

Thai Rice Soup

Jane Arp
Santa Fe, NM

3/4	cup left-over pork or chicken, cut in small pieces
3	cups water
1 1/2	cups cooked rice
1	medium onion, chopped
1	tablespoon fish sauce (found in Oriental food section)
1/2	teaspoon pepper
1	tablespoon fresh ginger, chopped
1	tablespoon celery leaves
	Parsley sprigs (1 per soup bowl)

Bring water and meat to a boil. Add rice, onion, fish sauce, pepper, and ginger. Cook 10 minutes on medium heat. Put in soup bowls and garnish with celery and parsley. (4-6 servings.)

This is a very common Thai dish, served for breakfast or lunch, or as a refreshment after an evening program.

Cioppino

Hugh W. Frey
Indianapolis, IN

2	large onions, diced (1 1/2 to 2 cups)
2 to 4	cloves garlic, minced
1	green bell pepper, chopped (about 1 cup)
2	cups tomato juice or tomato juice cocktail (V-8)
2	potatoes, peeled, diced
2	carrots, sliced
1	can tomatoes, undrained (28 oz.)
1/2	cup red wine
1	tablespoon fresh minced parsley or 1 teaspoon dried parsley
1	teaspoon dried oregano
1/2	teaspoon dried basil
1/4	teaspoon ground pepper
1	pound halibut (or other firm fish), cut in chunks

Put the onions, garlic, green pepper and tomato juice into a large pot. Cover and cook 10 minutes. Add potatoes and carrots; cook until vegetables are cooked but potatoes and carrots are still firm. Add tomatoes, wine, parsley, oregano, basil and pepper; cover and cook 10 minutes. Add fish; cover and cook for 15 minutes; uncover and cook for 5 minutes. (6 servings.)

Boston Clam Chowder

Mildred Lee Rydell
Tigard, OR

4	slices bacon
2	medium onions, chopped (about 1 cup)
2	cups boiling water
2	cups instant mashed potato flakes or granules
1	quart milk (4 cups)
1	pint minced clams, drained (16 oz.)
	Salt and pepper

Cook bacon in a medium saucepan; remove and reserve. Drain almost all of the drippings. Add onions to saucepan and cook over medium heat until wilted, about 3 minutes. Add water and potatoes. Cook until potatoes are done. Crumble reserved bacon and add to potato mixture. Add milk and clams. Simmer for 45 minutes over low heat; do not boil. (6 servings.)

This recipe was given to me by a family who emigrated from Finland to Boston.

Arizona Chowder

Linda Stitt
Tucson, AZ

8	slices bacon
1/2	cup chopped celery
1	cup sliced green onions with tender green tops
3	medium red potatoes, unpeeled, diced (about 1lb.)
1	can tomato sauce (8 oz.)
1	cup chicken broth
4	cans chopped clams, drained (6 1/2 oz. each)
1	cup half-and-half cream
1	cup milk
	Pepper to taste

Cook bacon in large pot until crisp. Remove and reserve bacon; drain drippings. Add celery, onions, potatoes, tomato sauce and chicken broth to pot. Bring to a boil over high heat. Reduce heat; cover and simmer until potatoes are tender, about 15 minutes. Stir in clams, half-and-half, milk and pepper. Heat until steaming but not boiling. (Makes 2 1/2 quarts — 5 to 6 servings.)

Mexican Tortilla Soup

Paula B. Trefz
Sharon, CT

2	cups water
1	can beef broth (14 1/2 oz.)
1	can chicken broth (14 1/2 oz.)
1	can tomatoes, undrained, cut up (14 1/2 oz.)
1/2	cup chopped onion
1/4	cup chopped green bell pepper
1 1/2	pounds chicken breast, skinned and boned, cut into large pieces
1	can whole kernel corn, drained (8 3/4 oz.)
1	teaspoon chili powder
1/2	teaspoon ground cumin
1/8	teaspoon pepper
3	cups tortilla chips, broken into pieces
4	ounces Monterey Jack cheese, shredded (about 1 cup)
1	avocado, peeled, seeded, cubed (optional)
	Fresh cilantro, chopped (optional)

Heat first 6 ingredients to boiling in a medium saucepan. Add chicken. Reduce heat; cover and simmer for 10 minutes. Add corn, chili powder, cumin and the pepper. Cover and continue cooking for 10 minutes. To serve. Place about 1/2 cup tortilla chips in each of 6 bowls. Ladle soup over tortilla chips. Sprinkle with cheese. Garnish with avocado and cilantro, if desired. (6 servings.)

In 1990, we visited Mexico City in search of Aztec ruins. While we were there, we ate in a tiny out-of-the-way restaurant that served a soup similar to this.

Tortilla Soup

Janis Payne Simmons
Dallas, TX

2	tablespoons vegetable oil
1	medium onion, or green onions, chopped (about 1/2 cup)
1	jalapeño pepper, seeds and stems removed, chopped*
2	cloves garlic, minced
2	cups cooked chicken (or stew meat), chopped
1	can tomatoes, undrained (14 1/2 oz.)
1	can tomatoes with green chilies (Rotel brand), undrained (10 oz.)
1	can beef broth (10 1/2 oz.)
1	can chicken broth (10 3/4 oz.)
1	can tomato soup (10 3/4 oz.)
1 1/2	soup cans water
1	teaspoon salt
1	teaspoon ground cumin
1	teaspoon chili powder
2	teaspoons Worcestershire sauce
1/2	teaspoon lemon-pepper seasoning
4	corn tortillas, cut in 1" square
1/4	cup shredded Cheddar cheese (about 1 oz.)
1	avocado, chopped (optional)
	Tabasco sauce (optional)

Heat oil in a large pot. Saute onion, jalapeño pepper, garlic and chicken until onion is tender. Add remaining ingredients except the tortillas and cheese; cover and simmer 50 minutes over medium heat. Add tortillas and cook 10 minutes. Serve topped with cheese and avocado, if desired. Pass the Tabasco sauce. (6 servings.)

* Handle jalapeño peppers carefully. Use rubber gloves; avoid contact with eyes.

Savory Southwestern Soup

Suzanne Reininga
Hinsdale, IL

1	pound ground chuck
1	medium onion, chopped (about 1/2 cup)
	Salt and freshly ground pepper
2	celery stalks, chopped
2	carrots, sliced
1	small zucchini, sliced (optional)
1	can peeled tomatoes, undrained, broken up (28 oz.)
1	can beef bouillon (10 1/2 oz.)
1	soup can water
1	small can whole kernel corn, drained (about 6 oz.)
1	tablespoon chili powder

Cook beef with onion and salt and pepper in large pot until meat is no longer red. Drain fat. Stir in remaining ingredients. Heat to boiling; reduce heat and simmer for 30 minutes. (6 servings.)

Serve with sourdough bread or cornbread and a salad of greens that includes fresh apple and orange slices and a sprinkling of sunflower seeds.

Chicken Posole Soup

Linda Stitt
Tucson, AZ

6	cups chicken broth
3	carrots, sliced
2	onions, chopped
2	cloves garlic, minced
1	tablespoon oregano
1/2	teaspoon ground cumin
1	can hominy, drained (29 oz.)
1	can chicken (10 oz.)
2	cans diced green chilies, drained (4 oz. each)
1	can sliced ripe olives, drained (2 1/4 oz.)

Heat chicken broth in large pot. Add carrots, onions, garlic, oregano and cumin. Cook until vegetables are tender. Add remaining ingredients. Heat to boiling; reduce heat, cover and simmer 10 minutes. (6 servings.)

Sopa de Fideo

Cordelia Coronado
Medanales, NM

1	tablespoon vegetable oil or lard
1	bag thin coiled noodles (vermicelli) (10 oz.)
1/2	cup chopped onion (1 medium onion)
1	clove garlic, mashed
1	can (15 oz.) tomato sauce (or 1 1/2 cups chopped fresh tomatoes)
6	cups water
1	beef bouillon cube
1	teaspoon celery salt
	Salt to taste

Heat oil in large saucepan. Cook noodles and onion in hot oil until light brown, stirring constantly. Add garlic, tomato sauce and water. Heat to boiling. Add bouillon cube and celery salt; season to taste with salt. Reduce heat and simmer over medium heat until noodles are tender but not mushy, 5 to 10 minutes. (6 to 8 servings.)

Note: 1/2 pound ground beef may be added and browned with the noodles. Add more water if you like the soup thinner.

editor's note: Cordelia, or "Cordy" as she is known by family and friends, has taught weaving at Ghost Ranch for many years. In 1991, she was named a "Santa Fe Living Treasure." Cordy has been a treasure to us for a long time!

Tish's Low-Fat Green Chili Soup/Stew

Tish Varney
Littleton, CO

1/4	cup olive oil
6 to 8	large Anaheim chilies, roasted, peeled, seeded, chopped (about 2 cups)
1-1 1/2	pounds lean pork, cut into 1/2"-cubes (boneless pork loin preferred)
1	large onion, diced (about 3/4 cup)
4	cloves garlic, minced
1	can (16 oz.) tomatoes, whole, sliced or chopped, undrained
4	cups (32 oz.) chicken broth
1	red bell pepper, chopped (optional)
2	fresh or dried cayenne peppers (about 2" long), seeded, chopped
1	tablespoon minced cilantro or 1 tablespoon mixed dried summer savory and dried tarragon
1	tablespoon fresh coarsely ground black pepper
1	teaspoon ground cumin
1	teaspoon Cajun spice (such as Paul Prudhomme's)

Thickener:

Thin: 1 teaspoon cornstarch dissolved in 1/4 cup water.

Thick: 1 tablespoon cornstarch dissolved in 1/2 cup water.

Heat olive oil in 12" skillet or large cast-iron pan. Add meat and brown carefully over high heat, stirring constantly and scraping bottom. Remove and place meat in slow cooker. Let pan cool slightly. Add onion to hot skillet. Cook, covered, over medium heat, stirring occasionally, until onion is transparent — do not add fat or liquid. Add garlic and saute briefly before adding remaining ingredients, except thickener. Heat to boiling; add to meat in slow cooker. Cook on low setting for 8 hours. Best if made a day ahead. When ready to serve, reheat and thicken to desired consistency. (4 to 6 servings.)

If you can find fresh New Mexico (Anaheim) chilies roasted on the spot by the seller, you'll have a great head start. We package our fresh roasted chilies in 2-cup packages after we peel them and remove the seeds. Then we freeze them. Slightly frozen chilies are easier to chop, so it all works out. Canned green chilies can be substituted for the fresh or frozen ones.

Taco Soup

Sue Hall
Oklahoma City, OK

2	pounds ground beef
1	medium onion, chopped (about 1/2 cup)
1	package taco seasoning mix (1 1/4 oz.)
2	cans stewed tomatoes (14 1/2 oz. each)
1	can Mexican-style stewed tomatoes (14 1/2 oz.)
1	can pinto beans, drained, rinsed (about 16 oz.)
1	can (about 16 oz.) pinto beans with jalapeño peppers, drained, rinsed (or 1 16 oz. can pinto beans + 4 oz. can chopped green chilies)
1	can whole kernel corn with juice (17 oz.)
2	corn cans of water

Brown ground beef and onion in large pot until beef loses its red color; drain fat. Stir in remaining ingredients; heat to boiling. Reduce heat; cover and simmer 1 hour. (12 to 14 servings.)

Chili Soup

Carrel Prey
Verona, WI

1	tablespoon vegetable oil
2	medium onions, chopped (about 1 cup)
3	stalks celery, chopped
1	green bell pepper, chopped (about 1 cup)
2	large cans tomatoes, undrained (28 oz. each)
2	cans kidney beans, undrained (14 oz. each)
1	can mushrooms, undrained (8 oz.)

Any two of the following to make 2 to 3 cups:

1/2	head cauliflower, cut in chunks
1	pound Brussels sprouts
1/2	pound broccoli, trimmed and cut in chunks
2	bay leaves
1 1/2	tablespoons chili powder
	Salt and pepper to taste

Heat oil in large pot. Cook onion, celery and green pepper in hot oil until tender. Add tomatoes, beans and mushrooms. Stir in fresh vegetables and seasonings. Heat to boiling; reduce heat, cover and simmer over low heat 1 hour. Remove bay leaves before serving. (8 servings.)

Scott's Hot Chili

Scott Winnette
Ghost Ranch volunteer

1	pound dried kidney or pinto beans, washed, sorted (use mix if you wish)
2	quarts water
1	pound ground beef or turkey
1	roll spicy sausage (16 oz.)
1	large onion, chopped (about 3/4 cup)
1	green bell pepper, chopped (about 1 cup)
1	can stewed tomatoes (14 1/2 oz.)
1	can refried beans (16 oz.)
2	tablespoons chili powder
1	tablespoon cayenne pepper

Soak beans in water overnight. Drain. Brown beef or turkey and sausage with onion and pepper in large pot; drain fat. Add remaining ingredients. Heat to boiling; reduce heat and simmer until beans are tender, about 2 hours.

New West Turkey Chili

Jan and Wil Hufton
Saginaw, MI

2	tablespoons vegetable oil
1	large onion, chopped (about 3/4 cup)
1	small green bell pepper, finely chopped (about 3/4 cup)
2	turkey thighs (about 1 1/2 lbs. each), skinned, boned, cut into 1/2" cubes
1	can tomatoes, undrained (28 oz.)
1/4	cup soy sauce
2	cloves garlic, pressed or minced
2	teaspoons chili powder
1	can kidney beans, rinsed, drained (15 1/2 oz.)
	Hot cooked rice

Heat oil in dutch oven or large pot. Saute onion and green pepper in hot oil until soft. Stir in turkey; cook until no longer pink. Stir in tomatoes, soy sauce, garlic and chili powder; cover and simmer 30 minutes, stirring occasionally to break up tomatoes. Stir in kidney beans; simmer uncovered until turkey is tender, about 15 minutes. Serve over hot rice. (6 servings.)

Marleen's White Chili

Jan and Wil Hufton
Saginaw, MI

1	tablespoon olive oil
1	whole chicken breast (about 2 lbs.), boned, skinned, cut into bite-size pieces
1	jar pre-cooked great northern beans, drained (48 oz.)
1	jar mild salsa (8 oz.)
2	teaspoons ground cumin
8	ounces Monterey Jack cheese, shredded (about 2 cups)
	Corn chips

Heat oil in 3-quart pot. Brown chicken in hot oil until it turns white, about 10 minutes. Add beans, salsa and cumin. Cook uncovered, stirring occasionally, about 10 minutes. Add cheese; stir constantly until melted, about 7 minutes. Serve with corn chips. (6 to 8 servings.)

Vegetarian Green Chili Sauce

Ghost Ranch

1	tablespoon vegetable oil
1	tablespoon all-purpose flour
3	cups water
2	cups chopped, frozen green chilies*
1	cup chopped tomatoes (8 oz.)
2	cloves garlic, chopped
1	teaspoon dried oregano
	Salt to taste

Heat oil in a large heavy sauce; add flour. Cook, stirring constantly, over medium-high heat until flour browns. Watch carefully! Gradually stir in water. Add chilies, tomatoes, garlic and oregano. Heat to boiling; reduce heat and cook, covered, 20 minutes. Add salt to taste. (Makes about 4 cups.)

*Note: May use canned green chilies if fresh or frozen chilies are not available.

Green Chili Stew

Benny Chavez
Plaza Resolana staff

3	tablespoons vegetable oil
2	pounds lean beef or pork, cut into 1/2" pieces
1/2	cup chopped onion (1 medium onion)
1	large clove garlic, minced
3	tablespoons all-purpose flour
1	pound fresh or frozen green chilies, roasted, peeled, chopped (or canned)
4	cups water or beef broth
1	teaspoon salt

Heat oil in large skillet or pot. Add meat; cook over lowest possible heat, stirring frequently, until meat is brown and tender. Add onion, garlic and flour. Cook and stir 2 minutes. Add chili, water and salt. Heat to boiling; reduce heat, cover and simmer 30 minutes. (8 to 10 servings.)

*May substitute canned tomatoes in liquid for some of the water.

Green Chilies with Beef or Pork

Ghost Ranch

2	tablespoons vegetable oil
1/2	pound ground beef or pork
1	tablespoon all-purpose flour
2	cups chopped fresh or frozen green chilies (may use canned)
1	cup chopped fresh tomatoes
2	cloves garlic, chopped
4	cups water
	Salt to taste
	Posole (hominy) or beans

Heat oil in large pot. Cook beef over medium heat until it is no longer red; drain excess fat. Add flour; cook and stir 2 minutes. Stir in chilies, tomatoes, garlic and water. Heat to boiling; reduce heat and simmer, covered, 20 minutes. Add salt to taste. Serve with posole or beans. (8 servings.)

Solamente Para Divirtirnos Chili ("Just For Our Own Fun Chili")

Norman Cash and Ken Miller
Wichita, KS

Zapata's Hot Oil:

2	ounces crushed dried red pepper (about 1/2 cup)
1	cup peanut or other vegetable oil
4	ribeye steaks, cubed (8 oz. each)
2	tablespoons bacon drippings
12	ounces cooked pork, shredded by hand (about 1 1/2 cups)
3	hot links, cooked, sliced 3/8" thick then quartered
1 1/2	green bell peppers, diced (about 1 1/2 cups)
1 1/2	medium onions, diced (about 1 1/2 cups)
3	cans plum tomatoes, crushed (28 oz. each)
3	cans stewed tomatoes (14 1/2 oz. each)
3	cans chili with no beans, Ellis brand preferred, (15 1/2 oz. each)
3	cans diced green chilies, drained (4 oz. each)
3	tablespoons chili powder
1 1/2	teaspoon cayenne pepper
1 1/2	teaspoon minced garlic
1 1/2	teaspoon salt
3/4	teaspoon black pepper
3/4	teaspoon dried oregano
1/2	teaspoon ground cumin

Make Zapata's hot oil by soaking red peppers in oil for 24 hours. Drain oil and add to beef in non-metallic container. Cover and marinade in refrigerator 24 hours. Remove beef from marinate and brown it in a large pot over medium heat with a little bacon drippings. Add remaining ingredients. Reduce heat; simmer "til you can't stand it any longer." (Makes 12+ servings.)

editor's note: This recipe, formulated by Norman and Ken, beat out 24 other entrants for top honors in a chile cook-off held by the Wichita State University Alumni Association.

Turner Chili

Carol Mackey
Pampa, TX

3	pounds beef chuck, trimmed, cut into small strips or pieces
1	cup hot water
1	can tomatoes, undrained (14 1/2 oz.)
1	can tomatoes with green chilies, Rotel preferred, undrained (10 oz.)
3	packages chili mix (French's preferred)
2	teaspoons cumin seed
1	pound lean ground meat (beef, pork, turkey)
1	large onion, chopped (about 3/4 cup)
	Salt and pepper to taste

Cook beef chuck in hot water in slow cooker on low setting overnight (8 hours). Mash canned tomatoes and add to crock pot with chili mix and cumin. Cook on low setting 4 to 5 hours. Brown ground meat and onion in skillet over medium heat; drain and add to crock pot. Continue cooking on low for 3 hours, adding water as needed. Season to taste with salt and pepper. Best when cooked 16 to 20 hours. (8 servings.)

This recipe comes from a Presbyterian minister with a strong liking for 'hot' dishes. He even raises his own pequin peppers. This chili is not very hot, however. It has been served at so many youth fundraisers, we sometimes call it "Presbyterian Chili."

Mulligatawny Soup

Ghost Ranch

3	boneless chicken-breast halves, diced into 1/2" pieces
4	tablespoons butter
3	stalks celery, sliced
1	large potato, peeled and diced
2	large onions, chopped
4	cloves garlic, smashed
2	carrots, diced
1	tablespoon curry powder
1/4	teaspoon ground cumin
1/4	teaspoon ground clove
1/4	teaspoon ground ginger
	Dash of cayenne pepper
	Salt and pepper to taste
8	cups chicken broth
3	cups cooked rice
2	Granny Smith apples, peeled, cored, shredded
2	tablespoons lemon juice
1	cup plain yogurt

Melt butter in stockpot. Cook chicken in hot butter until no longer pink, about 5 minutes. Remove chicken and set aside. In remaining butter, saute celery, potato, onion, garlic, carrot, and spices for 5 minutes. Add chicken broth and chicken breasts, simmer 20 minutes. Return chicken to pot with apples and lemon juice. Add rice to soup, reheat. Add a dollop of yogurt to each bowl. Serves 8.

Coyote's Giant Pinto Bean Soup

Elizabeth Berry
Santa Fe, NM

1	pound giant pinto beans
1/2	pound smoked bacon, diced
1	medium white onion, diced
6	cloves garlic, minced
6	Roma tomatoes, halved & roasted in a 350° oven for 1/2 hour
2	tablespoons chipotle chile en adobo
1/2	cup olive oil
2	tablespoons fresh marjoram, chopped
	Salt

Cook beans in 1 1/2 gallons water for 2 hours. Drain. While beans are cooking, saute bacon in olive oil over medium heat for 5 minutes. Add garlic and onions and cook 5 more minutes. Add tomatoes and chipotle sauce. Stir in 2 quarts water and cook for 1/2 hour to blend flavors and beans become soft. Add marjoram and season with salt. Serve with crema and "green" tortillas.

Note: For a slightly thicker soup, pulse 2 cups of soup in food processor and return to soup. For a spicier soup, add more chipotles.

Crema:
Mix 1 cup sour cream with 1 tablespoon lime juice.

Green Tortillas:

1	tablespoon basil
1	tablespoon cilantro
1	tablespoon parsley
1/2	cup olive oil
1/2	cup water
1	tablespoon dried jalapeno or serrano chiles
	Flour tortillas

Process ingredients in food processor. Rub mixture on one side of flour tortillas and bake in 350° oven until crisp. Cut into triangles.

editor's note: These dishes were designed for Elizabeth Berry by Mark Kiffin, head chef at the Coyote Cafe in Santa Fe. Elizabeth Berry owns the Gallina Canyon Ranch (just north of Ghost Ranch), where she grows organic heirloom vegetables (endangered varieties) for several restaurants in northern New Mexico. She had these tips for cooking beans:

I prefer pre-soaking beans, usually overnight, to lessen cooking time and enhance flavor. Never boil beans rapidly, always simmer. Always keep beans covered with water when cooking. Add salt at end of cooking to prevent toughness and shrivelling. To hasten cooking time, pressure cook at 15 lbs. pressure. Allow longer cooking time at higher altitudes. Beans and further information are available from: Elizabeth Berry, 144 Camino Escondido, Santa Fe, NM 87501

This & That

Microwave Cucumbers

John and Barbara Decker
Hutchinson, KS

2	cucumbers, unpeeled, thinly sliced
1 to 2	onions, cut in rings
1	cup sugar
1/2	cup vinegar
1/2	teaspoon salt
1/4	teaspoon tumeric
1/4	teaspoon celery seed
1/4	teaspoon mustard seed

Combine all ingredients in large, microwave-safe container. Microwave uncovered on High (100%) 5 minutes. Stir and microwave uncovered 5 minutes more on High. Cool and pack in jars. Store in refrigerator.

Green Tomato Pickles

'Becca May
Ghost Ranch staff

7	pounds green tomatoes, thin-sliced
2	gallons water
3	cups lime

Syrup:

5	pounds sugar
3	pints cider vinegar
1	tablespoon whole cloves
1	tablespoon whole allspice
1	tablespoon celery seed
1	tablespoon mace
1	cinnamon stick

Dissolve lime in water; soak tomatoes for 24 hours. Drain, soak for 4 hours in clean water, changing water every hour. Drain well. To make syrup, combine ingredients in a large saucepan and heat to boiling. Cool. Pour syrup over pickles and let stand overnight. Boil all gently for 1 hour, pack in hot, sterile jars and seal. Don't open for several weeks.

Dilled Squash

Helen Hall
Ghost Ranch staff

3	pounds zucchini, unpeeled, thinly sliced
3	pounds summer squash, unpeeled, thinly sliced
2	cups sliced celery
2	cups chopped onions (3 to 4 medium onions)
1/3	cup salt
	Ice cubes
2	cups sugar
2	cups white vinegar
2	tablespoons dill seeds
	Garlic cloves, peeled

Combine zucchini, summer squash, celery, onions and salt in large bowl. Place a layer of ice cubes on top. Cover and let stand at room temperature 3 hours; drain. Combine sugar, vinegar and dill seeds in large pot; heat to boiling, stirring constantly. Stir in vegetables; heat to boiling, stirring occasionally. Remove from heat. Spoon into hot sterile jars. Put garlic clove in each jar. Process in water bath 10 minutes.

Crunchy Pickles

Nola Scott
Ghost Ranch staff

1	jar (32 oz.) whole dill pickles (not Kosher)
2 1/2	cups sugar
1/2	cup vinegar
1/2	cup water

Drain pickles; cut each pickle in quarters, lengthwise. Place in large, non-metallic container. Combine sugar, vinegar and water in medium saucepan; heat to boiling. Pour over pickles. Cover and refrigerate at least 24 hours.

Fresh Pickled Vegetables

Ghost Ranch

Pickling liquid:
2	teaspoons basil
4	teaspoons sugar
1 1/3	teaspoons salt
1/3	cup white wine vinegar
1	small garlic clove
	Cheesecloth

Vegetable choices:
1	small bunch celery, sliced
3	medium carrots, sliced
2	cups cauliflower, broken into flowerets
3	small zucchini, sliced
1	package frozen green beans (9 oz.)
1	can small white onions

Place basil in cheesecloth and tie with string. In a pint jar place vinegar, sugar, salt, and minced garlic; stir until salt dissolves. Add spice bag and one of the vegetables; cover and refrigerate overnight. Makes enough liquid for 1 pint of vegetables. To serve, remove vegetables from liquid.

Hot Pickled Pepper

Helen Hall
Ghost Ranch staff

1 pound red, green and yellow hot peppers, (about 8 cups)
4	heads fresh dill or 2 tablespoons dill seed (optional)
3	cups water
1	cup white vinegar
2	tablespoons pickling salt
1	tablespoon sugar
2	cloves garlic, minced
1/2	teaspoon crushed dried red pepper flakes

Make 2 small slits in each hot pepper. Pack peppers into hot, sterile pint jars. If using dill, put 1 1/2 teaspoon in each jar. Combine remaining ingredients in medium saucepan; heat to boiling. Pour over peppers. Seal and process in water bath for 10 minutes.

Red Chile Jam

Criselda Dominguez
Ghost Ranch staff
Abiquiu, NM

12	large fresh red chiles
	Cider vinegar
2	lemons, quartered
3	cups sugar
	Paraffin

Remove seeds from chiles, grind and cover with water. Boil 5 minutes and drain. Cover with cider vinegar, add lemons. Simmer 30 minutes. Remove lemons, add sugar. Boil 10 minutes. Pour in jar and cover with paraffin. Serve with meat.

Jalapeño Jam

Cal Graham
Sacramento, CA

3	green bell peppers, seeds and stems removed, coarsely chopped
2 or 3	jalapeño peppers, seeded, chopped
1 1/2	cups white vinegar, divided
6 1/2	cups sugar
1	teaspoon cayenne pepper
1	bottle liquid pectin (6 oz.)

Place bell and jalapeño peppers and 1 cup of the vinegar in blender or food processor; cover and process until pureed. Place pepper puree in large saucepan. Add the remaining 1/2 cup vinegar, the sugar and cayenne pepper; heat to rolling boil. Add pectin; boil one minute, stirring constantly. Remove from heat and skim off foam. Pour into hot sterile jars and seal. (Makes 5 or 6 half-pint jars.)

Great with meat or as an appetizer with cream cheese on bland crackers. Put it on anything but apple pie! (editor's note: I've had it on apple pie and I love it there too!)

Texas Pepper Jelly

Carolyn Sanders
Dallas, TX

1	cup jalapeño peppers, seeds and stems removed
1/2	cup chopped red or green bell pepper*
1 1/2	cups white vinegar, divided
6	cups sugar
1	bottle liquid pectin (6 oz.)
	Red or green food coloring (optional)

Grind peppers in blender with 1/2 cup of the vinegar. Use more jalapeño peppers for hotter jelly. Cover and refrigerate in non-metallic container 8 hours or overnight. Place pepper mixture in large saucepan; add sugar and remaining 1 cup vinegar. Heat to full rolling boil. Remove from heat; let stand exactly 5 minutes. Skim off foam. Add pectin and food coloring, if desired. Pour in hot sterile jars; let stand to jell before sealing. Seal with melted paraffin. (Makes 6 to 7 half-pint jars.)

*Use red peppers for red jelly; green peppers for green jelly.

A jar of red jelly and a jar of green jelly in a basket with a bow is a good Christmas gift for neighbors. Serve over cream cheese and spread over crackers. Good also with cold sliced ham or turkey.

Pickled Green Chili

Betty Sallee
Santa Fe, NM

1/2	cup sugar
1/2	cup vinegar
1	teaspoon salt
1	teaspoon dill seed
1/2	teaspoon mustard seed
1	clove garlic, minced
3 or 4	cans (4 oz. each) whole green chilies or 2 cups fresh roasted, peeled green chilies

Combine sugar, vinegar, salt, dill and mustard seed and garlic in small saucepan. Heat to boiling; reduce heat and cook, stirring frequently, until mixture is a thin syrup consistency. Pour over chilies in non-metallic container. Cover and refrigerate 3 days before servings.

Fresh Mango Chutney

Judy Shibley
Ghost Ranch staff

2	medium mangoes, fairly firm, peeled, seeded, cut in wedges*
1	serrano pepper, stemmed, seeded, cut crosswise into very thin rings
3	tablespoons fresh cilantro
1/2	teaspoon salt
1/4	teaspoon ground red chili powder or cayenne pepper

Cut mango wedges into thin slices; place in medium bowl. Add remaining ingredients; toss gently. Let stand for at least 1 hour before serving. Cover and store refrigerated, up to 3 days.

*Tip: Place mangoes in freezer for 1 hour before preparing. The slightly frozen fruit is then easy to peel, remove from the seed and slice. If left in freezer longer, let stand a few minutes before peeling.

Apricot Chutney

Nancy Noyes
Santa Fe, NM

8	cups apricots, halved and pitted
1	lemon, chopped
1/2	cup dried currants
1/4	pound candied ginger, chopped
4	yellow onions, sliced thin
2	cloves garlic, minced
2	cups brown sugar
1	cup white sugar
1 1/2	cups red wine vinegar
2	tablespoons mustard seed
1	teaspoon powdered ginger
2	teaspoons salt
3	dried Japanese chiles, seeds removed, finely minced
1	teaspoon ground red pepper

Place apricots, lemon, currants, candied ginger, onions and garlic in a stainless steel pan. Add sugars and wine vinegar, bring to a boil. Add mustard seed, powdered ginger, salt, Japanese chiles, and red pepper. Simmer uncovered for 1 1/2 hours. Pack and seal in sterilized jars.

Richard M. and Dorothy Stern lived in Haiti at the beginning of his writing career. She obtained this recipe, originally for mangoes instead of apricots, in Haiti. She gave it to me for use with my apricots.

Flavored Vinegar

Judy Shibley
Ghost Ranch staff

White cider vinegar

Combinations (choose one set of combinations):

2	cups fresh tarragon leaves, 2 whole cloves, 1/2 small garlic clove
or,	
1	cup fresh tarragon leaves, 2 cups fresh lemon balm
or,	
1	cup fresh tarragon leaves, 2 cups fresh basil leaves, 2 cups fresh chives, 2 cups fresh burnet
or,	
1	cup fresh thyme, 1 cup fresh chives, 1 cup fresh basil leaves
or,	
2	cups fresh mint, spearmint or other mint leaves

Wash herbs; crush slightly. Place in 1/2 gallon glass container. Add spices and vinegar to fill jar. Cover and let stand 24 hours. Remove garlic, if used. Cover and let stand in a cool, dark place 2 weeks. Strain into sterile bottles; cover tightly.

Helen Hall shared this recipe with me the summer Jim and I grew dozens of different herbs and had a zucchini patch that could have fed all of China!

Sweet 'n Hot Mustard

Arlene Walsh
Ft. Collins, CO

1	cup sugar
2/3	cup dry mustard (2 oz. can)
3	eggs, beaten
2/3	cup white vinegar

Combine sugar and mustard in medium saucepan. Stir in eggs. Add vinegar. Cook over low heat, stirring constantly with wooden spoon until thickened. Cool slightly; spoon into containers. Cover and refrigerate up to 2 months. (Makes about 2 cups.)

Bar-B-Que Sauce for Chicken

Muriel Simm
Paullina, IA

1	egg
1	cup vegetable oil
2	cups vinegar
4	teaspoons salt
1	tablespoon poultry seasoning
1	teaspoon pepper

Beat egg well; by hand, beat in oil. Beat in remaining ingredients. Pour into squirt bottle. Use when grilling chicken, basting every time chicken is turned except the last 10 minutes. Grill chicken over high heat for 1 hour. (Enough sauce for 5 chickens.)

Barbeque Sauce

Criselda Dominguez
Ghost Ranch staff
Abiquiu, NM

1/4	cup shortening or meat drippings
2	tablespoons onion, chopped
1/4	cup celery, finely chopped
1/4	cup vinegar
1/4	cup tomato puree or tomato paste
1	tablespoon Worcestershire sauce
1/2	teaspoon garlic salt
2	tablespoons sugar
1/2	cup water
1/4	teaspoon pepper
1/2	teaspoon salt

Melt shortening in a skillet. Add onion and celery, and saute until tender. Add vinegar, tomato puree, Worcestershire, garlic salt, sugar, pepper, and salt. Simmer 10 minutes. (Makes about 2 cups.)

Red Chili Sauce (with or without meat)

Molly Martinez
Ghost Ranch staff
Abiquiu, NM

1/4	cup vegetable oil
1/4	cup flour
1/2	cup red chili powder
4	cups water
1	teaspoon salt
1	teaspoon garlic powder or 1 garlic clove
1/2	pound ground beef (optional)

Put vegetable oil in skillet, mix in flour and brown. Mix in chili powder, add water and mix well. Let it simmer for 20 minutes, stirring occasionally. Brown ground beef in separate skillet, drain excess fat. Mix in sauce, add salt and garlic. (8-10 servings.)

Mornay Sauce

1/4	pound butter
1	cup flour
4	cups milk
2	pounds Velveeta cheese
1	can beer

Melt butter and add flour. Cook until bubbly. Add milk, cook until smooth. Boil for 1 minute. Cut cheese in small pieces and beat into mixture. Add beer to desired consistency. Great served over broccoli.

Tomato Sauce

2	gallons tomatoes, chopped
2	cups celery, chopped
3	cups onion, chopped
14	bay leaves
1/2	cup sugar
1/2	cup flour or cornstarch
2	tablespoons salt

Combine tomatoes, celery, onion and bay leaves. Simmer for 1 hour or so. Run through colander. Combine dry ingredients, add to tomatoes. Simmer until thickened. Freeze in pint containers. (Makes about 4 pints.)

Taco Seasoning Mix

1	tablespoon red chili powder
2	teaspoons onion powder
1	teaspoon ground cumin
1	teaspoon garlic powder
1	teaspoon paprika
1	teaspoon ground oregano
1	teaspoon sugar
1/2	teaspoon salt

Mix all ingredients together. 3 tablespoons of this mix equals 1 package of commercial mix.

Winter Bird Food

Natalie Owings
Los Alamos, NM

1-2	cups dry bread (not moldy)
1	cup cornmeal
1	cup cooked chicken skin (optional)
3/4	cup peanut butter
	Egg shells and eggs

Combine ingredients in blender or food processor, process until crumbly. This is a nutritious and sustaining munchy for hungry birds in the winter. Put it on platform feeders or on the edges of regular bird feeders for all sizes to enjoy. It should be out of reach of dogs who also enjoy it immensely.

Since I feed all sizes of birds on seven different feeding places, I wanted to prevent squabbles and to keep everyone happy. It works! Ravens, crows, magpies and jays don't need to crowd out any of the tiny finches, sparrows, and juncos. I live in the Pojoaque Valley...lots of birds here.

Christmas Aromatics

'Becca May
Ghost Ranch staff

16	whole cloves
3	sticks cinnamon
1 1/2	tablespoons pickling spice
1	teaspoon ground allspice
	A few star anise pods

Combine ingredients. Store in jar or plastic bag. To activate, add contents of jar or packet to quart of water and simmer, uncovered. Once the mixture has perfumed the house, let it cool, put it in a covered quart jar in the refrigerator, and store until you want its magic again.

Desserts

Apple Dessert

Mom Boliek
Hemet, CA

	Peeled, tart apple slices (Jonathan, McIntosh preferred)
1	cup sugar
1	cup all-purpose flour
1	teaspoon baking powder
1	egg, beaten
	Ground cinnamon
	Ground nutmeg
	Butter
1/4	cup water

Fill an 11 x 17" baking pan with apple slices. Combine sugar, flour, baking powder and egg in medium bowl. Stir together until the consistency of corn meal; sprinkle over apples. Dust with cinnamon and nutmeg; dot with butter. Sprinkle with water. Bake at 400°F until brown, 25 to 30 minutes. Good warm or cold. (6 to 8 servings.)

editor's note: Mrs. Boliek is the mother of Ghost Ranch's Chad Boliek.

Apple Crisp

Joan and Myrv DeLapp
Swarthmore, PA

9 to 10	apples, peeled, cored, sliced in thin wedges
3	tablespoons lemon juice
1	cup all-purpose flour
1	cup packed light brown sugar
1/2	cup margarine (scant)
1 1/2	teaspoons ground cinnamon
1/2	teaspoon ground cloves
1/8	teaspoon salt
	Non-dairy whipped topping or frozen yogurt (optional)

Place apples in a 9 x 13" baking pan. Sprinkle with lemon juice. Place remaining ingredients in medium bowl. Work with fingers to crumbly consistency; spread over apples. Bake at 350°F for about 45 minutes. Serve warm (or cold), topped with non-dairy topping or frozen yogurt. (10 or more servings.)

Peach Cobbler

Betty Finlayson
Harrisonburg, VA

	Peeled, sliced peaches
3	tablespoons vegetable shortening
1 1/4	cups sugar, divided
1/2	cup milk
1	cup all-purpose flour
1	teaspoon baking powder
1/2	teaspoon salt
1	tablespoon cornstarch
1	cup fruit juice or boiling water

Make a thick layer of peaches in a greased 8 x 8" pan. Cream shortening and 3/4 cup of the sugar in medium bowl; add dry ingredients; spread over peaches. Combine remaining 1/2 cup sugar and the cornstarch in small bowl; sprinkle over batter. Pour fruit juice or boiling water over the top. Bake at 350°F for 1 hour.

Note: Cherries or apples can be substituted for the peaches.

Peach Cobbler

Edith Huebert
Alamogordo, NM

2	cups peeled, sliced peaches
2	cups sugar, divided
1/2	cup margarine or butter (1 stick)
3/4	cup all-purpose flour
1	teaspoon baking powder
1/8	teaspoon salt
3/4	cup milk
	Cream or whipped cream (optional)

Combine peaches and 1 cup of the sugar in medium bowl; let stand while preparing rest of recipe. Melt margarine in a 2-quart ovenproof pan; reserve. Combine the remaining 1 cup sugar, flour, baking powder and salt in medium bowl; stir in milk. Pour batter over melted margarine — do not stir. Spoon peaches on top of batter — do not stir. Bake at 350°F until tooth pick comes out clean when inserted in middle, about 45 minutes. (6 to 8 servings.)

Cherry Delight Dessert

Gretchen Bush
Las Vegas, NM

3/4	cup margarine or butter, melted (1 1/2 sticks)
50	Ritz crackers, crushed
1/2	cup lemon juice
1	can sweetened condensed milk, Eagle Brand preferred (14 oz.)
1	container non-dairy whipped topping (9 oz.)
1	can cherry pie filling (21 oz.)

Stir margarine into crackers in medium bowl; press firmly into 9 x 13"
pan. Bake at 350°F for 10 minutes; cool. Gradually stir lemon juice into
condensed milk in medium bowl. Fold into whipped topping. Spread
over cooled cracker crust. Spoon cherry pie filling over lemon mixture.
Refrigerate until ready to serve. (12 servings.)

Cherry Oatmeal Bars

Rose Marie Christison
Aurora, CO

1	cup packed brown sugar
1/2	cup margarine or butter (1 stick)
1	cup milk
1	cup quick-cooking rolled oats
1	cup all-purpose flour
1/4	teaspoon ground cinnamon
1/4	teaspoon baking soda
1/2	teaspoon baking powder
1	can cherry pie filling (21 oz.)

Cream brown sugar and margarine with electric mixer in large bowl
until light and fluffy. Add remaining ingredients, except pie filling, one
at a time, beating on medium speed after each addition. Spread half the
batter in bottom of greased 9 x 14" pan. Spread all of the pie filling over
the batter; top with remaining batter. Bake at 350°F for 40 minutes. (20
servings.)

Vinegar Egg Pastry

Ghost Ranch

3	cups all purpose flour
1	cup shortening
1	teaspoons salt
1	large egg
1/2	cup cold water
1	teaspoon vinegar

Sift flour and salt. Cut in shortening. Beat egg, add water and vinegar. Add to flour mixture. Knead 20 times. Roll out on flour board. (4 crusts.)

Apple Dumplings

Ghost Ranch

1	cup sugar
1	cup water
1/8	teaspoon cinnamon
1/8	teaspoon nutmeg
2	tablespoons butter
2	cups all purpose flour
2	teaspoons baking powder
1	teaspoon salt
2/3	cup shortening
1/2	cup milk
6	small whole apples, pared and cored

Combine sugar, water, cinnamon, and nutmeg in a saucepan: bring to boiling point. Add butter to hot syrup. Cool. Sift together flour, baking powder, and salt; cut in shortening. Add milk all at once and stir until flour is just moistened. Roll 1/4 inch thick on lightly floured surface; cut with pastry wheel or knife into 6" squares. Place 1 whole apple in the center of each pastry square.

Sprinkle each apple with sugar, cinnamon, and nutmeg; dot with butter. Moisten edges of pastry square; fold corners to center and pinch edges together securely. Place dumplings 1" apart in greased 11x7x1" dish. Pour syrup over dumplings, sprinkle with sugar. Bake at 375°F for 35 minutes. (6 dumplings.)

Apple Pie

Lynda Prim
Ghost Ranch staff

Two-Crust Pastry:
2	cups unbleached or all-purpose flour
1/2	teaspoon salt
2/3	cup butter, cut in pieces
1 1/2 to 3	tablespoons ice water

Apple Pie:
5 or 6	firm, tart-sweet apples (6 to 7 cups), peeled, cored, quartered
1/2	cup honey or maple syrup
1 1/2	tablespoons flour
1	teaspoon ground cinnamon
1	teaspoon ground nutmeg
	Juice of half a lemon (1 to 1 1/2 tablespoons)
1	tablespoon milk, cream or beaten egg

To make two-crust pastry: Combine flour and salt in medium bowl. Add butter; blend with pastry blender or 2 knives until the texture of coarse corn meal. Add water gradually, just until dough can be gathered into a ball. Refrigerate, wrapped in waxed paper or plastic wrap, for at least 30 minutes before rolling out.

To make apple pie: Roll out half of pastry on lightly floured surface; fit in 9" pie plate. Reserve other half of dough. Combine apples, honey, flour, cinnamon and nutmeg with hands. Mound into prepared pie plate. Roll out second half of dough to about 12" in diameter; place on top of apple mixture. Press rim of top pastry into bottom pastry to seal. Cut small slits in the top of the pastry to allow steam to escape. Brush top pastry with milk, cream or egg. Bake at 450°F for 10 minutes; reduce heat to 400°F and continue baking 35 to 50 minutes.

Pecan Pie

Ghost Ranch

1	cup corn syrup
3	eggs, beaten
1/2	teaspoon salt
1	teaspoon vanilla
1	cup sugar
2	teaspoons magarine, melted
1	cup pecans
1	9" pastry shell

Mix all ingredients, adding pecans last. Pour into pastry shell, bake at 400°F for 15 minutes. Reduce heat to 350°F for 30-35 minutes longer. When pie is done, center will be slightly soft.

Lemon Meringue Pie

Jean Hord
Plaza Resolana volunteer

Filling:

1 1/2	cups sugar
3	tablespoons cornstarch
3	tablespoons all-purpose flour
1/8	teaspoon salt
1 1/2	cups hot water
3	egg yolks, slightly beaten (reserve egg whites)
2	tablespoons butter or margarine
1/2	teaspoon grated lemon peel
1/3	cup lemon juice

Baked single-crust 9" pie shell, cooled

Meringue:

3	egg whites
1	teaspoon lemon juice
6	tablespoons sugar

To make filling: Combine sugar, cornstarch, flour and salt in heavy medium saucepan. Gradually stir in hot water. Heat to boiling over high heat, stirring constantly. Reduce heat; cook, stirring constantly for 8 minutes. Stir small amount of hot mixture into egg yolks; gradually add egg yolk mixture to hot mixture. Heat to boiling; cook, stirring constantly, for 4 minutes. (The stirring makes the filling smooth and creamy.) Add butter and lemon peel. Slowly stir in the 1/3 cup lemon juice. Pour into prepared pie shell. Cool to room temperature. (If filling is warm, it will ruin the meringue.)

For meringue: Beat egg whites and 1 teaspoon lemon juice with electric mixer until soft peaks form. Gradually add sugar, beating until stiff peaks form and sugar is dissolved. Spread meringue over cooled filling. Seal over the edges of the crust, down to the edge of the pan so it won't shrink when baked. Bake at 350°F until meringue is lightly browned, 12 to 15 minutes. Cool before serving.

Note: To make "Mile High Lemon Pie," make 3 recipes and divide evenly between 2 pies. The big, thick and high slices look better, but can be cut into smaller pieces.

Glazed Strawberry Pie

Maria Torres Knox
San Antonio, TX

	Baked single-crust 8" pie shell, cooled
1	quart strawberries, hulled
3	tablespoons cornstarch
1/2	cup water
1	cup sugar
1/4	teaspoon salt
1	tablespoon lemon juice
	Whipped cream (optional)

Place half the strawberries, whole, in pie shell. Place remaining berries in medium saucepan. Mix cornstarch and water and add to strawberries; crush (a potato masher or pastry blender works well). Add sugar, salt and lemon juice. Cook over medium heat, stirring constantly, until mixture thickens, about 5 minutes. Pour over whole berries in pie shell. Refrigerate until cold. Top with whipped cream, if desired.

Pumpkin Chiffon Pie

Phoebe and Arthur Pack
former owners of Ghost Ranch

3	eggs, separated
1	cup sugar
1/2	cup milk
1 1/4	cups canned pumpkin
1/2	teaspoon salt
1/2	teaspoon nutmeg
1/2	teaspoon ginger
1/2	teaspoon cinnamon
1	tablespoon Knox gelatin
1/4	cup cold water

Beat egg yolks slightly, add 1/2cup sugar, milk, pumpkin, salt and spices. Cook until thick in a double boiler. Soften gelatin in cold water, add to hot mixture. Stir thoroughly and cool. When the mixture begins to stiffen, fold in stiffly beaten egg whites to which has been added the remaining 1/2 cup sugar. Pour into a pie crust made from mixing ginger cookie crumbs and butter and top with a very thin layer of whipped cream.

editor's note: This recipe was part of the Pack's cookbook put out in the 1930's. Current advice warns against eating uncooked eggs. Eat uncooked, organically grown eggs from a known source at your discretion.

Heavenly Pie

Ghost Ranch

4	egg whites
1/4	teaspoon cream of tartar
1	cup sugar
1/2	pint whipping cream

Lemon custard:

4	egg yolks
1/2	cup sugar
	Juice and rind of 1 lemon

Beat whites frothy. Add cream of tartar and beat until stiff. Add sugar gradually; beat until it stands in peaks. Spread into greased 9" pie pan. Bake for 20 minutes at 275°F, then 40 minutes more at 300°F. Cool. Whip cream stiff. Spread half of cream on merringue shell, then lemon custard, and spread remaining whipped cream on top. Refrigerate overnight.

For lemon custard: beat yolks with sugar and juice of lemon rind. Cook in double boiler until thick, about 10 minutes. Cool before spreading on pie.

Opal's Key West Lime Pie

Kerby Goforth
Medanales, NM

Filling:

	Juice of 3 limes
	Zest (peel) from 3 limes, grated
1	can sweetened condensed milk
2	eggs, separated *
5	tablespoons sugar

Crust:

1	cup all purpose flour
1/4	cup oil
1/8	cup cold milk
1/8	teaspoon salt

For filling, separate eggs. Beat yolks. Add sweetened, condensed milk, grated zest, and lime juice. Pour into partially baked crust (see below). Beat egg whites until stiff but not dry, add sugar one tablespoon at a time. Lightly, deftly, gaily place on top of the pie into peaks and valleys. Bake 15-20 minutes at 350°F, until meringue is golden. Opal and Jean's oil crust (for a single 9 inch crust): mix crust ingredients together with as few strokes as possible (too much makes it tough, not light and flakey). Make into a ball. Flatten and roll between waxed paper. Place deftly onto pie pan. Crimp and bake at 425°F. Bake 10 minutes for the open-faced pies that will bake some more, and 13-15 minutes for open-faced pies that require no further baking.

editor's note: Current advice warns against eating uncooked eggs. Eat uncooked, organically grown eggs from a known source at your discretion.

Rich Chocolate Pie

Nola Scott
Ghost Ranch staff

8	ounces cream cheese
1	box instant chocolate pudding
1	can sweetened condensed milk
1	cup milk
	Graham cracker crust

Soften cheese. Combine milks with pudding mix. Add cheese, blend well, and pour into graham cracker crust. Chill. Garnish with whipped cream, if desired.

Mixed Fruit Pie

Mary F. English
Houston, TX

1	can apple pie filling (20 oz.)
1	can cherry pie filling (20 oz.)
1	can crushed pineapple, drained (20 oz.)
1/2	cup raisins
1/2	cup flaked coconut
1/4	cup chopped pecans
1	box yellow cake mix
1/2	cup butter, cut in thin slices (1 stick)
	Non-dairy whipped topping

Spread fillings and pineapple in a 9 x 13" baking dish. Sprinkle with raisins, coconut and pecans; stir to combine. Spread dry cake mix over filling as evenly as possible. Cover with butter slices. Bake at 350°F until brown on the edges, about 30 minutes. Serve with whipped topping. (8-10 servings.)

Eastern Hills Pineapple Pie

Sylvia J. Deaver
Gainesville, TX

2 1/2	cups crushed pineapple, undrained (20 oz.)
1/2	cup sugar
2	tablespoons all-purpose flour
1	teaspoon vanilla extract
2	tablespoons butter, melted
	Pastry for double-crust 9" pie

Combine pineapple, sugar, flour, vanilla and butter in medium bowl. Pour in pie plate lined with pastry; place top pastry over filling. Seal; punch holes in top pastry to vent. Bake at 350°F for about 1 hour.

My husband, Earl, enjoyed this pie while teaching at Eastern Hills High School in Fort Worth. He asked and asked for the recipe, but was told that it was mixed in such large quantities that the recipe for one pie was unknown. After much insistence and continued compliments to the cooks, he was given the recipe at lunch one day.

Pineapple Cheese Dessert

Gertrude Anderson
Boulder, CO

Crumb Crust:
1 1/4	cups fine crumbs (graham crackers, vanilla wafers)
1/4	cup sugar
1/4	cup butter or margarine, at room temperature (1/2 stick)

Pineapple Filling:
1	package orange, pineapple or lemon-flavored gelatin (3 oz.)
1 1/4	cup boiling water
1	can crushed pineapple in heavy syrup, drained, syrup reserved (8 3/4 oz.)
1	package cream cheese, at room temperature (3 oz.)
1/4	teaspoon orange or lemon peel
3	tablespoons sugar
1/2	teaspoon vanilla extract
1	cup sour cream

To make crumb crust: Combine crumbs, sugar and butter in medium bowl. Press firmly in bottom and up sides of 9" pie plate or on bottom of 8 x 8" pan. Refrigerate 1 hour.

To make pineapple filling: Dissolve gelatin in boiling water. Add reserved pineapple syrup; cool slightly. Beat cream cheese, orange or lemon peel, sugar and vanilla with electric mixer until smooth. Combine 1/2 cup of the gelatin mixture and the pineapple; reserve. Gradually beat remaining gelatin into cheese mixture. Fold in sour cream. Pour into prepared Crumb Crust. Refrigerate until set but not firm. Spoon on reserved pineapple mixture. Refrigerate until firm. (Makes 8 or 9 servings.)

Fruit Pie on a Tortilla

Marj Nienstaedt
Morelia, Michoacan, Mexico

2 to 3	tablespoons butter or margarine, at room temperature
8	flour tortillas
4	teaspoons sugar
1	teaspoon ground cinnamon
1	can sliced canned peaches, drained (16 oz.)
1	cup sour cream (8 oz.)
	Shaved semi-sweet chocolate

Lightly butter both sides of tortillas. Combine sugar and cinnamon; sprinkle over buttered tortillas. Place on baking sheets; bake at 350°F for 12 minutes; cool. Put sliced peaches on top of each baked tortilla; top with sour cream and grated chocolate. (8 servings.)

I found this recipe in a small-town newspaper in northern Wisconsin. I brought it to Mexico where I've lived for 6 years. It is an easy, quick dessert and the Mexicans love it. Buena suerte!

English Trifle

Midge Pinkerton
Columbia, MO

1	package yellow cake mix
1	cup raspberry jam
1	can ready-to-eat vanilla pudding (16 oz.)
1/3	cup orange juice
2	tablespoons sherry extract or sherry
1	carton non-dairy whipped topping or 1 cup heavy cream, whipped (8 oz.)

Bake cake as directed on package in 13 x 9 x 2" pan. Cut cake in half; freeze half for future use unless doubling recipe. Cut first half in 8 pieces. Split pieces horizontally. Arrange half the pieces in a 2-quart glass bowl. Spread half the jam over the cake. Spoon half the pudding over the jam; repeat. Combine orange juice and sherry; pour over cake mixture. Cover and refrigerate 6 to 8 hours. Spread whipped topping or whipped cream over the top just before serving. (8 servings.)

When we visit our relatives in England and Scotland, they usually serve us trifle. We love it! I serve it for special occasions — wedding showers, summer parties, etc. When I double the recipe, I put it in a glass punch bowl.

Cheesecake

Mary Thompson
Swarthmore, PA

Crumb Crust:
1/2	package zwieback, crushed (6 oz. pkg.)
2	tablespoons sugar
4	tablespoons butter or margarine, melted

Filling:
3	packages cream cheese, at room temperature (8 oz. each)
4	eggs
1	cup sugar, divided
1	teaspoon vanilla extract
2	cups sour cream (16 oz.)

To make crumb crust: Combine zwieback crumbs, sugar and butter. Press on bottom and up sides of 9" springform pan.

To make filling: Beat cream cheese, 3/4 cup of the sugar and the vanilla with electric mixer in large bowl until smooth. Add eggs, one at a time, beating well after each addition. Pour over crumbs in pan. Bake at 350°F for 30 minutes. Combine sour cream and remaining 1/4 cup sugar; spread over cheesecake. Return to oven and continue baking for 10 minutes. Cool completely. Refrigerate at least 2 hours before serving. (12 to 14 servings.)

Danny's Pineapple Delight Dessert

Daniel M. O'Keefe
Mount Prospect, IL

1	cup hot milk
1	pound marshmallows, cut in small pieces
12	graham crackers, crushed, divided
2	cans crushed pineapple, drained (8 3/4 oz. each)
2	cups heavy cream, whipped (1 pint)

Pour hot milk over marshmallows in medium bowl; cool. Cover bottom of 9 x 13" pan with 2/3rds of the graham cracker crumbs. Fold pineapple and whipped cream into cooled marshmallow mixture. Spoon into cracker-lined pan. Sprinkle remaining graham cracker crumbs on top. Cover and refrigerate. Cut in squares. (12 servings.)

The Next Best Thing to Robert Redford

Frances and Scott D. King
Indianapolis, IN

1 2/3	cup all-purpose flour
1/2	cup chopped nuts
3/4	cup butter, melted
1	package cream cheese, at room temperature (8 oz.)
1	cup confectioners' sugar
1	cup non-dairy whipped topping, divided
1	package instant vanilla pudding (3 oz.)
1	package instant chocolate pudding (3 oz.)
3	cups milk
1	cup shaved chocolate or toasted coconut

Combine flour, nuts and butter in medium bowl; press firmly in bottom of 9 x 13" pan. Bake at 350°F for 15 minutes; cool. Beat cream cheese and confectioners' sugar until smooth. Stir in 1/2 cup of the whipped topping. Spread over baked layer. Mix puddings and milk; spread over cream cheese mixture. Top with remaining 1/2 cup whipped topping. Cover and refrigerate 8 hours or overnight. (15 servings.)

Pfeiffer's Suet Pudding

Georgene Morrison Shank
Ames, IA

Pudding:

1	cup finely chopped suet (available in meat department)
1	cup molasses
1	cup sour milk or buttermilk*
1	teaspoon baking soda
1	cup raisins
1	egg
3 1/2	cups all-purpose flour
1	teaspoon each: Ground cloves, nutmeg, cinnamon and salt

Pudding Sauce:

2	tablespoons cornstarch
1	tablespoon cold water
1	cup sugar
2	cups boiling water
4	tablespoons butter
	Ground nutmeg and salt to taste
	Vanilla extract, rum or brandy to taste

To make pudding: Combine ingredients in large bowl; pour into greased tube pan or pudding mold. Cover and steam 3 hours. Serve with pudding sauce.

To make pudding sauce: Combine cornstarch and cold water to form a paste; mix with sugar in medium saucepan. Gradually stir in boiling water, stirring until smooth. Heat to boiling over medium heat; reduce heat. Boil for 5 minutes; remove from heat. Add remaining ingredients. Does not keep well. Also good on apple pie or apple dumplings.

*To make sour milk, add 1 tablespoon lemon juice or vinegar to 1 cup milk; let stand in warm place 5 minutes.

Family legend says that this recipe was given to Elizabeth McNett Pfeiffer (born late 1800s in Buffalo, NY) by her mother-in-law who brought it from Germany and, on her deathbed, whispered it to Lib. It is always served at our family Christmas dinner.

Noodle Kugel

Gael Faulkner-Gonzalez
Tustin, CA

1/2	cup butter or margarine, at room temperature (1 stick)
1/2	cup granulated sugar
5	eggs
4	cups buttermilk (1 qt.)
	Grated peel of 1 orange
1/2	teaspoon vanilla
1	package medium noodles, parboiled, drained (12 oz.)
1	cup corn flakes
1/4	cup butter or margarine, melted (1/2 stick)
1/2	cup packed brown sugar
1/2	teaspoon ground cinnamon

Beat soft butter and sugar with electric mixer in large bowl; add eggs, one at a time, beating well after each addition. Gradually add buttermilk. Stir in orange peel and vanilla. Stir in noodles. Spoon into greased 9 x 13" baking pan. Toss corn flakes with melted butter, brown sugar and cinnamon. Sprinkle over noodle mixture. Cover and refrigerate overnight. Bake at 350°F until a knife comes out clean when inserted in center, about 1 hour. Cut in squares. (12 to 15 servings.)

Pineapple Bread Pudding

Mike and Elaine Fry
Newville, PA

7	tablespoons butter or margarine
1	cup sugar
5	eggs
1/2	teaspoon salt
1/2	cup milk
1	can pineapple chunks in syrup, undrained (20 oz.)
4	cups soft bread crumbs or cubes, divided

Beat butter, sugar and eggs with electric mixer in large bowl. Beat in salt and milk. Stir in pineapple and 3 1/2 cups of the bread. Spoon mixture into greased 2 1/2-quart baking dish. Top with remaining bread. Bake at 375°F for 45 minutes. Good hot or cold. (10 servings.)

Note: Pineapple bread pudding makes an nice accompaniment to baked ham.

Panocha Sprouted Wheat Dessert

Criselda Dominguez
Ghost Ranch staff
Abiquiu, NM

5	cups sprouted wheat flour
2 1/2	cups whole wheat flour
9	cups boiling water
2	cups caramelized sugar
1	cup boiling water
4	tablespoons butter

The flour may be prepared at home or bought already prepared. To sprout wheat, wash and drain, but do not dry. Place in a cloth bag in a warm place to sprout. When the wheat has sprouted, dry in sun. Grind into flour.

Mix the whole wheat and sprouted wheat flour thoroughly, add 1/2 of the boiling water, and stir well. Set aside and cover. Let stand for 15 minutes; then add the rest of the water. (To caramelize sugar, place 2 cups sugar in heavy skillet over medium-low heat. Heat until sugar liquifies.) To caramelized sugar add 1 cup of boiling water, and when blended, add to flour mixture. Boil mixture gently for 2 hours, add butter, and place uncovered in 350°F oven for 1 hour or until it is quite thick and deep brown. Some people prefer to leave sugar out, as the sprouted wheat has its own sugar.

editor's note: During Holy Week, from Wednesday to Saturday, the Penitentes keep a vigil in the morada, or little chapel, in preparation for Easter Sunday. This is a time of prayer and contemplation. The Penitentes are a Catholic religious organization in northern New Mexico. People from the community bring food to the Penitentes during their seclusion. Panocha is one of the traditional foods for this special time.

Sopa (Indian Bread Pudding)

Ghost Ranch

1 1/2	cups sugar
3	cups water
2	tablespoons margarine or butter
1 1/2	teaspoons ground cinnamon
1/2	teaspoon ground nutmeg
1	tablespoon vanilla extract
6	slices whole wheat bread, toasted, cubed
1 1/2	cup shredded longhorn Cheddar cheese
1	cup raisins
1/2	cup chopped nuts
	Non-dairy whipped topping or whipped cream (optional)

Brown sugar in a medium heavy skillet or pan over low heat until golden brown. Remove from heat. Slowly add water, stirring until sugar is dissolved. Stir in margarine, cinnamon, nutmeg and vanilla; reserve. Combine bread, cheese, raisins and nuts in 2-1/2 quart baking dish. Pour sugar mixture over bread mixture; let stand 10 minutes. Serve with whipped topping or whipped cream. (8 servings.)

Natillas

Rebecca Martinez
Ghost Ranch staff
Canjilon, NM

6	cups milk
1	cup all-purpose flour
2	eggs, separated
1	cup water
1 1/2	cups sugar
	Grated peel of 1/2 orange (or 2 teaspoons vanilla)
1/4	cup sugar
1/2	teaspoon nutmeg
1	teaspoon cinnamon

Boil milk. Combine flour, egg yolks and water. Add to hot milk. Add sugar, cook until thick, stirring constantly. Add flavoring of choice. Beat egg whites until stiff, gradually adding 1/4 cup sugar. Carefully spoon egg whites over hot custard. Spoon a little of the hot custard over whites, sprinkle with nutmeg and cinnamon. Cover until ready to serve. The heat from the custard will cook the whites. Serve warm.

editor's note: Rebecca's grandmother made this recipe often when she was growing up. Because her family had cows and chickens, they always had an abundance of milk and eggs. Her grandmother never had vanilla in the house, so desserts were flavored with orange peels. This brings back many happy memories and is a favorite with Rebecca's family.

Capirotada o Sopa

Carmen Chavez
Plaza Resolana staff

1	cup sugar
2	cups boiling water
1/2	cup sherry
1/8	teaspoon cinnamon
8	slices bread, toasted, cut in 1" pieces (whole wheat preferred)
3/4	cup pinon nuts or chopped walnuts
1	cup shredded Cheddar cheese
3/4	cup raisins (optional)

Place sugar in heavy skillet or pan. Stir over low heat until light golden brown and liquified. Add water; stir constantly until sugar is dissolved. Add sherry and cinnamon; reserve. Cook, stirring constantly, 3 to 5 minutes. Layer bread and nuts in 1 1/2-quart greased baking dish. Pour sugar mixture over bread and nuts; top with cheese. Cover and bake at 350°F for 30 minutes. (8 servings.)

This recipe has been passed down from my grandmother to my mother and then to me.

Fruity Pizza

Carmen Chavez
Plaza Resolana staff

Sugar cookie dough (your own, a mix, or prepared refrigerated dough)
1   cup sour cream (8 oz.)
2   cups heavy cream, whipped
2   tablespoons sugar
1   teaspoon vanilla, almond or rum extract
        Fresh fruit slices and berries (bananas, strawberries, kiwi, blueberries, etc.)

Roll out cookie dough into large circle. Place on pizza pan or baking sheet. Bake at 375°F for 8 to 10 minutes. Remove and cool. Fold sour cream into stiffly beaten whipped cream in medium bowl; stir in sugar and vanilla. Spread sour cream mixture over cooled cookie crust; arrange fruit slices on top. (12 servings.)

Great recipe to make with kids!

Lemon Pudding

Ghost Ranch

1	cup sugar
6	tablespoons butter (almost 1/2 cup)
1/2	teaspoon salt
3	egg yolks, beaten
3	egg whites, stiffly beaten
6	tablespoons all purpose flour
	Juice and rind of 1 lemon
1 1/2	cups milk

Cream together sugar and butter; add salt, egg yolks, flour, lemon juice, grated rind and milk. Mix well, then fold in beaten egg whites. Place in greased casserole, set in pan of water, bake 1 hour at 300°F. (6 servings.)

Cream Puffs

Ghost Ranch

1	cup margarine
2	cups boiling water
2	cups all-purpose flour
2	teaspoons salt
8	eggs
	Fillings: Ice cream, pudding, fresh fruit
	Toppings: Chocolate sauce, fresh fruit, whipped topping, confectioners' sugar

Combine margarine and water in medium pan. Heat to boiling over high heat; reduce heat. Add flour and salt, all and once; stir vigorously with wooden spoon until ball forms in the center. Cool slightly. Add unbeaten eggs, one at a time, beating well after each addition. Mixture will be very stiff. Drop by tablespoonfuls on greased baking sheet. Bake at 450°F for 15 minutes. Reduce heat to 350°F and continue baking 30 minutes. Cool before slicing and filling. (8-10 puffs.)

Easy Does It Doughnuts

Criselda Dominguez
Ghost Ranch staff
Abiquiu, NM

1/3	cup sugar
1/2	cup milk
1	egg
2	tablespoons vegetable oil
1 1/2	cups all-purpose flour
2	teaspoons baking powder
1/2	teaspoon salt
	Oil for deep frying

Mix together sugar, milk, egg, and oil. Combine flour, baking powder, and salt. Then add to liquid mixture; stir lightly. Drop by teaspoon into deep oil fryer heated to 365°F. Fry 3 to 4 minutes. Drain on paper towel. (Makes 1 1/2 dozen.)

Sour Cream Doughnuts

Criselda Dominguez
Ghost Ranch staff
Abiquiu, NM

1	egg
1	cup sugar
1	cup light cream, soured
1	cup buttermilk or sour milk
2	teaspoons baking powder
1	teaspoon baking soda
1 1/2	teaspoons nutmeg
1	teaspoon salt
4 1/2	cups all-purpose flour, approximately

Beat egg and gradually add sugar. Add milk, cream, and sifted dry ingredients. The dough should be as soft as can be handled. The amount of flour needed will depend upon thickness of sour cream and milk. Place about 1/3 of dough on well-floured pastry canvas. Round up. Work in a little flour if necessary. Roll approximately 3/8" thick and cut with doughnut cutter. Drop in hot (360-375°F) oil. There should be enough oil to float doughnuts. When browned on one side, turn and brown other side. Drain on absorbent paper. Sprinkle generously with powdered sugar mixed with cinnamon (1 tablespoon cinnamon to 1 cup sugar). (Makes 3 to 4 dozen doughnuts.)

Ray Woods' Cherries Jubilee

Rebecca Martinez
Ghost Ranch staff
Canjilon, NM

1	can black Bing cherries, drained, juice reserved (16 oz.)
1	tablespoon cornstarch
1/4	cup sugar
1	tablespoon water or cherry juice
1	tablespoon butter
2	tablespoons Kirschwasser
2	tablespoons brandy
	Vanilla ice cream
	Cognac (optional)

Bring 1 cup of the reserved juice (add water if necessary to make 1 cup) to a boil in small saucepan. Mix cornstarch, sugar and 1 tablespoon water or juice; add to hot juice. Heat to boiling; boil 1 minute. Add cherries. Remove from heat; add butter, kirchswasser and brandy. Serve hot over vanilla ice cream. To ignite, pour good cognac over cherries and light. (6 servings.)

This is a very old recipe that was introduced to us by Ray Woods, a long-time friend of the Ranch. Ray made this for the college staff's annual Fourth of July picnic. I remembered it and thought I'd put it in for him.

Cranberry Sorbet

Grace May
Ghost Ranch kid

2	quarts cranberries
2	quarts water
4	cups sugar
6	tablespoons lemon juice
2	egg whites, beaten stiff *
1/2	teaspoon salt

Cook cranberries in water until they stop popping. Strain, discard pulp. Add sugar and salt to liquid, bring to boiling point. Cool; add lemon juice. Freeze partially in ice cream maker. Remove dasher—fold in egg whites and continue freezing until done. (Makes 2 quarts sorbet.)

Six Threes Ice

Jean Rutledge
Manhattan, KS

3	cups milk
3	cups heavy cream*
3	cups sugar
	Juice of 3 lemons
	Juice of 3 oranges
3	bananas, mashed

Mix milk and cream. Heat 1 cup of the milk mixture in medium saucepan. Add sugar; cook, stirring constantly over medium heat, until sugar is dissolved. Add remaining milk mixture. Freeze in ice cream freezer until mushy. Add fruit juices and bananas and freeze until firm. Remove dasher and pack for 4 hours or less (or follow manufacturer's directions for your ice cream maker). (Makes 1 gallon.)

* Whole milk or half-and-half cream can be substituted for the heavy cream.

This is a recipe my family made frequently on Sunday afternoons when I was growing up in Dallas, TX. Usually a great aunt and uncle would drive over from Ft. Worth and join us. We would all sit around in the yard enjoying this cool, refreshing dessert.

Peach or Orange Sherbet

Carol E. Davies
Louisville, KY

Peach Sherbet:
6	bottles peach-flavored soft drink, such as Nehi (16 oz. each)
1	cup fresh peaches, peeled, pitted, crushed
1	can sweetened condensed milk, such as Eagle Brand (14 oz.)

Orange Sherbet:
6	bottles orange-flavored soft drink, Orange Crush preferred (16 oz. each)
1	can crushed pineapple, undrained (8 3/4 oz.)
1	can sweetened condensed milk, such as Eagle Brand (14 oz.)

Combine ingredients in large bowl. Pour into freezer container of electric or manual freezer. Process according to manufacturer's instructions. (Makes 1 gallon.)

This recipe was given to me at a party in Independence MO. We were celebrating a man's release from Kansas State Prison. All present were involved in the M-2 (Monto Mon) prison program in the late '70s and '80s.

Homemade Ice Cream

Hanna, Darcy, and Cahalen Morrison
Ghost Ranch kids

3	tablespoons all purpose flour
2	cups sugar
1/2	teaspoon salt
3	eggs, beaten
1	tablespoon vanilla
3	quarts milk (approximately)

Combine flour, sugar, and salt in a saucepan and mix well. Add 1 quart milk and mix until the sugar dissolves. Add the eggs and stir well. Heat slowly, stirring constantly until it begins to thicken. Pour into cannister of ice cream maker, add cold milk to fill line. Add vanilla. Freeze until you can't crank any more. (Makes 4 quarts.)

Variations (substitute volume for milk):

   Mashed ripe peaches or nectarines, strawberries, raspberries, blackberries.

   Substitute 1 tablespoon peppermint extract for vanilla and add 1 cup chopped chocolate chips later when the mixture has begun to freeze a little.

   Add 1/4 cup instant coffee crystals, a little at a time, to the mixture when beginning to heat.

   Add 1 cup chopped walnuts and 1 cup chocolate chips when mixture is partially frozen.

No-Cook Ice Cream

Judy Shibley
Ghost Ranch staff

1/2	gallon milk
2	cans sweetened condensed milk, such as Eagle Brand (14 oz. each)
1	cup heavy cream, whipped

For vanilla:

2	tablespoons vanilla extract
1	teaspoon lemon juice

For peppermint:

1	package hard peppermint candy (8 oz.)

Combine milk and sweetened condensed milk. For vanilla ice cream, add whipped cream; stir in vanilla and lemon juice. Freeze in 1 1/2 gallon ice cream maker, following manufacturer's instructions. For peppermint ice cream, heat 3 cups milk mixture with the candy until candy melts. Cool, then add to remaining milk and whipped cream (omit vanilla and lemon juice). Freeze in 1 1/2 gallon ice cream maker according to manufacturer's instructions.

Praline Sundaes

Ghost Ranch

1/3	cup water
1/3	cup brown sugar
1	cup light corn syrup
1	cup pecans, chopped
1/8	teaspoon rum extract
1/8	teaspoon maple extract
10	servings vanilla ice cream

Combine water, sugar and corn syrup in saucepan. Cook slowly until mixture comes to a boil. Add nuts and flavorings. Cool. Cover and refrigerate. (Makes 1 pint of sauce.) To serve, spoon sauce over ice cream.

Fudge Topping for Ice Cream

Mimi Tharp
Ghost Ranch staff

1/2	cup butter
1/2	cup cocoa
1/2	teaspoon salt
1/4	cup light corn syrup
3	cups sugar
1	can evaporated milk (12 oz.)

Mix cocoa, salt and corn syrup and place over low heat, then slowly add sugar and evaporated milk. Continue heating until smooth, stirring constantly, being careful not to burn. Refrigerate unused topping. (Makes 1 1/2 pints.)

Chocolate Ice Box Dessert

Eleanor Pack Liddell
Albuquerque, NM

1/2	cup butter
2	tablespoons cocoa
2	cups powdered sugar
2	eggs, separated
1/2	teaspoons vanilla
	Vanilla wafer crumbs

Cream butter, add cocoa and sugar. Mix well. Add egg yolks and vanilla. Whip egg whites until stiff and fold into creamed mixture. Line 9 x 5" loaf pan with vanilla wafer crumbs. Add chocolate mixture, crumbling a few more wafers on top. Freeze several hours. May double the recipe.

Note: Current advice warns against eating raw eggs. Eat organically grown raw eggs from a known source at your discretion.

When our family had company, this dessert was often served, made in metal ice trays. My sister, Peg, and I were only allowed a thin sliver. We swore that when we grew up we'd make a whole tray and eat it all ourselves! We did make it, but soon found out that all we could manage was maybe two thin slivers.

editor's note: Eleanor is the daughter of Arthur Pack.

CAKES

Editor's note: In the interest of conserving natural resources, we have not called for preheating your oven in this book. With cakes, however, a preheated oven is essential.

Chocolate Sheet Cake

Christeen Moore
Las Cruces, NM

Chocolate Sheet Cake:
2	cups granulated sugar
2	cups all-purpose flour
1/2	cup margarine or butter
1/2	cup vegetable shortening
4	tablespoons cocoa powder
1	cup water
1	teaspoon baking soda
1/2	cup buttermilk
2	eggs, slightly beaten
1	teaspoon vanilla extract

Frosting:
1/3	cup milk
4	tablespoons cocoa powder
1/2	cup margarine or butter
1	box confectioners' sugar, sifted (1 pound)
1	cup chopped nuts
1/2	teaspoon vanilla extract

To make cake: Sift granulated sugar and flour into large bowl. Place margarine, vegetable shortening, cocoa and water in medium saucepan. Heat to boiling; stir into dry ingredients. Dissolve baking soda in buttermilk; add to chocolate mixture. Beat in eggs and vanilla. Pour into greased 12 x 17" pan. Bake at 400°F for 20 minutes. Spread with frosting while still warm. (Makes 12 servings.)

To make frosting: Gradually stir milk into cocoa in medium saucepan; add margarine. Heat to boiling. Remove from heat; stir in confectioners' sugar, nuts and vanilla. Spread over warm sheet cake.

Chocolate Cherry Cake

Opal N. Kingsbury
Madison, WI

Cake:
2	eggs
1	package devils food or chocolate cake mix
1	can cherry pie filling (21 oz.)
1	teaspoon almond extract

Frosting:
1	cup sugar
5	tablespoons butter or margarine
1/3	cup milk
1	package chocolate chips (6 ounces)

To make cake: Beat eggs in large bowl. Stir in cake mix, pie filling and almond extract by hand. Pour in greased 9 x 13" pan. Bake at 350°F for 35 minutes. Frost while warm.

To make frosting: Combine sugar, butter and milk in medium saucepan. Heat to boiling; boil 1 minute. Remove from heat; stir in chocolate chips. Stir until smooth. Spread immediately over warm cake.

Chocolate Chip Kahlua Cake

Molly Parker
Los Alamos, NM

1	package devils food cake mix (18.5 oz.)
4	eggs
1	cup Kahlua
1	cup sour cream
3/4	cup vegetable oil
1	package semi-sweet chocolate chips (6 oz.)
	Whipped cream or ice cream (optional)

Place first 5 ingredients in large bowl; beat with electric mixer on medium speed until smooth, 3 to 5 minutes. Stir in chocolate chips. Pour in greased and floured bundt pan. Bake at 350°F for 50 to 60 minutes. Let stand 5 minutes; remove and cool completely on rack. Serve with whipped cream or ice cream, if desired.

Gus's Famous Chocolate Fudge Cake

Joyce Sherrod
Midland, TX

Chocolate Fudge Cake:

2	cups granulated sugar
2	cups all-purpose flour
1	teaspoon salt
1	teaspoon baking powder.
1	cup margarine or butter (2 sticks)
4	tablespoons cocoa powder
1	cup water
1	cup sour cream
2	eggs
1	teaspoon vanilla extract

Frosting:

6	tablespoons buttermilk
3	tablespoons cocoa powder
1/2	cup margarine or butter
1	box confectioners' sugar (1 pound)
1	teaspoon vanilla extract
1/2	cup finely chopped pecans

To make cake: Combine dry ingredients in large bowl. Place margarine, cocoa and water in small saucepan; heat to boiling. Stir cocoa mixture into dry ingredients; add sour cream, eggs and vanilla. Pour into greased 9 x 13" baking pan. Bake at 350°F for 20 minutes. Frost while warm.

To make frosting: Gradually stir buttermilk into cocoa in medium saucepan; add margarine. Heat to boiling; remove from heat. Stir in remaining ingredients. Spread immediately over warm cake.

Gus was the cook on a fishing boat that took a group to see the gray whales off Baja, CA. He created this masterpiece in his pitching galley during a "little blow".

Aunt Katie's Cake

Laurie Baur
Philadelphia, PA

1	package German chocolate cake mix
1	can (14 ounces) sweetened condensed milk (such as Eagle Brand)
3/4	cup (12 ounces) caramel fudge sauce (Mrs. Richardson's pre ferred)
1	container (9 ounces) non-dairy whipped topping
2 to 3	Heath bars, crushed

Prepare cake in 13 x 9" pan, according to package directions. When it has cooled about 30 minutes, make holes with a knife, 2 to 3" apart, on top of cake. Pour condensed milk over the cake. Pour fudge sauce (use less for less-rich cake) over the cake. Cover and refrigerate 8 hours or overnight. Top with whipped topping and crushed Heath bars. (Makes 12 servings.)

My Aunt Katie Doty, a member of the Sturgis Presbyterian Church in Sturgis, MI, is a great cook!!! We have left her recipes all over the country and feel privileged to share one with Ghost Ranch.

Chocolate Chip Cake

Ghost Ranch

1/2	cup margarine
1	cup sugar
1	teaspoon vanilla
2	eggs
1/4	teaspoon salt
1	cup sour cream
1	teaspoon baking powder
1	teaspoon baking soda
2	cups all purpose flour
1	package chocolate chips (6 oz.)

Cream margarine, vanilla, eggs and sour cream. Combine dry ingredients, add to liquids. Bake in greased tube or bundt pan for 45 minutes at 350°F. (10-12 servings)

Chocolate Date Torte

Polly McClure
Peoria, AZ

1	cup boiling water
1	cup chopped pitted dates
1	cup butter (use half margarine, if desired)
1	cup sugar
2	eggs
1 1/2	cups all-purpose flour
2	tablespoons cocoa
1	teaspoon baking soda
1/4	teaspoon salt
1	teaspoon vanilla extract
1	cup chopped nuts
	German chocolate frosting, ice cream or whipped cream

Pour boiling water over chopped dates in small bowl; let stand 5 minutes. Beat butter, sugar and eggs with electric mixer in large bowl until light and fluffy. Combine dry ingredients; gradually beat into creamed mixture. Stir in dates, vanilla and nuts. Pour in greased 9 x 13" pan or two 8 x 8" pans. Bake at 350°F until tester inserted in center comes out clean, 35 to 45 minutes. When cool, frost with German chocolate frosting, or serve with ice cream or whipped cream. (16 to 18 servings.)

Mississippi Mud Cake

Evelyn King
Chattanooga, OK

Brownies:

1	cup margarine or butter, melted (2 sticks)
1/2	cup cocoa powder
4	eggs (or egg substitute)
2	cups granulated sugar
1 1/3	cups all-purpose flour
1/8	teaspoon salt
1 1/2	cups chopped pecans
1	jar marshmallow creme (7 oz.)

Frosting:

1/2	cup cocoa powder
1/4	cup (1/2 stick) margarine or butter, melted
1	teaspoon vanilla extract
1	box (1 pound) confectioners' sugar, sifted
1/2	cup milk

To make brownie: Place melted butter in large bowl; stir in cocoa. Stir in eggs, sugar, flour and salt; add nuts. Pour in greased 9 x 13" baking pan. Bake at 325°F for 30 minutes. Turn off oven; spread marshmallow creme evenly over the top. Put back in oven until creme melts. Cool; frost.

To make frosting: Stir cocoa into melted margarine in medium bowl. Stir in vanilla; gradually add confectioners' sugar and milk; beat until smooth. Spread over cooled cake.

Delhi Chocolate Chip Oatmeal Cake

Patty Colson
Emmaus, PA

1	cup rolled oats
1 3/4	cups boiling water
1	cup granulated sugar
1	cup packed brown sugar
1/2	cup margarine or butter
2	eggs
1 3/4	cups all-purpose flour
1	teaspoon baking soda
1/2	teaspoon salt
1 to 2	tablespoons cocoa powder
1	cup chocolate chips
	Chopped walnuts (optional)
	Chocolate chips for frosting (optional)

Combine oatmeal and water in large bowl; let stand 10 minutes. Stir in sugars and margarine. Stir in eggs. Sift dry ingredients and add to batter. Stir in chocolate chips and nuts if desired. Pour in greased 9 x 13" baking pan. Bake at 350°F for 40 minutes. If desired, sprinkle another cup of chocolate chips on hot cake; spread when melted. (Makes 16 to 20 servings.)

This cake often appeared at picnics and suppers in our church, United Ministry of Delhi, NY. It travels well and can be baked in two 9"-round pans to freeze one and eat one or share one with a friend.

Oatmeal Cake

Carmen Chavez
Plaza Resolana staff

Cake:

3	cups boiling water
2	cups rolled oats
2	cups granulated sugar
2	cups packed brown sugar
1	cup vegetable shortening
4	eggs, slightly beaten
3	cups all-purpose flour
1	tablespoon ground cinnamon
2	teaspoons baking soda
1/2	teaspoon salt
2	teaspoons vanilla extract

Topping:

11	tablespoons (1 1/3 stick) margarine or butter, at room temperature
1	cup packed brown sugar
1/2	cup heavy or half-and-half cream
2	teaspoons vanilla extract
2	cups flaked coconut, toasted

Pour boiling water over rolled oats in medium bowl; let stand 20 minutes. Cream sugars and shortening with electric mixer in large bowl until light and fluffy. Add eggs, one at a time, beating well after each addition. Sift dry ingredients; add gradually to creamed mixture. Stir in oatmeal and vanilla. Pour in greased 12 x 17" pan. Bake at 350°F until tester inserted in center comes out clean, 40 to 50 minutes. Spread with topping while warm. (30 servings.)

To make topping: Combine all ingredients; spread on warm cake. Broil just until bubbly, watching carefully.

Crazy Cake

Sylvia Edwards
Woods Hole, MA

1 1/2	cups all-purpose flour
3	tablespoons cocoa powder
1	cup (or less) sugar
1	teaspoon baking soda
5	tablespoons vegetable oil
1	teaspoon vinegar
1	teaspoon vanilla extract
1/2	teaspoon salt
1	cup water
	Vanilla ice cream or non-dairy whipped topping (optional)

Sift flour, cocoa, sugar and baking soda together directly into greased 8 x 8" pan. Make 3 holes in the dry ingredients. Put vegetable oil in one; vinegar in another; and vanilla into the third. Sprinkle salt on top; pour water over entire mixture. Mix well and bake at 350°F for 30 minutes. Best served warm with ice cream or whipped topping. (6 to 8 servings.)

My daughter found this recipe in the Sunday newspaper when she was a little girl. It's been a family favorite for 30 years!

1-2-3-4 Cake

Ruth M. Kraemer
Tulsa, OK

Cake:
1	cup vegetable shortening
2	cups granulated sugar
4	eggs, separated
1	teaspoon vanilla extract
3	cups all-purpose flour
3	teaspoons baking powder
1/4	teaspoon salt
1	cup milk

Creamy Icing:
1	cup milk
5	tablespoons all-purpose flour
1/2	cup butter or margarine
1/2	cup vegetable shortening
1	cup superfine granulated sugar (not confectioners'!)
2	teaspoons vanilla extract

To make cake: Cream shortening and sugar with electric mixer in large bowl until light and fluffy. Add egg yolks (reserve whites) and vanilla. Sift dry ingredients; add alternately with milk. Beat reserved egg whites in large bowl until stiff; fold into creamed mixture. Spoon into 3 waxed paper-lined, greased 8" round layer pans. Bake at 350°F for 30 minutes. Let stand 5 minutes; remove and cool completely on racks. Frost with creamy icing.

To make creamy icing: Gradually stir milk into flour in small saucepan. Cook and stir over medium heat until slightly thick; cool. Beat remaining ingredients with electric mixer in large bowl until light and fluffy (about 15 minutes). Beat in cooled flour mixture. Freezes well. (Makes enough for 3-tiered cake.)

My family has been making this cake for 3 generations. We always use it for special birthday cakes, since it's good for carving into original cakes for theme parties. I have made a Cinderella's castle, United Nations building, cowboy boot, shoeskate, trains on a licorice track, Mickey Mouse, gingerbread man, Easter bunny, and doll cake using the basic recipe.

Lane Cake and Filling

Donnalee Van Zante
Eddyville, IA

Cake:

1	cup butter or margarine
2	cups sugar
3 1/2	cups cake flour
2	teaspoons baking powder
1	teaspoon vanilla extract
1	cup milk
8	egg whites, stiffly beaten (reserve yolks for filling)

Filling:

8	egg yolks
1	cup sugar
1/2	cup butter or margarine
1	cup raisins
1	cup flaked coconut
1	pound pecans, chopped (optional)
1	teaspoon vanilla extract

To make cake: Cream butter and sugar with electric mixer in large bowl until light and fluffy. Sift dry ingredients 2 times; add vanilla to milk. Alternately add dry ingredients and milk mixture to creamed mixture. Fold in egg whites. Spoon into 2 greased and floured 9" cake pans. Bake at 350°F until tester inserted in center comes out clean, 25 to 30 minutes. Let stand 5 minutes; remove and cool completely on racks. Spread filling between cooled layers. (16 to 18 servings.)

To make filling: Beat egg yolks slightly in top of double boiler; add sugar and butter. Cook over hot water, stirring constantly, until thick. Remove from heat; add remaining ingredients. Spread between cooled cake layers.

This recipe is from one of the cookbooks published by Will and Marlyn Smith of Memphis, TN. The Smiths donate proceeds from the sale of their books to St. Jude Children's Research Hospital in Memphis. (To order, call 1-800-858-3364)

Prince of Wales Cake

Marion Sweet
Verona, WI

Cake:

1/2	cup butter (no substitutes)
1	cup sugar
1	tablespoon molasses or brown sugar
2	eggs
2	cups all-purpose flour
1	teaspoon baking powder
1	teaspoon ground cinnamon
1/2	teaspoon ground nutmeg
1/4	teaspoon ground cloves
1	teaspoon baking soda
1	cup sour milk or buttermilk*
1/2	cup raisins, plumbed in hot water, drained

Filling:

1	cup sugar
3	tablespoons all-purpose flour
2	eggs, slightly beaten
2	cups milk
1/2 to 1 cup chopped nuts
1/2	teaspoon vanilla extract

To make cake: Preheat oven to 375°F. Cream butter and sugar with electric mixer in large bowl until light and fluffy. Beat in molasses. Add eggs, one at a time, beating well after each addition. Sift dry ingredients; stir baking soda into buttermilk. Add dry ingredients alternately with milk mixture to creamed mixture. Stir in raisins. Pour into 2 greased and floured 9" cake pans. Bake at 375°F until tester inserted in center comes out clean, about 30 minutes. Let stand 5 minutes; remove and cool completely on rack. When cool, spread filling between layers.

To make filling: Combine sugar and flour in top of double boiler. Stir in eggs and milk. Cook, stirring frequently, over hot water until quite thick. Cool, then add nuts and vanilla. Spread between and on top of cake layers.

*To make sour milk, add 1 tablespoon vinegar or lemon juice to 1 cup warm milk; let stand 5 minutes.

From my mother, Olga Blum, who used to make this cake 60 years ago.

Queen Elizabeth Cake

Betty Farrell
Arlington, TX

Cake:
1	cup boiling water
1	cup chopped, pitted dates
1	teaspoon baking soda
1	cup sugar
1/4	cup margarine or butter (1/2 stick)
1	egg, beaten
1	teaspoon vanilla extract
1 1/2	cups all-purpose flour
1	teaspoon baking powder
1/2	teaspoon salt
1/2	cup milk

Topping:
5	tablespoons packed brown sugar
5	tablespoons whole or half-and-half cream
2	tablespoons margarine or butter
	Chopped nuts (optional)
	Flaked coconut (optional)

To make cake: Pour boiling water over dates and soda in small bowl; let stand 5 minutes. Cream sugar and butter with electric mixer in large bowl. Add egg and vanilla. Sift flour with baking power and salt; add alternately with milk to creamed mixture, beating until smooth. Stir in date mixture. Pour into greased and floured 9 x 12" baking pan. Bake at 350°F until tester inserted in center comes out clean, about 25 minutes. Spread topping over cake while warm.

To make topping: Combine brown sugar, cream and margarine in small saucepan; heat to boiling. Reduce heat; cook, stirring constantly, 5 minutes. Spread over warm cake. Sprinkle with nuts and coconut, if desired.

When my grandfather died, Texas hospitality and warmth brought many wonderful dishes into the house for the gathered family. The thoughtful neighbors and friends attached recipes to each dish. This has always been known in our house as "Grandaddy's Funeral Cake."

Momma's Gumdrop Cake Squares

Sylvia J. Deaver
Gainesville, TX

4   eggs
2 1/2   cups packed brown sugar
1/2   cup margarine or butter, at room temperature (1 stick)
1   teaspoon vanilla extract
2   cups all-purpose flour, divided
1/2   teaspoon salt
1   cup chopped pecans
1   cup gumdrops
        Confectioners' sugar

Beat eggs with electric mixer in large bowl until foamy. Beat in brown sugar, butter and vanilla. Beat 1 cup of the flour and the salt into the egg mixture. Toss remaining flour with pecans and gumdrops; stir into batter. Batter will be very stiff. Pour into greased and floured 9 x 18 x 2" baking pan. Bake at 350°F for 45 minutes. Sprinkle top with confectioners' sugar. (24 servings.)

My momma, Anne Dane, made this dessert years ago. It's very chewy — excellent for people who 'dunk'. It smells good when it's baking, and since it is usually made at holiday time, it always brings family holiday memories to mind.

Neiman Marcus Cake

Judy Shibley
Ghost Ranch staff

Crust:
1   package sour cream cake mix (Duncan Hines preferred)
4   eggs, divided
2   teaspoons vanilla, divided
1/2   cup margarine or butter, melted
1   box confectioners' sugar (1 pound)
1   package cream cheese, at room temperature (8 ounces)
3/4   cup chopped pecans

Combine cake mix, 1 egg, 1 teaspoon of the vanilla and the melted margarine in large bowl; press firmly in 9 x 13" baking pan. Beat confectioners' sugar, cream cheese, the remaining 3 eggs and 1 teaspoon vanilla with electric mixer in large bowl until smooth. Pour over crust; sprinkle with pecans. Bake at 300°F for 1 hour. (Makes 20 servings.)
Neiman Marcus is a famous department store that caters to people who willspend exorbitant amounts of money, thus the name for this very rich cake.

Stack Cake

Lynn Ann and Edwin J. Best
Maryville, TN

1/2	cup vegetable shortening
1	cup granulated sugar
1	egg, beaten
1	teaspoon vanilla extract
4	cups all-purpose flour
1	teaspoon baking powder
1/2	teaspoon salt
1/4	teaspoon baking soda
1/4	cup milk
1/4	cup buttermilk
4	tablespoons butter or margarine, melted (1/2 stick)
2 1/2	cups apple filling, heated (recipe follows)

Apple Filling:

1	pound dried apples
1	cup packed brown sugar
1/2	cup granulated sugar
2	teaspoons ground cinnamon
1/2	teaspoon ground cloves
1/2	teaspoon ground allspice

Cream shortening and sugar; add egg and vanilla. Sift dry ingredients; add alternately with milks to creamed mixture. Cover and refrigerate. For filling: combine ingredients in saucepan. Cook over low heat, mashing apples as they soften, to the consistency of thick applesauce. Filling should be a little lumpy. Keep filling warm while preparing the dough. Divide dough in 6 equal parts. Pat dough portion onto bottom of greased 9" pie plate. Repeat with remaining dough portions. Bake at 400°F until light brown, about 12 minutes. Remove from pan and brush with melted butter. Spread hot apple filling between each layer (not the top). Cover and refrigerate at least 12 hours, until moistened throughout.

Stack cake was a favorite on the frontier. There was some competition among cake bakers to see how many layers they could have. A 'real stack cake' might have 10 or 12 layers and would take several days to moisten.

Applesauce Cake

Marta Rivera
Ghost Ranch staff

1/2	cup butter
1	cup sugar
1	egg, well beaten
1/8	teaspoon salt
1	teaspoon vanilla
1 1/2	cups applesauce
2	cups all purpose flour
1/2	teaspoon cinnamon
1/2	teaspoon cloves
2	teaspoon baking soda
1	cup nuts, chopped
1	cup raisins
1	cup dates, chopped

Cream butter and sugar. Add egg, salt, vanilla and applesauce. Add dry ingredients and put in nuts, raisins, and dates. Bake in greased, floured 9 x 13" pan at 350°F for 50-60 minutes.

Grandma Hattie's Applesauce Cake

Jacqueline McCalla Smith
Newton, KS

1	cup butter or margarine or 1 cup vegetable oil
2	cups packed dark brown sugar
2	eggs
3 1/2	cups whole wheat flour
2	teaspoons baking soda
1	teaspoon salt
1	teaspoon ground cinnamon
1	teaspoon ground cloves
2	cups applesauce
2	cups raisins
2	cups chopped pecans or walnuts
	Grated peel of 1 orange

Cream butter and brown sugar with electric mixer in large bowl until light and fluffy. Beat in eggs. Sift dry ingredients together; stir into creamed mixture. Stir in remaining ingredients. Pour into 2 greased 9 x 9" square baking pans. Bake at 350°F until tester inserted in center comes out clean, about 40 minutes. (Makes 2 cakes, 12 servings each.)

My tiny Ohio Grandma Hattie kept scrapbooks of her folk hero, Johnny Appleseed (John Chapman, 1776-1845). He was a houseguest at her grandparents' farm in the 1820s. Johnny's gravesite is in nearby Ft. Wayne, IN.

Applesauce Cake

Karen I. Kudia
Ipswich, MA

1/2	cup vegetable shortening
1 1/2	cups sugar
1	egg
1 1/2	cups applesauce
2 1/2	cups flour
1/2	teaspoon each: salt, ground cinnamon, ground allspice, ground cloves
1	cup raisins
1/2	cup chopped walnuts (optional)
2	teaspoons baking soda
1/2	cup boiling water

Cream shortening and sugar with electric mixer in large bowl until light and fluffy. Beat in egg, then applesauce. Sift dry ingredients; add to creamed mixture. Stir in raisins and nuts. Dissolve baking soda in boiling water; add gradually to batter. Pour into greased 9 x 13" baking pan. Bake at 350°F until tester inserted in center comes out clean, about 45 minutes.

My mum's delicious cake!

Spring Cake

Ghost Ranch

1	package yellow cake mix
2	eggs
1/2	cup oil
1/2	cup water
1	small can Mandarin orange with juice (8 oz.)

Topping:
1	package instant vanilla pudding
1	can crushed pineapple, not drained (16 oz.)
1	carton whipped topping (8 oz.)
	Coconut
	Nuts

Combine first five ingredients, mix for 2 minutes. Bake in a greased 9 x 13" pan for 35 minutes at 350°F. Cool. Stir first two topping ingredients until thick, then fold in carton of whipped topping. Spread on cooled cake. Sprinkle with coconut and chopped nuts, if desired.

Strawberry Cake

Ghost Ranch

1	package of strawberry jello (3 oz.)
1	cup boiling water
	One box white cake mix.
3	tablespoons all purpose flour
4	eggs
1	cup oil
1	box of frozen strawberries, thawed (10 oz.)

Frosting:
1	pound powdered sugar
1/2	stick margarine

Dissolve strawberry jello in water. Let cool. Stir flour into cake mix. Add eggs beaten until foamy. Add oil. Combine ingredients, blend well and add 1/2 box of strawberries (1/2 cup). Bake at 350°F for 45 minutes in a 9 x 13" or about 20 minutes in a jelly roll pan. Combine powdered sugar, margarine and balance of strawberries. Spread on cooled cake.

Ruthie's Banana Cake

Betty J. Beasley
Pagosa Springs, CO

1/2	cup butter or margarine (1 stick)
1	teaspoon vanilla extract
1 1/2	cups sugar
2	eggs
1 1/2	cups all-purpose flour
1/2	teaspoon each: salt, baking soda, ground nutmeg
1	cup mashed ripe bananas (2 to 3 bananas)
3	tablespoons buttermilk
	Chopped nuts (optional)

Cream butter and vanilla with electric mixer in large bowl. Beat in sugar; add eggs and beat well. Sift dry ingredients; add gradually to batter. Add bananas and buttermilk. Spread evenly in greased 9 x 9" pan. Bake at 350°F for 45 minutes.

An Air Force wife next door to us at Loring AFB, Maine in the early '50s shared this recipe with us. We've lost track of Ruthie, but her cake has been enjoyed by many friends and relatives over the years!

Prune Cake

Judy Shibley
Ghost Ranch staff

Cake:

2	cups granulated sugar
3/4	cup vegetable shortening
3	eggs
1 1/2	cups buttermilk
3	cups all-purpose flour
1	cup chopped nuts
1	cup cooked, drained prunes
2	ounces unsweetened chocolate, melted, slightly cooled
2	teaspoons baking powder
2	teaspoons vanilla extract

Topping:

1 1/2	cups granulated sugar (not confectioners' sugar)
1	cup heavy and half-and-half cream
1	cup chopped nuts
1	cup cooked, drained prunes

To make cake: Cream sugar and shortening with electric mixer in large bowl until light and fluffy. Add eggs, one at a time, beating well after each addition. Gradually beat in buttermilk. Stir in flour, nuts, prunes, chocolate, baking powder and vanilla; mix thoroughly. Pour into greased and floured 9 x 13" baking pan. Bake at 350°F until tester inserted in center comes out clean, 30 to 40 minutes. Cool, then spread with topping. (12 to 15 servings.)

To make topping: Place sugar and cream in medium saucepan; heat to boiling. Remove from heat; add nuts and prunes. Cool, then beat to spreading consistency (not sugary). Spread over cake.

My Nanny Smith (grandmother) cooked for oil workers in a wooden-floored tent in the boom town days of Borger, TX, before Borger was a town. After being invited to one of the bosses' homes for tea, she created this version of the prune cake she was served. It's my favorite cake!

Carrot Cake

Lidie Miller
Ghost Ranch librarian
Billings, MT

Cake:
2	cups sugar
1 1/2	cups vegetable oil
4	eggs
2	cups all-purpose flour
1/2	teaspoon baking powder
1	teaspoon ground cinnamon
1	teaspoon baking soda
1/2	teaspoon salt
1	teaspoon vanilla extract
3	cups shredded peeled carrots*
1	cup chopped nuts (raisins or coconut)
1/2	cup wheat germ
1	cup raspberry jam

Cream Cheese Frosting:
2	cups sifted confectioners' sugar
1	package cream cheese, at room temperature (8 ounces)
1/2	cup butter or margarine (at room temperature)
2	teaspoons vanilla extract
1/2	cup plain yogurt

To make cake: Beat sugar and oil with electric mixer in large bowl; add eggs, one at a time, beating well after each addition. Beat in remaining ingredients, adding wheat germ last. Pour into greased 9 x 13" baking pan (or 2 loaf pans or 8 x 8" pans). Bake at 350°F until tester inserted in center comes out clean, 45 to 55 minutes. Spread raspberry jam over warm cake; cool completely. Frost with cream cheese frosting. (Makes 12 to 15 servings.)

To make cream cheese frosting: Cream sugar, cream cheese, butter and vanilla with electric mixer in large bowl until smooth. Thin to spreading consistency with yogurt. Spread over baked cake.

*Reduce carrots to 2 cups and add 1 small can (8 3/4 oz.) drained crushed pineapple, if desired.

The topping of raspberry jam and cream cheese frosting was inspired by a dessert served at the Abiquiu Inn.

Cranberry Holiday Cake

Ghost Ranch

2	teaspoons baking powder
2	cups all purpose flour
1	cup sugar
1/2	teaspoon salt
2 1/2	cups whole raw cranberries
1	cup milk
3	tablespoons butter, melted

Sauce:

1	stick butter
1	cup sugar
3/4	cup whipping cream, unwhipped

Sift together dry ingredients. Add cranberries. Mix well. Combine milk and 3 tablespoons melted butter, add all at once to dry ingredients. Mix well by hand. (Don't use an electric mixer). Bake in a greased 9 x 13" pan at 375°F for about 40 minutes. Cake will not rise as high as regular cakes. Cut cake in squares with a sharp knife. Serve with warm sauce. (10-12 servings.)

Sauce: Combine butter, sugar and cream. Bring to a full boil. Boil for 3 minutes, stirring constantly or until slightly thickened. Serve warm.

Orange Cranberry Torte

Vera Lichty Kibbey
Sheffield, AL

Cake:
2 1/4	cups sifted all-purpose flour
1	cup sugar
1	teaspoon baking powder
1	teaspoon baking soda
1/4	teaspoon salt
1	cup chopped nuts
1	cup fresh or frozen cranberries
1	cup chopped pitted dates
	Grated peel of 2 oranges
2	eggs, beaten
3/4	cup vegetable oil
1	cup buttermilk

Topping:
1	cup orange juice
1	cup granulated sugar (not confectioners' sugar)
	Whipped cream (optional)

To make cake: Sift dry ingredients into large bowl. Stir in nuts, cranberries, dates and orange peel. Combine eggs, oil and buttermilk in small bowl; stir into flour mixture. Pour into greased 10" tube pan. Bake at 350°F for 1 hour. Remove and let stand until lukewarm. Pour topping over cake in the pan; let cool completely before removing. Serve with whipped cream, if desired. (Makes 12 to 16 servings.)

To make topping: Combine orange juice and sugar; stir until dissolved. Pour over warm cake.

Sock-It-To-Me Cake

Lidie Miller
Ghost Ranch librarian
Billings, MT

Cake:
1	package yellow cake mix (Duncan Hines preferred)
1/2	cup vegetable oil
1	cup sour cream or plain yogurt
1/4	cup water
4	eggs, beaten

Filling:
1	cup chopped pine nuts*
1/4	cup packed brown sugar
2	tablespoons ground cinnamon

Topping:
1	cup sifted confectioners' sugar
2	tablespoons milk

Combine cake mix, vegetable oil, sour cream, water and eggs in large bowl. Pour half of the batter in greased and floured bundt pan or 9 x 12" baking pan. Combine ingredients for filling; sprinkle over batter in pan. Top with remaining batter. Bake at 350°F for 35 to 45 minutes. Remove and let stand 5 minutes. Remove from pan. Combine ingredients for topping; drizzle over warm cake. (Makes 12 or more servings.)

*Pine nuts can be purchased ready-to-use. Roast fresh piñon nuts, and while they are hot, put them on a board, cover with a towel and press with a rolling pin to remove shells.

This recipe originated in "What's Cooking in the National Parks?" The late Dick Hull thought it was tops and calligraphed it for me.

Poppy Seed Cake

Ghost Ranch

2	ounces poppyseeds
1	cup buttermilk
1	teaspoon almond extract
1	cup butter
1 1/2	cups sugar
4	egg yolks
2 1/2	cups all purpose flour
1	teaspoon baking soda
1	teaspoon baking powder
1/2	teaspoon salt
4	egg whites
1/2	cup sugar
1	tablespoon cinnamon

Soak seeds in almond extract and buttermilk; set aside. Cream butter and sugar until light; add yolks and beat. Add poppy seed mixture. Sift dry ingredients together, add to creamed mixture. Beat egg whites stiff, fold into batter. Grease bundt pan, pour in half of batter, sprinkle sugar and cinnamon, add remaining batter. Bake at 350°F for 1 hour or more until done. Cool in pan. (10-12 servings)

Poppyseed Cake

Nancy and Ken Smith
Pueblo, CO

1	package white cake mix
1	package instant vanilla pudding (3.4 ounces)
1/2	cup orange juice
1/2	cup water
1/2	cup oil
1	tablespoon almond extract
2	tablespoons poppy seeds
5	eggs
3	tablespoons granulated sugar
1/2	teaspoon ground cinnamon
	Confectioners sugar

Combine cake mix, pudding mix, orange juice, water, oil, almond extract and poppy seeds in large bowl; beat with electric mixer until smooth. Add eggs, one at a time, beating well after each addition. Grease an angelfood cake pan; sprinkle with granulated sugar mixed with cinnamon. Pour batter into prepared pan. Bake at 375°F for 40 to 45 minutes. Let cool in pan; remove and sprinkle top with confectioners' sugar.

We got this recipe when we were dating in college. Now, each of our 4 children wants it for his/her birthday cake!

Grandma Gene's Fruitcake

Georgene Morrison-Shank
Ames, IA

1	cup light molasses
1/2	cup water
2 1/2	pounds raisin, ground
3/4	pound candied citron, sliced
1/2	pound candied cherries, sliced
1/2	pound candied pineapple, sliced
1/2	pound pecans, chopped
1/2	pound blanched almonds, chopped
2 1/4	cups all-purpose flour, divided
1 1/2	teaspoons ground cinnamon
3/4	teaspoon ground allspice
1/2	teaspoon ground cloves
1/4	teaspoon baking soda
1	cup butter or margarine
1 1/4	cups sugar
6	eggs, divided
1/2	cup brandy

Mix molasses and water in large roasting pan; heat to boiling. Reduce heat; stir in fruit and nuts. Cook and stir over low heat until all liquid is absorbed, about 5 minutes. Cool on large platters or baking sheets. When cool, toss with 1/4 cup of the flour. Cream butter and sugar with electric mixer in large bowl until light and fluffy. Add 3 eggs, one at a time, beating well after each addition. Sift remaining 2 cups flour with cinnamon, allspice, cloves and soda. Add 1 cup of the flour mixture to the creamed mixture. Add 3 more eggs, one at a time, beating well after each addition. Add remaining flour mixture alternately with the brandy. Stir in floured fruit. Line bottom and sides of 2 greased tube pans with heavy greased brown paper. Spoon batter evenly into pans. Bake at 275°F for 1 hour. Place pan of hot water on bottom rack of oven after 1 hour. Continue baking 2 hours. (Total baking time, 3 hours.) Let stand 15 minutes; remove and cool completely on racks. Store, wrapped in aluminum foil, in plastic bags, in air-tight containers for 3 months, to age before serving. Do not add additional rum or brandy during aging.

Mother used whole fruit, which has a much better flavor than cut fruit. You can buy whole candied fruit at fancy delicatessens like Goldberg-Bowen in San Francisco and Harrod's food court in London. Worth the trip!

Hot Milk Sponge Cake with Praline Topping

Opal N. Kingsbury
Madison, WI

Cake:

2	eggs
1	teaspoon vanilla or 1/2 teaspoon lemon extract
1	cup sugar
1	tablespoon butter or margarine
1/2	cup milk
1	cup cake flour
1	teaspoon baking powder
1/2	teaspoon salt

Praline Topping:

3	tablespoons butter or margarine
5	tablespoons heavy or half-and-half cream or evaporated milk
1/2	cup packed brown sugar
1/2	cup flaked coconut
1/4	cup chopped nuts

To make cake: Beat eggs with electric mixer in large bowl until light and lemon-colored. Add flavoring. Gradually add sugar; continue to beat until mixture is light and shiny. Add butter to milk and heat in small saucepan. While this heats, sift dry ingredients; add all at once to egg mixture. Fold in just until smooth. Add hot milk all at once and blend in quickly. (The batter is rather thin.) Pour immediately into greased 8 x 8" baking pan. Bake at 375°F for 10 minutes; reduce heat to 350°F and continue baking until cake shrinks from sides of pan, about 20 minutes. Remove and let cool in the pan. Spread praline topping over warm cake.

To make praline topping: Place butter, cream and brown sugar in small saucepan; heat to boiling. Add remaining ingredients; spread over cake. Broil until bubbly, watching carefully.

In the early 1960's, my son Tom was on college staff at Ghost Ranch. One of the ladies in the kitchen made this cake for his birthday. Ghost Ranch is still a favorite place for our family!

Meringue Cake

Peg Pack McKinley
Santa Fe, NM

4	egg whites
1	cup sugar
1/8	teaspoon cream of tartar
1/2 to 1	teaspoon vanilla extract
1	cup heavy cream, whipped
4 or 5	small Heath bars, crushed

Preheat oven to 300°F. Beat egg whites and cream of tartar with electric mixer in large bowl until stiff. Gradually add sugar while beating; fold in vanilla. Spread on brown paper-lined baking sheets to 2 dinner plate-sized circles. Bake at 300°F until firm and just beginning to brown, about 1 hour. Peel from paper and let cool completely on racks. To serve, place one meringue layer on plate; top with half the whipped cream and half the crushed Heath bars; repeat.

Variation: Add sugar and vanilla to whipped cream; replace candy bars with sliced strawberries and garnish with whole berries.

editor's note: Peg is the daughter of Arthur Pack.

Gingerbread

Ghost Ranch

1	cup vegetable shortening
1/4	cup sugar
2	eggs
2	cups dark molasses
2	cups boiling water
4 1/2	cups all-purpose flour
1 1/2	teaspoons baking soda
1	teaspoon salt
1	teaspoon ground ginger
2	teaspoons ground cinnamon
	Whipped cream or non-dairy whipped topping

Preheat oven to 325°F. Cream shortening, sugar and egg with electric mixer in large bowl. Gradually add molasses and water. Sift dry ingredients; gradually beat into molasses mixture until smooth. Pour into greased 9 x 13" baking pan. Bake at 325°F for 50 minutes. Serve warm with whipped cream or whipped topping. (15 servings.)

Ice Box Gingerbread

Ghost Ranch

1	cup sugar
1	cup shortening
1	cup molasses
1	cup buttermilk
2	eggs
4	cups all purpose flour
2	teaspoons ginger
1	teaspoon baking soda
1/2	teaspoon cinnamon
1/2	teaspoon cloves
1	cup raisins
1	cup nuts
3/4	teaspoon salt

Cream sugar and shortening. Add molasses, buttermilk and eggs. Combine dry ingredients, add to creamed mixture. Add nuts and raisins. Bake in 325°F oven. Keep in ice box and bake as much at a time as desired, either in a 9 x 13" pan (45 minutes) or muffin tins (20-25 minutes). Especially good served warm with whipped cream. (Makes one cake or 24 muffins.)

Sour Cream Icing

Judith Snyder
Boulder, CO

2	cups sugar
1	pint sour cream
6	eggs
1	cup ground walnuts
1	teaspoon almond extract (or to taste)

Put sour cream in skillet. Add sugar. Beat eggs well. Add eggs and mix on medium heat, stirring constantly as mixture thickens. Add almond to taste. Remove from heat and add ground nuts.

I am offering a recipe which I have never seen in print. It comes by way of my maternal grandmother, Anna Cristina Royal Goehring, ne Ley. It is a disgustingly cholesterol-filled, delicious tasting icing, which I have made in a "healthier" version using egg substitutes and low fat sour cream. The second version is not too bad and if you put it on angel food cake you needn't feel quite so guilty.

This is the one recipe which I have never shared when requests came to me for a recipe for cookbooks. Only Ghost Ranch is dear enough to my heart to pry this one loose. This recipe has warmed the hearts of my family for several generations as only a tradition could.

COOKIES

Biscochitos

Charlie Carrillo
Santa Fe, NM

2	cups lard (traditional) or shortening (for diet-conscious people)
1 1/2	cups sugar
3-6	teaspoons anise seed
4	cups all-purpose flour
1	teaspoon salt
2	teaspoons baking powder
2	cups whole wheat flour
3/4	cup water (or use juice, brandy, etc.)
3	eggs
2	tablespoons vanilla

Cream lard or shortening. Add sugar, stir in anise. Sift together flour, salt, and baking powder. Stir mixture into creamed mixture. Stir in water (or juice). On floured surface roll dough out 1/4 to 1/2 inch thick, cut into fancy shapes. Sprinkle with sugar and cinnamon. Bake until lightly brown, 10-15 minutes, at 350°F. (Makes 5 dozen cookies.)

This is a traditional family recipe. Since colonial times in New Mexico, Hispanic and Native American people have made biscochitos. In my childhood these cookies were made either in traditional outdoor ovens known as hornos or in modern ovens. I remember that the biscochitos were specifically made for important or festive occasions. I can, however, remember the thick biscochitos made by my grandmother, Ignacia Carrillo, for everyday consumption. My favorite biscochitos were those my mother, Loretta Carrillo, made. They are thin and crispy with just the right amount of anise seed. The smell of hot biscochitos is one of love and brings back memories of Christmas at home!

Prune Pastelitos

Philadelfia Leyba
Rebecca Martinez' grandmother

Filling:

2	pounds dry pitted prunes
2	cups sugar
1	small can sweet yams, drained (12 oz.)
1	teaspoon cinnamon

Crust:

3	cups all-purpose flour
1	teaspoon salt
2	tablespoons sugar
1	teaspoon baking powder
1	cup warm water
1	cup shortening

Cook prunes until soft and tender, drain all excess juice. Smash them by hand, add sweet yams, sugar, and cinnamon. To make crust: mix all crust ingredients, adding water slowly. Make dough. Let set for about 10 minutes and roll out. Either make a pie or use a cookie sheet, putting a layer of dough, then filling, then another sheet of dough on top. Sprinkle a little brown sugar on top if desired. Cook at 350°F for 25-30 minutes. Let cool. Cut into small squares and serve.

This recipe I learned from my Grandma. When I was a little girl, she would make them in the horno oven all the time.

Special Goodies

Dorothy Craft
Claremont, CA

12	Honey graham crackers (about 3 x 6")
1	stick (1/2 cup) butter
1	stick (1/2 cup) margarine
1/2	cup sugar
1	cup chopped nuts

Separate graham crackers into units (4 each). Place on foil-lined baking sheet with sides (or shallow pan). Place butter, margarine and sugar in medium pan; heat to boiling. Boil exactly 2 minutes; pour over graham crackers. (It may seem like too much, but spread it around.) Sprinkle nuts evenly on top. Bake at 375°F for exactly 10 minutes. Cool; then break apart. (Makes 48 cookies.)

This is a favorite with Head Start nurses in the Norwalk-LaMirada School District, CA.

editor's note: Viola L. Shelby Doty, of El Reno OK, submitted a recipe for "Toffee Squares" that is very similar to the recipe above. Mrs. Doty omits the nuts and sprinkles chocolate chips over the toffee-topped graham crackers as they come out of the oven. When they have melted, she spreads the chocolate evenly and then sprinkles finely-chopped pecans on top.

Lebkuchen (German Hazelnut Bars)

Judy Minnich Stout
San Diego, CA

3/4	cup + 2 tablespoons granulated sugar
1 1/3	cups butter
1 1/4	cups honey
3 1/3	cups flour
1	teaspoon ground cinnamon
1/8	teaspoon ground cloves
1 1/4	cups ground hazelnuts
1	egg
1	teaspoon baking powder*
1	tablespoon milk
1	cup sifted confectioners' sugar
3	tablespoons lemon juice
	Decorative colored sugar

Heat granulated sugar, butter and honey in large saucepan. Sift flour and spices; add to honey mixture. Stir in nuts and egg. Cover and refrigerate 8 hours or overnight. Mix baking powder with milk and add to dough. Roll out onto a greased 15 x 10" baking sheet with sides. Bake at 350°F until firm, 25 to 30 minutes. Cut in diamond shapes. Mix confectioners' sugar and lemon juice; pour over cookies. Sprinkle with colored sugar. Remove and cool completely on wire racks. Store tightly covered.

*Original recipe calls for 10 grams of potash and 5 grams of cream of tartar.

Lebkuchen is sometimes translated "gingerbread" which is a misnomer, since this recipe calls for no ginger. Maria Frey of Freiburg im Breisgau gave me this recipe in German with the quantities in grams. I've been making it for 20 years. The students in my German classes voted it 'BEST'.

Linzer Bars

Ghost Ranch

1	cup applesauce
3/4	cup raspberry preserves
1	cup whole almonds
3/4	cup sugar, plus 2 tablespoons sugar
1/2	cup butter, softened
1	egg
1/2	teaspoon lemon peel, grated
1 1/2	cups all-purpose flour
1/4	teaspoon salt
1/2	teaspoon cinnamon
1	egg white, lightly beaten

Line 9 x 13" pan with foil, grease foil. Cook applesauce down on low heat until most of liquid evaporates (25 minutes). Stir in preserves. Set aside. In food processor, grind almonds and 2 tablespoons sugar until fine. In a bowl, beat butter until light and fluffy; gradually add 3/4cup sugar. Beat in egg and lemon. Combine flour, salt, cinnamon; stir into butter mixture. Stir in almond-sugar. Set aside 1/4 of dough. Pat remaining dough in pan. Bake 20 minutes; spread with fruit filling. Add egg white to remaining dough. Spoon into pastry bag with #1 plain tube. Pipe dough over filling in lattice pattern. Bake at 375°F for 30 minutes. Cut into 2 x 1" bars. (Makes 54 bars)

Shortbread

Kay Taybe
Sun City, AZ

1/2	pound butter
1	cup sugar
1/4	teaspoon vanilla extract
2 1/2	cups sifted all-purpose flour (scant rather than generous)

Cream butter and sugar with electric mixer until light and fluffy; add vanilla. Fold in flour by hand or with mixer on lowest speed. Roll dough to 1/4" thickness between sheets of waxed paper. Place dough, between sheets of waxed paper, on 12 x 15" baking sheet. Refrigerate until firm. Peel off top paper; cut in desired shapes. Remove from bottom sheet of waxed paper; place on baking sheet(s), leaving space between. Bake at 300°F just until beginning to brown, about 35 minutes. Watch carefully! Overdone cookies lose their delicate flavor.

A friend made me 2 wooden strips to put on either side of the dough on top of the waxed paper. The strips are exactly 1/4" thick. Each cookie is the same thickness and thus they bake evenly.

Original Scottish Shortbread

Ghost Ranch

1	pound butter (room temperature)
1 1/2	cups superfine sugar
4	cups all-purpose flour
1/2	cup cornstarch
1/8	teaspoon salt

Cream together butter and sugar. Mix flour, cornstarch and salt; add to butter mixture (you may use a dough hook). Mix with floured hands. Spread onto large (11 x 17) ungreased cookie sheet. Prick with fork all over dough. Cook at 325°F for 30-40 minutes—watch till dough gets golden brown. Cut into squares while warm.

Polenta Anise Shortbread

Kimberly Sweet
Plaza Resolana staff

1	cup butter (2 sticks)
2	teaspoons anise seed, lightly toasted, ground*
1	teaspoon vanilla extract
2/3	cup sifted confectioners' sugar
1 1/2	cups all-purpose flour
1/2	cup corn meal
1/4	teaspoon salt

Beat butter, anise and vanilla until smooth and creamy. Beat in sugar. Combine flour, corn meal and salt; add to butter mixture. Roll out on lightly-floured surface and cut with cookie cutters, or form into a roll, wrap and refrigerate and cut into rounds. Bake at 300°F until firm but not brown, 10 to 15 minutes. (Makes 24, 2" cookies.)

* Tip: Grind anise seed in electric coffee grinder.

Forget 'Ems

Ghost Ranch

3	egg whites, room temperature
3/4	cup sugar
1	teaspoon vanilla
6	ounces chocolate chips
	Chopped nuts if desired

Preheat oven to 350°F. In grease-free bowl beat egg whites until stiff. Very gradually add sugar, beating all the while. Fold in vanilla and chocolate chips. Drop by teaspoons on paper-lined cookie sheets. Turn oven off, put cookies in and forget 'em. (3-4 hours or overnight).

Pecan Macaroons

Dorothy Hyatt
Alamogordo, NM

2   egg whites
1   cup sifted confectioners' sugar
1   cup packed brown sugar (no lumps)
2   cups pecans, ground (measure before grinding)
        Non-stick vegetable oil spray

Beat egg whites with electric mixer in large bowl until very stiff. Gradually beat in confectioners' sugar. Stir in brown sugar and pecans. Line baking sheets with foil; spray foil with vegetable oil spray (essential!). Drop batter by teaspoonfuls, 1" apart. Bake at 325°F just until firm, 20 to 25 minutes. Allow to cool completely before peeling cookies from the foil. (Makes 3 to 4 dozen cookies.)

These cookies look modest, like oatmeal cookies, but every first-time taster says, "Wow!" The recipe came from Germany, where they probably used hazelnuts instead of pecans.

Note: To grind oily nuts such as pecans, walnuts and peanuts, in blender or food processor, first place a small amount of flour in bottom to absorb excess oils, otherwise they will become nut butter. Drier nuts like hazelnuts and almonds can be ground without flour.

Hazelnut Cookies

Richard and Susan Moore
San Rafael, CA

7   egg whites
2   cups packed dark brown sugar (no lumps)
1   teaspoon vanilla extract
1   pound unblanched hazelnuts, ground
1/4   cup granulated sugar

Beat egg whites with electric mixer in large bowl until very stiff. Gradually add brown sugar, beating constantly. Beat in vanilla. Fold in ground nuts. Shape in 1" balls; roll in granulated sugar. Place on greased baking sheets. Bake at 325°F for 10 to 20 minutes. Remove from baking sheet immediately. (Makes 4 dozen cookies.)

Aunt Pauline's Cookies

Mary Ellen Epting
Moneta, VA

1/2	cup butter or margarine
1/2	cup granulated sugar
1/2	cup packed brown sugar
1	egg
2	tablespoons water
1/2	teaspoon vanilla extract
1/2	teaspoon almond extract
1 1/4	cups all-purpose flour
1/2	teaspoon salt
1/2	teaspoon baking soda
1	cup quick-cooking rolled oats
1/2	cup each: raisins, chopped nuts, All-Bran, coconut flakes

Cream butter and sugars with electric mixer in large bowl until light and fluffy. Beat in egg, water, vanilla and almond extract. Sift flour, salt and soda; add to batter. Stir in remaining ingredients. Drop by teaspoonfuls on greased baking sheets. Bake at 350°F on top shelf of oven until light brown, about 10 minutes. (Makes 6 dozen cookies.)

Oatmeal Raisin Cookies

Barbara L. Hutchison
Richwood, WV

1	cup margarine or butter (2 sticks)
1	cup granulated sugar
1	cup packed brown sugar
2	eggs, beaten
1	teaspoon vanilla extract
1/2	cup chopped nuts
1 1/2	cups all-purpose flour
3	cups quick-cooking rolled oats
1	teaspoon salt
1	teaspoon baking powder
1	cup raisins

Cream margarine and sugars with electric mixer in large mixer bowl until light and fluffy. Beat in eggs and vanilla; add nuts. Combine flour, oats, salt and baking powder in medium bowl; add flour and raisins to batter. Drop by teaspoonfuls onto baking sheet, leaving about 2" between. Bake at 350°F for 10 to 12 minutes. Remove and cool on racks. (Makes 4 to 5 dozen cookies.)

World's Best Cookies

John May
Albuquerque, NM

1	cup butter
1	cup sugar
1	cup brown sugar
1	egg
1/2	cup oil
1	cup regular rolled oats
1	cup cornflakes, crushed
1/2	cup shredded coconut
1/2	cup nuts, chopped
3 1/2	cups all-purpose flour
1	teaspoon baking soda
1	teaspoon salt
1	teaspoon vanilla

Cream butter and sugars. Add egg, then oil, mixing well. Add oats, cornflakes, coconut and nuts, stirring well. Add flour, soda, and salt. Form into balls the size of walnuts and place on greased cookie sheet. Flatten with fork dipped in water. Bake 12 minutes at 325°F. Allow to cool on cookie sheet a few minutes before removing. (Yields 90-100 with small "ice cream" dipper.)

Raisin Drop Cookies

Flora Garcia
Ghost Ranch staff
Canjilon, NM

1/2	cup butter or margarine
1/2	cup sugar
2	eggs
1	cup all-purpose flour
1	teaspoon baking powder
1/4	teaspoon salt
1	teaspoon vanilla
1/2	cup moist raisins

Cream together butter, sugar and eggs. Combine dry ingredients, add to creamed mixture. Scoop or spoon cookie dough on greased cookie sheet, bake at 350°F for 10-12 minutes. Don't overbake or they will be dry. (Makes 3 dozen.)

Crispy Oatmeal Cookies

Ann W. Nichols
Tucson, AZ

1	cup butter
1	cup margarine
1 1/2	cups granulated sugar
2	cups packed brown sugar
4	eggs
2	teaspoons vanilla extract
3	cups all-purpose flour
2	teaspoons salt
2	teaspoons baking powder
2	teaspoons ground cinnamon
6	cups rolled oats ("old-fashioned" preferred)
1 1/2	cups flaked coconut
1	cup finely chopped nuts, raisins or chocolate chips (optional)

Cream butter, margarine and sugars with electric mixer in large bowl until light and fluffy. Beat in eggs, one at a time, beating well after each addition; add vanilla. Combine flour, salt, baking powder and cinnamon; add gradually to creamed mixture. Stir in rolled oats, coconut and nuts (raisins or chocolate chips). Drop by teaspoonfuls, 2" apart, on baking sheets. Bake at 350°F, 10 to 15 minutes. (Makes 14 dozen cookies.)

Once, I had a secretary who submitted her resignation when she was expecting a baby. However, she refused to leave until I had given her this recipe. I'm an absent-minded professor and kept forgetting — until she nearly had her baby in the office! I make these cookies for my students on exam days. Many claim they owe their good grade to the sustenance of these oatmeal cookies.

Raggedy Ann Cookies

Opal N. Kingsbury
Madison, WI

1/2	cup butter
1	cup packed brown sugar
2	tablespoons granulated sugar
2	eggs, beaten
1 1/2	cups all-purpose flour
1	teaspoon baking soda
1/4	teaspoon salt
1	teaspoon vanilla
1	cup chopped dates
1/2	cup raisins (golden raisins preferred)
1/2	cup flaked coconut
1/2	cup chopped nuts
3	cups "Special K" cereal, measured, then coarsely crushed

Cream butter and sugars with electric mixer in large bowl until light and fluffy. Stir in eggs. Sift flour, soda and salt; add to creamed mixture. Stir in vanilla, dates, raisins, coconut and nuts. Lastly, stir in cereal. Drop by teaspoonfuls on ungreased baking sheets. Bake at 375°F until firm, about 10 minutes. Cookies should not overbake — they may look a little wet on top, but still be done. Adjust oven to 350°F, if cookies bake too fast.

We had finished a delicious dinner in the home of an old friend when she brought out a plate of these cookies. I thought they were the best drop cookie I had ever eaten. I copied the recipe and have baked them many times since.

Salted Peanut Crisps

Sarah Bradford
Cortez, CO

1	cup shortening (part butter or margarine)
1 1/2	cups brown sugar, packed
2	eggs
2	teaspoons vanilla
3	cups all-purpose flour
1/2	teaspoon baking soda
1	teaspoon salt
2	cups salted peanuts

Mix shortening, sugar, eggs, vanilla thoroughly. Blend flour, baking soda, salt; stir into sugar mixture. Add peanuts. Drop by rounded teaspoonfuls about 2" apart on lightly greased cookie sheet. Flatten with bottom of glass dipped in sugar. Bake at 375°F for 8-10 minutes, or until golden brown.

Chocolate Raisin Nut Cookies

Janet Clark
Denver, CO

1/2	cup vegetable shortening
1	cup sugar
2	eggs
3	squares unsweetened chocolate, melted
1/2	cup milk
1/2	teaspoon vanilla extract
2	cups all-purpose flour
1	teaspoon baking powder
1/2	teaspoon salt
3/4	cup chopped walnuts
3/4	cup raisins

Cream shortening and sugar with electric mixer in large bowl until light and fluffy. Beat in eggs, chocolate, milk, and vanilla. Sift flour, baking power and salt; add gradually to creamed mixture. Stir in nuts and raisins. Drop by teaspoonfuls on greased baking sheets. Bake at 350°F, 15 minutes; let stand one minute before removing to rack.

Chocolate Truffle Cookies

Nancy Deever
Plaza Resolana volunteer

4	ounces unsweetened chocolate
6	tablespoons butter
2	cups semisweet chocolate chips, divided (12 ounces)
3	eggs
1	cup sugar
2	teaspoons vanilla extract
1/2	cup all-purpose flour
2	tablespoons unsweetened cocoa powder
1/4	teaspoon baking powder
1/4	teaspoon salt

Melt unsweetened chocolate, butter, and 1 cup of the chocolate chips in double boiler or microwave; reserve. Beat eggs and sugar with electric mixer in large bowl until smooth and lemon-colored, about 2 minutes. Add vanilla and reserved chocolate mixture. Combine flour, cocoa, baking powder and salt; add gradually to batter. Stir in remaining 1 cup chocolate chips. Cover and refrigerate for 1 hour. Drop by teaspoonfuls on ungreased baking sheets. Bake at 350°F for 8 to 10 minutes. (Makes 30 to 40 cookies.)

Best Brownies

George and Margaret Wolf
Hudson, IL

4	squares unsweetened chocolate
1	cup margarine or butter (2 sticks)
2	cups sugar
4	eggs
1 1/2	cups all-purpose flour
1	teaspoon baking powder
1/2	teaspoon vanilla extract
1	cup chopped nuts (optional)

Melt chocolate and margarine in double boiler over hot water; remove from heat. Beat in sugar; add eggs one at a time, beating well after each addition. Sift flour and baking powder; stir into chocolate mixture. Add vanilla and nuts. Pour in greased 9 x 13" pan. Bake at 350°F for 30 minutes. When cool, frost with favorite frosting. (Makes 24 large squares.)

$250 Cookie Recipe

Emily Brudos
Albuquerque, NM

2	cups butter
2	cups granulated sugar
2	cups packed brown sugar
4	eggs
2	teaspoons vanilla extract
4	cups all-purpose flour
5	cups rolled oats, ground to a fine powder in blender or food processor
2	teaspoons baking powder
2	teaspoons baking soda
1	teaspoon salt
24	ounces chocolate chips (4 cups)
1.8	ounce chocolate bar, grated (Hersheys preferred)
3	cups chopped pecans

Cream butter and sugars with electric mixer in large bowl until light and fluffy. Add eggs, one at a time, beating well after each addition. Add vanilla. Combine flour, oatmeal, baking powder, baking soda and salt; stir into creamed mixture. Stir in chocolate chips, grated chocolate and nuts. Form in 1" (or larger) balls and place 2" apart of ungreased baking sheet. Bake at 375°F until set, 6 to 10 minutes.

The story (supposedly) behind this recipe: A woman had lunch one day at a famous Dallas department store and was served this cookie. She asked if the recipe was available and was told that it was, for a small charge of two-fifty. She told them she would like the recipe, and just to charge it to her account. When she got the bill, it was for $250. She called to inform them of their error and was told that there was no mistake. She vowed to get back at them by giving the recipe to everyone she possible could.

Judy's Soft Ginger Cookies

Bruce and Anne Hunt
Hawthorn Woods, IL

3/4	cup margarine or vegetable shortening
1 1/4	cup sugar
1	egg
4	tablespoons molasses
2 1/2	cups all-purpose flour
2	teaspoons each: baking soda, ginger, ground cinnamon, ground cloves

Cream margarine and 1 cup of the sugar with electric mixer until light and fluffy. Beat in egg and molasses. Combine flour with baking powder and spices; beat gradually into creamed mixture. Form into 1" balls; roll in remaining 1/4 cup sugar. Place on greased baking sheets, 2" apart. Bake at 350°F until top is crackled all over (do not overcook). Let stand for 5 minutes before removing to rack. (Makes 2 to 3 dozen cookies.)

Our senior year at the College of Wooster, we got married and lived in $45-a-month barracks built for World War II vets returning to school. A number of married students that year were active in school organizations, so there were many meetings in the old Taylor Units. This recipe, from our Taylor neighbor, Judy McCullough, was often served at those gatherings. We're still going to meetings and making these cookies 35 years later!

Polish Tea Cookies (Ciastka z Konserwa)

Katherine H. Harper
Española, NM

1/2	cup butter
1/2	cup sugar
1	egg, separated
1/2	teaspoon vanilla
1	cup all-purpose flour
1/2	teaspoon salt
2	cups finely chopped nuts (can be done in blender)
	Preserves

Cream butter and sugar with electric mixer in large bowl until light and fluffy. Beat egg yolk slightly; add to creamed mixture with the vanilla. Sift flour with salt; add to creamed mixture. Form balls about 3/4" in diameter; roll in beaten egg white then in chopped nuts. Place on greased baking sheet. Press the center down with a thimble, dipped in flour between indentations. Bake at 325°F for 5 minutes; press down again with thimble. Continue baking until edges begin to color slightly, 10 to 15 minutes (do not overbake). Remove from oven and fill each indentation with preserves while still warm. (Makes 50 small cookies.)

From Treasured Polish Recipes (1948). This is my favorite of all cookies and is so delicate and buttery that guests always comment. They make an exceptionally nice gift for someone who has given you the preserves!

Grandma Anderson's Jam Cookies

Betty Farrell
Arlington, TX

2	cups sugar, divided
1	vanilla bean, cut up
1	pound (4 sticks) butter (not margarine)
3	cups sifted all-purpose flour
1/2	pound ground blanched, skinned almonds
	Raspberry preserves or jam

Several days ahead, combine 1 cup sugar and the vanilla bean in air-tight container. Shake several times to insure evenly flavored sugar.

To make cookies, combine the remaining 1 cup sugar, the butter, flour and almonds. Roll out very thin on floured surface. Cut in tiny 1 to 1 1/4" circles. Bake at 350°F until golden brown, 5 to 10 minutes, watching carefully. Sandwich two cookies together with preserves or jam. When set, roll in vanilla-flavored sugar. Store in air-tight container.

Our bridge club meets on New Year's Eve for dinner. We became friends at First Presbyterian Church in the early 1950's and have gathered each year since. It wouldn't be "right" without Grandma Anderson's Jam Cookies.

Rum Balls

Ghost Ranch

3	cups rolled vanilla wafers
1	cup powdered sugar
1 1/2	cups nuts, finely chopped
1 1/2	tablespoons cocoa
2	tablespoons light corn syrup
1/2	cup rum

Mix all ingredients thoroughly and form small balls. Roll in powdered sugar. Keep refrigerated in tightly covered container. Great for Christmas holidays.

Whiskey Balls

Vera Clark
Alpine, NJ

1	cup ground pecans
1 1/2	cups confectioners' sugar, divided
2	teaspoons dry cocoa powder
1/2	cup rum
3	tablespoons bourbon or brandy
3	tablespoons light corn syrup

Combine pecans, 1 cup of the sugar and the cocoa in large bowl. Stir in rum and whiskey. Drip in the corn syrup. Mix well. Form into 1" (or smaller) balls; roll in reserved confectioners' sugar. Store tightly covered. Roll again in confectioners' sugar just before serving.

At a Christmas tea at the First Presbyterian Church, Englewood, NJ, I asked who had made these delicious cookies and was directed to a tall dignified lady, Mrs. Edna Clark. Mrs. Clark sent me the recipe on December 23, 1966. Two years later, my husband died, leaving me with 2 young children. The minister asked Dr. Graham Clark, Mrs. Clark's son and an elder in the church, to help us. Dr. Clark taught at Ghost Ranch in the summers. He encouraged me to go to Ghost Ranch, and I did sign up for the following summer. However, this never happened because I became engaged to and married Graham's brother, LeRoy Clark, Jr., who was also a widower, and 22 years later, we are still enjoying life together. I would still like to visit Ghost Ranch one of these days!

Mimi's Sliced Cookies

Norma J. Weiner
Hilton Head, SC

2	cups butter
2	cups sugar
4	cups all-purpose flour
1/2	teaspoon baking soda
1/2	teaspoon ground nutmeg
1/4	teaspoon ground cloves
1/8	teaspoon salt
1/2	cup sour cream
1/2	cup sliced almonds

Cream butter and sugar with electric mixer in large bowl until light and fluffy. Sift together flour, soda, nutmeg, cloves and salt; add slowly to creamed mixture. Add sour cream; fold in almonds. Form in rolls, approximately 10 x 2". Refrigerate, wrapped in waxed paper or plastic wrap until firm, up to 2 weeks. Slice 1/8" thick and place on ungreased baking sheets. Bake at 350°F until lightly browned, 10 to 12 minutes. (Makes 8 to 10 dozen cookies.)

This was one of my mother's favorite recipes. It had no name, so we named it in her honor!

Ice Box Cookies

Mozelle Neill
Midland, TX

1	cup granulated sugar
1	cup packed brown sugar
3/4	cup butter (1 1/2 sticks)
3/4	cup vegetable shortening
2	eggs
1	teaspoon vanilla extract
1	teaspoon baking soda
2	teaspoons water
3 1/2	cups all-purpose flour
1/2	teaspoon salt
1	cup chopped pecans

Cream sugars, butter and shortening with electric mixer in large bowl until light and fluffy. Add eggs, one at a time, beating well after each addition. Beat in vanilla; add baking soda, dissolved in 2 teaspoons water. Add flour and salt; stir in pecans. Form into rolls; wrap in waxed paper or plastic wrap. Refrigerate until firm. Slice and place on ungreased baking sheets. Bake at 375°F until brown, about 12 minutes. (Makes 144 cookies.)

I have made these cookies for well over 50 years.

Sand Tarts

Ghost Ranch

1	pound butter
6	tablespoons powdered sugar
1	teaspoon vanilla
1	tablespoon water
4	cups all-purpose flour
2	cups pecans, grated or finely chopped

Combine ingredients in order listed. Dough will be stiff. Roll dough in 1" balls, bake on ungreased sheet in 300°F oven for 45 minutes. Roll in powdered sugar while warm.

My Mother's Biscotti

Edythe Pizio Campodonico
Redwood City, CA

2	cups sugar
1	cup butter or margarine, melted, cooled
4	tablespoons anise seed
4	tablespoons amaretto
2	teaspoons vanilla
2	tablespoons water
5	eggs
5 1/2	cups all-purpose flour
1	tablespoon baking powder
2	cups coarsely chopped almonds

Combine sugar, butter, anise seed and amaretto. Mix vanilla and water and add to sugar mixture. Beat in the eggs. Combine flour and baking powder and add to sugar mixture. Stir in almonds. Cover and refrigerate at least 2 hours. Shape dough to form 2 loaves, 1/2" high x 3" wide x about 16" long. Place on greased jelly-roll pan. Bake at 375°F on top rack; change to bottom rack after 10 minutes and bake until golden brown, about 10 minutes more. Remove from oven and cool a little. Remove loaves to a cutting board with a spatula. Cut 1/2" slices diagonally. Place cookies close together on their sides in the baking pan. Bake at 375°F for 10 minutes, changing from top to bottom rack after 5 minutes. Watch carefully as they brown quickly. Cool on racks; store in tightly-covered container. (Makes about 9 dozen cookies.)

My mother brought this recipe with her from Pinerola, Italy in the province of Piemonte, in the north near the Alps. I have been helping make these since I was very young.

Almond Torte Cookies

Barbara Bowen Moore
Atlanta, GA

1	cup almonds, ground
1	cup rolled oats, ground in blender or processor (natural, unproc essed oats preferred)
1	cup brown rice flour
1/4	teaspoon ground cinnamon
1/4	teaspoon salt
1/2	cup vegetable oil (Hain cold-pressed safflower oil preferred)
1/2	cup maple syrup
1/2	teaspoon almond extract
	Fruit spread (jam made with colorful fruit, sweetened with fruit juice)

Combine almonds, rolled oats, brown rice flour, cinnamon and salt in large bowl. Combine and add oil, maple syrup and almond extract. Form in 1" balls and place about 2" apart on 2 greased baking sheets. Dent top of each ball with a finger and place about 1/4 teaspoon fruit spread in the dent. Bake in 350°F oven on middle rack until slightly brown on top, about 25 minutes. Check after 15 minutes to see if baking sheets should be shifted to ensure even browning. (Makes 30 to 35 cookies.)

In an effort to revise my way of life and cooking, I attended the Natural Gourmet Institute for Food and Health (48 W. 21st Street, New York, NY 10010) in the summer of 1986. These cookies were my favorite recipe from the course. The founder and director, Annemarie Colbin, has 2 books, The Book of Whole Meals and The Natural Gourmet.

French Cookies

Elsa Snuggs
Tulsa, OK

2	cups packed brown sugar
3	cups all-purpose flour
1	teaspoon baking soda dissolved in 1 cup hot water
1	teaspoon ground cinnamon
1	teaspoon baking powder
2	eggs
1	cup butter or margarine, at room temperature
1	cup raisins
	Confectioners' sugar icing (optional)

Put all ingredients in large bowl. Do not stir until everything is added. Stir; divide evenly between 2 greased jelly-roll sheets, 14 x 17" each. Bake at 350°F until done, 30 to 45 minutes. Frost with confectioners' sugar icing, if desired. Cut in squares.

This was a favorite of my mother when she wanted to serve a large group, such as a church luncheon or tea. I use it for church circle luncheons.

Nola's Storybook Cookies

Nola Scott
Ghost Ranch staff

1/2	cup butter, at room temperature
1/4	cup sugar
1/8	teaspoon almond extract
	Food coloring (yellow, red, green, orange)
1 1/4	cups all-purpose flour

Cream butter, sugar, almond extract and food coloring with electric mixer until light and fluffy. Beat in flour. Repeat full recipe for each food color. Form fruits and vegetables, using food pick for creases. Apply "blush" (apricots, peaches, pears) with small clean brush and diluted food coloring. Roll strawberries in red decorator's sugar. Use green dough for leaves and stems. Place formed pieces on ungreased baking sheet. Refrigerate at least 30 minutes. Bake at 300°F until firm but not brown, 30 minutes more or less, depending on size.

Storybook cookies were a Christmas tradition at our house. I made them for my boys every year. We gave away tons of them. Now, I make them for my grandchildren. Don't make these if you are in a hurry. It takes about 2 hours to get one tray ready to be baked! The dough can also be molded into animals.

Hypocrites

Joan and Chad Boliek
Ghost Ranch staff

	Enough pie crust dough for a two crust pie
2	tablespoons melted margarine
1/4	cup sugar
1	tablespoon cinnamon

Form dough into a ball. Roll out on floured surface into a rectangle. (The longer and narrower the rectangle, the smaller round the hypocrites.) Spread surface with a very light coating of margarine. Sprinkle sugar and cinnamon over all. Roll, starting from long end, as tightly as possible. Moisten other side of long end so that it will stick to the roll. With a sharp knife, slice the roll into 1/2 to 3/4" slices. Place on cookie sheet, cut side down, about an inch apart. Bake at 425°F for about 10 minutes or until golden brown on the bottom. Cool before removing from pan. (Makes about 3 dozen.)

Webster's defines hypocrite as a pretender; a person who pretends to be what he or she is not. Thus, these hypocrites pretend to be cinnamon rolls but they're not. These became a traditional treat for the Annual Ghost Ranch Christmas Tree Outing when one year, I made cookies and burned them. In a panic, I remembered Chad's mother's recipe for hypocrites. I had a box of pie crust mix on hand and quickly mixed it up and took hypocrites on the outing. We've been doing it every year since!

The Annual Ghost Ranch Christmas Tree Hunt

Lesley Poling-Kempes
Christmas tree hunter of 17 years
Abiquiu, NM

As early as Arthur Pack's days at Ghost Ranch there was a Christmas tree hunt in the mountains near the ranch. Jim Hall and Joe Keesecker continued the tradition in true cowboy style: Ranch families and friends are led up Mesa de las Viejas in snow, rain, or blazing sunshine.

The faces and names have changed over the decades, but basically the Ghost Ranch Christmas Tree Hunt, held as close to Christmas as possible, has included the same ingredients year after year: staff, friends, and family out for the day, come what may, on top of Mesa de las Viejas; vans, pickup trucks and jeeps, at least one of which sports some sort of four wheel drive to pull the others up the mountain; hats, coats, mittens, mufflers and boots, preferably the waterproof, not horse proof, variety;

vocal chords not embarrassed to sing a tune now and again whilst waiting for the vehicle ahead to be pulled through the mud or snow; sleds and toboggans on the chance there is enough snow on the Big Hill for a good hour of sledding; chains, matches, cameras, sunglasses, more chains, an axe, a saw or two, patience for waiting AGAIN while the vehicle ahead is pulled out from under a fir tree that was too close to the road anyway, and FOOD.

Food is the second most important ingredient on the Ghost Ranch Christmas Tree Hunt recipe for winter fun. The first is, of course, the four wheel drive vehicle: the point of the hunt is not to find Christmas trees, although a few are brought home (with their proper Forest Service tags) each year, but is to first reach and then stand upon Lookout Point, stare at the magnificent view of the Chama Valley, Pedernal and the Sangre de Cristo mountains, huddle over the fire, and finally crowd about the goodies on the back of one of the pickup trucks. There is an unspoken agreement amongst staff and friends that although everyone is nutritionally correct the rest of the year, the weeks before and after Christmas are a sugarfest of holiday eats.

So, if you want to imitate this ranch tradition in your home, here are some ideas from our table—actually, pickup truck bed—for use on yours:

Several tankards of black coffee, preferably not decaf. Cowboys simply never drink the stuff and remember you're going to be standing near a smoky fire with your feet curling with frostbite and your hands numbing fast.

One tin each of Hypocrites, chocolate chip cookies, sticky buns, donuts (homemade or not, they all taste the same in the winter wild), sugar cookies with icing, fudge brownies cut extra large, pound cake, white cake, chocolate cake, another tin of Hypocrites, raisin sweetrolls, glazed sweetrolls, and decorated Santa cookies.

Feel free to improvise with treats from your own bakery and recipe collection. What is important is to make a lot, eat a lot, and take a long day getting to and from the hunt. We recommend a snowball fight that lasts a good, long while, or until one of the wee ones gets ice down his or her back. This affords the hunters with exercise which alleviates the guilt acquired at the back of the pickup truck rifling through the tins of goodies. You can choose your own form of exercise: just include everyone, keep moving, and make sure there are a few tins of cookies left for the long drive home on the road that will most certainly have worsened during the intervening hours.

CANDY

Zurich Butter Truffles

Diane Arenberg
Mequon, WI

Filling:

2	cups heavy cream
1/2	cup unsalted butter, cut in 1/2" chunks
6	tablespoons sugar
1	pound semi-sweet chocolate (good quality)
6	tablespoons Grand Marnier
	Confectioners' sugar

Coating:

1 1/2	pounds semi-sweet chocolate, chopped in pea-size pieces

To make filling: Heat cream almost to boiling in top of double boiler over medium heat. Add butter and sugar; stir until dissolved. Chop 1 pound chocolate into peas-sized pieces; add to cream mixture. Stir until smooth. Remove from heat and add Grand Marnier. Pour into jelly roll pans; freeze 2 hours. Put thickened chocolate into pastry bag with wide round tip; squeeze 3/4" balls or kisses onto waxed-paper coated baking sheets. Return to freezer until firm, 1 1/2 to 2 hours. Dust hands with confectioners' sugar; roll kisses into smooth balls. Return to freezer.

To make coating: Fill a large pot with hot water. Put the 1 1/2 pounds chocolate into a metal bowl that will fit into the pot of hot water. Immerse metal bowl in water, being careful not to get any water into the chocolate. Scrape chocolate off sides as it melts, until all is melted and "tempered." If the chocolate gets too hot for your hands, it is too hot!

Remove chocolate balls from freezer. Coat hands with tempered chocolate. Roll balls in chocolate in your hands. Place them on waxed paper-lined baking sheets. Let stand until chocolate coating hardens; repeat until truffles have 2 or 3 coats of chocolate. Cover and store in refrigerator. (Makes about 72 truffles.)

This recipe is from the head pastry chef at the Drake Hotel in Chicago, IL. He claimed they sold for $50 a pound in Paris.

Golden Fudge

Jan Myers
Arvada, CO

3	cups sugar
1/4	cup light corn syrup
3	tablespoons butter or margarine
1/2	teaspoon salt
1	cup evaporated milk
1/2	cup water
2	teaspoons vanilla extract

Combine sugar, corn syrup, butter, salt, evaporated milk and water in a large heavy saucepan. Heat to boiling over medium heat, stirring constantly. Cook rapidly, stirring several times, to 238°F on candy thermometer (a teaspoonful will form a soft ball when dropped in cold water). Remove from heat at once. Add vanilla, but do not stir. Cool in pan to 110°F (lukewarm). Beat 2 to 3 minutes, or until mixture begins to thicken and loses its gloss. Spread in buttered 8 x 8 x 2" pan. Let stand just until set, 2 to 3 minutes. Cut in squares.

From Family Circle magazine (about 1968). This fudge has been a family favorite at Christmas-time for about 20 years.

Peanut Butter Fudge

Ellen S. Kronkright
Grand Junction, CO

5	cups sugar
2	cups margarine or butter
1	can evaporated milk (12 oz.)
1	teaspoon vanilla extract
1	large jar marshmallow creme (13 oz.)
1 1/2	cups chunky or smooth peanut butter

Combine sugar, margarine and milk in large heavy saucepan. Heat to boiling; reduce heat and continue boiling, stirring constantly, 8 minutes. Remove from heat; stir in vanilla, marshmallow creme, and peanut butter. Pour into buttered 11 x 13" pan; cool. Cut in squares. (Makes about 140 1"-square pieces.)

Cherry Bombs

Rose Marie Christison
Aurora, CO

1/2	cup butter or margarine
1/4	cup sifted confectioners' sugar
1	teaspoon water
1 1/4	cup sifted all-purpose flour
1/4	teaspoon salt
24	maraschino cherries with stems, drained
	Red decorator sugar

Cream butter and sugar with electric mixer in medium bowl; add water. Add flour and salt; beat well. Shape equal portions of mixture around each cherry, leaving stem showing. Roll in red sugar; place on ungreased baking sheet. Bake at 325°F for 15 to 20 minutes. (Makes 24 candies.)

Pecan Clusters

Rose Marie Christison
Aurora, CO

1 to 2	pounds pecan halves, divided
1	cup butter (2 sticks)
2	cups packed brown sugar
1	cup corn syrup
1	can (14 oz.) sweetened condensed milk (such as Eagle Brand)
1	teaspoon vanilla extract
2	pounds molding chocolate discs, melted

Put bunches of 3 or 4 pecans, 2" apart, on waxed paper-lined baking sheets. Reserve about 75 halves for garnish. Melt butter in medium heavy saucepan over high heat, watching carefully so it does not brown. Reduce heat to medium; stir in brown sugar, corn syrup and condensed milk. Heat to boiling; reduce heat and cook to 235°F on candy thermometer. Remove from heat and gently stir in vanilla. Let this caramel mixture stand until slightly cool, 10 to 15 minutes. Spoon caramel mixture over pecan clusters. Spoon melted chocolate over caramel; top each cluster with one reserved pecan half. (Makes about 75 clusters.)

These are by far the best Pecan Clusters I have ever eaten! The recipe came from a dear friend who is no longer living. She would be pleased to know I'm passing it on.

Crunch Toffee

Jan Myers
Arvada, CO

2 cups butter or margarine (1 lb.)
2   cups sugar
1/4   cup water
2   tablespoons corn syrup
1 1/2 cups chopped peanuts
1   package semi-sweet chocolate chips (6 ounces)

Combine butter, sugar, water and corn syrup in large heavy saucepan; cook over medium heat, then low heat, stirring constantly, until bubbly. Continue cooking until mixture reaches 290°F (hard-crack stage) on candy thermometer. Remove from heat; quickly stir in peanuts. Spread mixture evenly on large baking sheet with sides. (Place a towel under the baking sheet). Remove excess oil with a paper towel. Sprinkle chocolate chips over hot toffee mixture. When melted, spread evenly. Let stand until cool and firm. Break into small pieces; store in airtight container. (Makes about 20 pieces.)

This has been a Myers family recipe for over 30 years.

Heidi's Mock Baby Ruth Bars

Marion Sweet
Verona, WI

2/3	cup margarine or butter
1	cup packed brown sugar
1/2	cup corn syrup
1/4	cup crunchy peanut butter
1	teaspoon vanilla
4	cups rolled oats (quick-cooking preferred)
1	package chocolate chips (12 oz.)
1	package butterscotch chips (6 oz.)
2/3	cup creamy peanut butter
1	cup salted Spanish peanuts

Melt margarine, brown sugar and corn syrup over medium heat in heavy medium saucepan. Stir in crunchy peanut butter and vanilla. Pour over rolled oats in large bowl; stir to combine. Press oat mixture in bottom of greased 9 x 13" baking pan. Bake at 375°F for about 12 minutes. Remove and let stand until cool. Melt chocolate and butterscotch chips in the saucepan. Stir in smooth peanut butter and peanuts. Pour over cooled oat crust. Cool and cut. Store in refrigerator.

Granola Bar for Diabetics

Mildred K. Yoder
South Bend, IN

1	envelope carnation hot cocoa mix made with NutraSweet
3	tablespoons water
2	tablespoons chunky peanut butter
1/4	cup sugar-free dry cereal (such as Grape Nuts Flakes, Nutra Grain)
2	tablespoons raisins, coconut or nuts (some of each or none, if desired)

Mix cocoa mix and water until smooth. Stir in peanut butter; fold in cereal, dried fruit and/or nuts. Form into bar, about 2 x 3"; wrap in aluminum foil and freeze 2 hours. (Makes 1 bar. Exchanges: 1 bread, 1 milk, 2 meat; 1 fruit, optional.)

Many people with diabetes crave chocolate. This helps answer the need. Instead of making into a bar, after mixing, I drop them by teaspoonfuls onto a foil-lined pan and freeze. I store the drops in the freezer and use them as a dessert treat, one after each meal. The drops are 'free' - no exchange necessary.)

An Invitation to Remember

Selena Petersen-Keesecker
Ghost Ranch

A memory
The scent of a small piñon fire
A roasting stick
Flat chocolate bars
Bag of marshmallows
Box of graham crackers

Prepare the fire and invoke the blessings of the evening with the scent of piñon. Break the graham cracker into two squares as you remember bread being broken at other tables. Place one or two marshmallows on your roasting stick. Kneel down beside the fire and slowly begin to roast the marshmallows. Listen to your heart as you watch the coals. If you are hasty, the marshmallows will catch on fire. Not to worry. When you sense the inside of the marshmallow is melted (or if you can't wait any longer) remove from the fire, place on chocolate covered graham cracker. Place the other half of the graham cracker on top and pull out your roasting stick. Take a breath and begin to eat as you remember times shared with friends. Remember times and places where you were changed and became something fresh and new as you were tempered in other fires. This is not a frivilous "s'more"; rather, it is a call to when you became someone more. May you celebrate who you are as you share this invitation to remember.

Selena is the wife of Ghost Ranch Director, Joe Keesecker.

More Friends

Cooking in the Ghost Ranch Kitchen
January 19 - 20, 1996

Each January for the last four years, I've flown from the icy snowstorms of upstate New York to the piquant warmth of the Ghost Ranch kitchen. Inspired by the Spanish women I work with - Molly and Rebecca, Flora, Mary, Doreen, Marta, Terri, and by Rosie (who is Navajo), I've learned to cook traditional New Mexican dishes. I've also invented dishes using the local ingredients and my own style.

Eight cooks who have worked together in the same kitchen for decades aren't always eager to learn from a newcomer! When my fellow cooks started taking small bowls of my food and saying to me in surprise, "Not too bad," I can tell you how good it felt!

On this weekend, there were 90 hungry college students and their instructors living at Ghost Ranch, taking photographs, making black pottery and turquoise jewelry, painting, hiking and writing for the "Jan" college term.

Here's what I was doing in the kitchen. I always start by seeing what's in season and what's locally available. That weekend, we had 20 pounds of organic sweet baby carrots grown by Ben and Ramoncita Garcia. We had onions grown by Amadeo Trujillo, dried red chiles from Cordelia Coronado, local chick peas (garbanzos) and garlic, calavacas (delicious lumpy orange native pumpkins), and even sweet corn from A.B. Valdez. There was pesto, made from Scott Markman's basil, frozen by a prudent Rebecca. We also had dried mitlas, an ancient variety of black beans, grown on the small farm at the Ranch.

Julie Jordan is a chef from Ithaca, NY. She owned and operated her own restaurant for 15 years. Julie has written two cookbooks, Wings of Life *and* Cabbagetown Cafe Cookbook. *She is currently working on* Julie Jordan's Great Vegetarian Cookbook, *to be published by Crossing Press of Freedom, CA .*

Julie's Menu for the Weekend

(recipes follow)

Friday, January 19

Lunch

Thick Tomato Soup with Green Peas and Marjoram
Couscous
Red Chile Chick Peas

Dinner

Butternut Squash Soup with Onions, Pan-Fried Sourdough
Piñon Pesto on "Bowties"
Oven-Roasted Broccoli and Baby Carrots

Saturday, January 20

Lunch

Clay Pot Black Beans with Cilantro, Toasted-Corn Polenta
Red Leaf Lettuce, Green Sunflower Dressing
Sourdough Bread

After cooking Saturday lunch, I had dinner off, so I headed up the Chimney Rock trail. After I cook, I love to hike. Moving through the sunny blue New Mexico air clears all the fatigue out of me. At the top, I spent more than a little time just looking out over the red and gold mudhills and the snow-covered Sangre de Cristos.

Thick Tomato Soup with Green Peas & Marjoram

Julie Jordan

1	quart or 1 can tomatoes, undrained (28 ounces)
2	cups water
2	cloves garlic, finely chopped
2	stalks celery, finely chopped
4	green onions with tender green tops, chopped
1	carrot, grated
1	tablespoon olive oil
2	teaspoons dried or 2 tablespoons fresh marjoram
1/2	teaspoon salt
	Few grinds fresh black pepper
1	cup green peas, fresh or frozen
	Couscous (recipe follows)
	Red Chile Chick Peas (recipe follows)

Blend tomatoes in a blender or food processor until smooth. Pour into a 4-quart pot; add water. Heat to simmer over medium heat. Add garlic, celery, green onions and carrot. Cover and simmer over medium heat, stirring occasionally, for 30 minutes. Add olive oil, seasonings and green peas. Cover and continue cooking for 30 minutes. Add more seasoning, if desired. (More pepper is often good.) Serve in a soup bowl with side dishes of Couscous and Red Chile Chick Peas, to be stirred into the soup as desired. (4 servings)

I've always made this soup with sour cream, but this time, I opened the walk-in refrigerator at 11:15, and we were out of sour cream! Peter, the long-time Jan-term Dean of Students, just happened to be there. "Jump into my car," he said. We raced to Bode's in Abiquiu, only to find one tiny half-pint container of sour cream in the dairy case. When we got back to the Ranch, I tasted the soup and realized I liked it much better without the sour cream. This shows how crazed a cook can become following a recipe, how Peter is gallant, and how a good dish can be simply the result of circumstance.

Couscous

1	cup couscous
1/2	teaspoon salt
	Black pepper
	Olive oil
2	cups water

Mix the couscous, salt and pepper in a medium saucepan. Drizzle a little olive oil over the top. Boil the water in a separate kettle. Pour boiling water over the couscous; heat to boiling over medium-high heat. Remove from heat; cover and let stand 15 minutes. Fluff with a fork before serving. (4 servings)

Couscous is a crushed grain product that originated in North Africa. Today, you can get white and whole wheat couscous. It's quick to make and delicious with soups and stews.

Red Chile Chick Peas

1	pound dry chick peas (garbanzos)
2	dried New Mexico red chiles
	Olive oil
	Whole black peppercorns
1	heaping teaspoon salt

Wash and sort the chick peas for stones. Place in a large pot and cover with water. Let stand 12 hours; drain. Cover generously with fresh water; heat to boiling. Boil uncovered 10 minutes; skim off the foam. (This step makes beans more digestible.) Cover and cook over medium heat until soft, about 2 hours.

Add the chiles. (Leave the seeds in for hot chick peas; remove the seeds for a milder dish.) Add a little olive oil, the peppercorns and 1 heaping teaspoon salt. (Always wait until beans are soft before adding salt. If you add salt too early, the beans will stay hard, no matter how long you cook them.) Cook and cook, covered, at least one hour more. It's a basic rule: You can't overcook a bean. Add more water, if necessary. The dish is ready then the chick peas are very soft and have a delicious rich flavor. Drain; serve warm or at room temperature. (About 5 cups)

One November, Doreen, Molly and I left the Ranch kitchen for a week to make clay cooking pots with Felipe. I use my clay pot at home every time I cook beans. It gives beans the best flavor and texture.

Butternut Squash Soup with Onions, Pan-Fried Sourdough

Julie Jordan

	Olive oil (divided)
1	butternut squash, cut in chunks (about 2 pounds)*
2	medium onions, cut in chunks
	Salt
2	cups water
	Fresh ground black pepper
	Green onions with tender green tops, chopped
	Sourdough bread, sliced

Pour a little olive oil into a large soup pot; add squash and onions. Sprinkle with salt. Cover and cook over medium heat, stirring occasionally, about 20 minutes. Watch closely so the vegetables don't dry out and burn. Starting the cooking without water develops the rich sweet flavors of the vegetables.

Add 2 cups water. Continue cooking until the vegetables are very soft, about 20 minutes. Puree in blender or food processor until smooth. Add a bit more water if the soup is too thick, but be careful since too much water knocks out the lovely rich flavor.

Taste and correct seasoning. If you have a good squash, you shouldn't need to do anything more, except perhaps add a pinch of salt. Heat the soup. Top each serving with a grind of black pepper and chopped green onions. Serve with thin slices of sourdough bread, pan-fried in the remaining olive oil until slight brown. (4 servings)

*All commercial squash needs to be peeled because their skins are waxed. Homegrown or organic squash with soft skins don't need to be peeled. Their skins soften entirely during cooking.

VARIATIONS: At the Ranch, we sometimes use mature New Mexico pumpkins called calavacas for this soup. As we cut up each pumpkin, we're careful to save the seeds for next summer's planting. Another variation is to cook one or two turnips or a rutabaga with the squash and onions.

Piñon Pesto on "Bowties"

Julie Jordan

	Big bunch of fresh basil
	(3 cups leaves and tender stems)
1/2-3/4	cup piñon nuts
1	teaspoon salt
2-3	cloves garlic
1/3	cup olive oil
1	package bowtie pasta (16 ounces)
	Fresh grated Parmesan cheese
	Fresh ground black pepper

Get that basil ready! Use all the leaves and the tender parts of the stems near the top. Toast piñon nuts and salt in small skillet over low heat, or in the oven. Be *very* careful as they brown in a matter of minutes. Pulse garlic and basil in food processor. Add the toasted piñon nuts and salt; pulse until blended. Add olive oil and pulse just until combined. Cook pasta; drain. Toss hot pasta with basil mixture. Serve with plenty of fresh Parmesan cheese and a grind of black pepper over each serving. (4 servings)

I think of being at the Ranch in the summer and that farm-healthy, sun-tanned Scott unloading big paper grocery bags of the fragrant basil leaves he's just picked. The classic "pine" nuts in pestos are the piñon nut from our friendly high-desert piñon trees. Piñon nuts used to be a major export crop from New Mexico.

Green Sunflower Dressing

Julie Jordan

1	cup sunflower seeds, toasted
1	medium bunch fresh parsley, coarsely chopped, stems and all
1	cup vegetable oil
	Juice of 2 lemons (about 1/2 cup)
1/4	cup water
2	tablespoons soy or tamari sauce
2	teaspoon dried dillweed
1	teaspoon dry mustard
1	teaspoon salt

Combine all ingredients in blender container or food processor. Process until smooth. Cover and store in refrigerator. (About 3 cups)

This was my first invention that was to become regular fare at the Ranch. Ed Davy, the librarian, loved it and pestered the cooks every morning until they started making it. The dressing is also delicious on pasta and vegetables.

Oven-Roasted Garden Vegetables

Julie Jordan

Good vegetables to roast:
> New Mexico calavacitas
> Baby or full-size summer squash
> Baby or full-size carrots
> Broccoli
> Cauliflower
> Leeks
> Mushrooms
> Sweet red peppers
> Eggplant

Seasonings:
> Olive oil, salt, garlic, rosemary, thyme, ground
> red chile, black pepper, lime or lemon juice

Leave baby vegetables whole; cut large vegetables into nice-looking chunks of a size you can spear with a fork and eat in one or two bites. If you're cooking large quantities of vegetables, cook each vegetable in a separate baking pan, so you can monitor the degree of doneness and seasoning of each. If you're just cooking a bit, do them all together.

Preheat oven to 425° F. Spread a little olive oil in each pan; add the vegetables. Sprinkle with salt. Bake until tender but not soft, about 15 minutes. If the vegetables are sticking, add a tiny bit of water. Usually, if you shake or stir them, they're okay without added water.

Add herbs and spices (totally by inspiration). The hotness of the red chile goes wonderfully with the sweetness of the squash soup. Continue cooking 10 minutes; test for doneness. You can add a sprinkle of salt and fresh lime or lemon juice just as vegetables are removed from the oven. Serve each vegetable separately, or mix them. (Servings vary depending on amount of vegetables and use - appetizer, entree, side dish.)

Each summer, as a support to the Ranch's continuing program of purchasing locally-grown produce, I've spent a month on the back porch behind the kitchen -- receiving and prepping the beautiful vegetables raised in the sweet red soil. At home, I'd steam fresh garden vegetables, but at the Ranch, we have these enormous gorgeous ovens going all the time, so I've started oven-roasting the produce. I love that slightly seared outside with a burst of flavor inside.

editor's note: If you prefer to use a lower baking temperature, cook the vegetables longer.

Clay Pot Black Beans with Cilantro

Julie Jordan

1	pound black turtle beans or mitlas
2	medium onions, chopped (about 1 cup)
	Olive oil
1	tablespoon ground cumin
	Salt and pepper
	Chopped fresh cilantro

Wash and sort the beans for stones. Place in large pot; cover with water and soak for at least 12 hours. Drain; cover generously with fresh water. Heat to boiling. Boil uncovered 10 minutes; skim foam. Reduce heat; cover and cook until soft, about 2 hours. Add chopped onions, a pour of olive oil, the cumin, salt and black pepper to taste. Cover; cook and cook, at least 1 hour -- the more the better -- adding water, if necessary. Add cilantro and cook a few minutes. Taste and correct seasoning. The beans should be melting, rich and succulent. (4 to 5 cups)

The first time I visited the Ranch, I took a tan plastic bowl of black beans from the gleaming stainless steel counter at the lunch line. Next, I had the astounding experience of tasting beans that were simply beans boiled in water with salt, but were by far the most succulent and flavorful beans I'd tasted in my whole lifetime of questing. I braved all the apparent sternness of the kitchen women, who would later become my good friends, to dash back and ask, "What are these?" "Just beans," answered Marta. It took me several days to discover that they were fresh mitlas just delivered by Susie VerKamp, manager of the High-Desert Research Farm on the Ranch. Make plenty and freeze the leftovers.

editor's note: The older dried beans are, the longer they take to cook. Shop in a busy market where you're more likely to get beans from the most recent fall harvest. Store beans in an airtight container in a cool place.

Toasted-Corn Polenta

Julie Jordan

2	cups cornmeal of choice
6	cups water or more
2	teaspoons salt
	Olive oil
	Chopped onions, fresh or frozen corn (optional)
	Black pepper
	Beans, red chile or tomato sauce

Heat the dry cornmeal in a heavy pot, stirring constantly until it just starts to brown and turn fragrant. Very slowly add the water, stirring vigorously after each addition, until the cornmeal absorbs the water and is smooth. If the mixture is really thick after adding 6 cups of water, gradually stir in up to 2 more cups of water. (The key to getting the water right for a really creamy polenta is a matter of inspiration and experience.) Add salt and a pour of olive oil. Add onion and corn, if desired. Continue stirring over medium heat until the mixture begins to shine. Taste and add more salt if necessary.

Pour into one or two shallow baking dishes, lightly coated with olive oil. Bake at 350°F until the cornmeal mixture developes a nice crust, one hour or more. If the top starts to get hard, drizzle it with a bit of olive oil. To serve, cut in large squares or wedges.

Serve baked polenta with beans or with a flavorful red chile or tomato sauce. Leftover polenta can be cut in slices and fried, then served with beans or sauce, or baked with the sauce or beans covering it. (6 to 8 servings)

Polenta has become a staple of my cooking. I make it with any type of cornmeal I can find wherever I am. In New Mexico, you can buy a specialty cornmeal called chaqueque *which is ground from toasted corn and is especially sweet and nutty. If you live outside of New Mexico, the farm associated with JoAnn's restaurant in Española specializes in mail-order New Mexican foods. Ranch-O-Casados, P.O. Box 1149, San Juan Pueblo, New Mexico, 87566.*

Sopaipillas

Angelitos Productions
Santa Fe, NM

2	cups flour
2	teaspoons baking powder
1	teaspoon salt
1	teaspoon sugar
1	tablespoon solid shortening
	Oil
	Warm water
	Honey, cinnamon sugar, confectioners' sugar

Mix flour, baking powder, salt and sugar in a medium bowl. Cut in shortening with a pastry blender or fork until it is the consistency of fine meal. Stir in just enough warm water to make a medium-soft dough, almost like pie crust dough. Cover and let stand for about 30 minutes at room temperature.

Roll the dough on a floured board to a thickness of 1/8". Cut into 3 to 4" triangles. Do not stack, as they will stick; cover with a damp cloth. Deep fry in hot oil (400°F) until puffed up and light golden brown. Remove and drain on paper towels.

Best served warm with honey or cinnamon-sugar (see editor's note) or sprinkled with confectioners' sugar. They are also good with beans and chile (red or green). They make great little pockets! (12 to 16 sopaipillas)

Angelitos Productions (David Manzanares, Daniel Manzanares, Andie Shay) is a full-service production company in Sante Fe. The company represents Ghost Ranch for print ads and catalogs, commercials, music videos and feature films. There has been a lot of action in recent years! The movies "City Slickers," "Wyatt Erp," and "Speechless" have scenes filmed at the Ranch. Directors, photographers, art directors, producers, cameramen and talent from New York to Los Angeles to London to Tokoyo are absolutely mesmerized with the taste of Sopaipillas. One art director of a high-style catalog ate them for breakfast, lunch and dinner. Along with schedules, call times and sunset shots, Sopaipillas go with a Ghost Ranch production.

David and Daniel Manzanares grew up in Abiquiu and learned to swim in the Ghost Ranch pool.

editor's note: To make cinnamon-sugar, place 1/2 cup sugar and 1 1/2 teaspoons cinnamon in a paper bag. Shake to mix. Place sopaipillas in bag just after removing from hot oil; shake to coat with cinnamon-sugar mixture.

More Friends 374

Fried Rice

Gary Salazar
Ghost Ranch

3	tablespoons olive oil
1 1/2	cups thinly cut pieces meat or poultry (your choice): chicken, pork, beef, Canadian bacon
1/2	cup each thinly cut pieces of: Carrots, broccoli, mushrooms, bell pepper, celery
1/2	cup frozen peas
1/4	cup chopped onion
4	cups cooked white rice
1/3	cup soy sauce
2	eggs, beaten

Combine olive oil and meat in hot deep skillet or wok. Cook over moderately-high heat until meat is brown. Add carrots and broccoli; cook and stir 2 to 3 minutes. Add remaining vegetables; stir to desired tenderness. Add rice and soy sauce; stir until rice is hot. Add eggs; cook and stir until mixture starts to separate and rice reaches desired moisture level, about 5 minutes. Great as a side dish with egg rolls. (4 servings)

Fried rice is one of my favorite dishes. For years, I only had fried rice when I ate at a Chinese restaurant. [Which wasn't often after Gary moved to the Ranch!] It wasn't until recently, after talking with my sister Debbie, that I realized how easy it is to make.

editor's note: Gary Salazar, who grew up in nearby Tierra Amarilla, is Manager of Conference Services at Ghost Ranch. He holds a degree in wildlife science -- good training for his current position!

Jean's Favorite Pasta

Jean Richardson
Ghost Ranch

1 1/2	pounds pasta
3	tablespoons olive oil
2	whole chicken breasts, skinned, boned, cut in 1" pieces
1/2	large onion, chopped (about 1/2 cup)
2	teaspoons chopped garlic
1/2	green bell pepper, chopped (about 1/2 cup)
1/2	sweet red bell pepper, chopped (about 1/2 cup)
1/2	cup chopped sun-dried tomatoes
1	cup crumbled feta cheese (4 oz.)
1/2	bunch chopped cilantro

Cook pasta. Meanwhile, heat olive oil in large skillet. Add chicken, onion and garlic; cook and stir over medium heat until chicken is white and onions are tender. Add peppers and tomatoes; cook and stir until peppers are crisp-tender. Drain pasta; toss with chicken mixture, cheese and cilantro. (4 to 6 servings)

I was tired but ecstatic as I boarded the plane in London with my newly adopted infant son from the Ukraine. The woman sitting in front of me offered to help as I struggled with bags, bottles and the baby. We began to talk. I told her I was not on my way home to San Francisco, but was going to Ghost Ranch in New Mexico to teach a class. (Adoption had not been on my schedule!) "What a wonderful place to take your baby! I have gone there for years," she exclaimed. "I'm a compadre." Her name was Janis Simmons. A gift of the Divine! Little did I know that almost to the day, a year later, we'd move to the Ranch and I'd become the Ranch Associate for Programs.

Grilled Salmon

Jean Richardson
Ghost Ranch

8	tablespoons unsalted butter (1 stick)
1/2	cup honey
1/3	cup packed brown sugar
2	tablespoons lemon juice
1	teaspoon natural liquid smoke flavoring
3/4	teaspoon dried red pepper flakes
1	center-cut salmon fillet, with skin (about 2 pounds)

Combine all ingredients except salmon in a small saucepan. Cook over medium heat, stirring until smooth. Cool to room temperature. Put salmon in nonmetallic pan; pour butter mixture over salmon. Let stand 30 minutes, turning once. Cook on oiled grill over hot coals 5 to 7 minutes on each side. (4 servings)

Rebecca's Chicken Loaf

Rebecca Martinez
Ghost Ranch

Chicken Loaf:

3	cups chopped cooked chicken
1	cup cooked rice
1/4	cup chopped pimientoes
1/4	cup margarine or butter, melted
2	cups chicken broth
1	cup milk
2	cups soft bread crumbs
3	whole eggs + 2 egg whites from the sauce (below), beaten
1 1/2	teaspoons salt

Mushroom Sauce:

4	tablespoons margarine or butter
5	tablespoons all-purpose flour
2	cups chicken broth
1	can mushrooms, drained (8 oz.)
1	teaspoon lemon juice
2	egg yolks
2 1/4	cups milk
	Salt to taste

To make chicken loaf: Combine chicken, rice, pimientoes and melted margarine in large mixing bowl. Gradually add broth and milk. Stir in bread crumbs. Fold in eggs and salt. Spoon into 9 x 9" baking pan. Bake at 350°F for 1 1/4 hours. Serve hot, with Mushroom Sauce. (6 to 8 servings)

To make sauce: Melt butter or margarine in medium saucepan over low heat. Stir in flour; cook and stir 2 minutes. Gradually add chicken broth; stir until smoooth. Stir in mushrooms and lemon juice. Cook and stir over medium heat until smooth and thick. Combine egg yolks and milk in small bowl. Stir a spoonful of the hot sauce into the egg mixture; add egg mixture to remaining hot sauce. Heat, but do not boil. Add salt to taste.

Goo Sammich

Philip Geissal
Ghost Ranch

Equal parts: honey (plain or flavored)
butter or margarine
peanut butter (smooth or crunchy)
Plain white bread, "98-grain," or any bread that suits your fancy

Mix equal parts of honey, butter and peanut butter in a bowl or on a large plate until a great "goo" is formed. Spread peanut butter mixture about 1/4" thick on one slice of bread. Top with another slice of bread or fold over for a richer taste. (1 sammich)

Children of the Geissal clan have grown up with this special treat prepared by their father. Even in today's health conscious climate, the next generation, consisting of six grandchildren, still find Grandpa's Goo Sammich quite a delicacy.

editor's note: Philip Geissal is National Ghost Ranch Foundation Director and Funds Development Director for Ghost Ranch and Plaza Resolana.

Chicken Supreme

Carol Ruth Geissal
Ghost Ranch

Serves 12		Serves 50	
1	large chicken (3 lbs.) or 6 split breasts (12 pieces)	12	pounds chicken or 25 split breasts (50 pieces)
4 - 5	cups water	1 1/4	gallons water (20 cups)
3 - 4	cups broth from cooked chicken	1	gallon chicken broth (16 cups)
1 1/2	cups diced celery	6	cups chopped celery
1/2	medium onion, chopped (1/4 cup)	4	medium onions, chopped (2 cups)
3	tablespoons butter or margarine	3/4	cup butter or margarine
8	oz. American or longhorn cheese, shredded (2 cups)	2	pounds cheese, shredded (8 cups)
1	can mushroom soup, undiluted (10 3/4 oz.)	4	cans (10 3/4 oz. each) mushroom soup
3	cups crushed Ritz crackers	12	cups (3 quarts) crushed Ritz crackers
4	eggs, unbeaten Salt and pepper to taste	16	eggs, unbeaten Salt and pepper to taste

Place chicken in large pot; cover with the water. Cover and cook slowly over medium heat until tender, about 2 hours. Refrigerate until cool enough to handle. Reserve broth; bone and chop the chicken. (When using chicken breasts only, leave meat in large pieces.) Combine meat and specified amount of reserved broth in a container large enough to hold all the remaining ingredients. Cook onion and celery in butter in a skillet until tender; add to chicken with remaining ingredients. Pour into greased baking pan or casserole. You will need one 13 x 9 x 2" pan for 12 servings; 4 pans this size or one large commercial pan for the 50-serving recipe. Bake at 350°F for 45 to 60 minutes. Let stand for 15 minutes. It will cut into nice squares for serving.

I was born in the kitchen -- on the kitchen table in my family home in Brookfield, Missouri. It has made a deep and lifelong impact on my life. I 've always loved food. I like to read about cooking. I try the old and create new and different recipes for my family and friends. Philip and I have worked in camps and conference centers and I have managed the foodservice and dining rooms. Philip has often said that if we feed our guests well, we'll be forgiven for other mistakes we might make. This recipe has always been a success with my family and with large groups, too. I usually serve it with a cranberry gelatin salad and a green vegetable. Enjoy!

editor's note: Carol Ruth Geissal works with her husband in the Ghost Ranch Foundation office.

To Preserve Children

Rebecca Martinez
Ghost Ranch

1/2	dozen young children
2 or 3	puppies
1	large grassy field
1	pinch of brook
	Some beautiful pebbles

Mix children and puppies together in a large grassy field, stirring constantly. Pour the brook over the pebbles. Sprinkle splashing water over the children and puppies. Bake in warm sunshine until brown. Remove children and set them in a cool bathtub. They are wonderful!

This is my favorite recipe because of all my grandchildren!

Pumpkin Cheese Roll

Mary Martinez
Ghost Ranch

Cake:

1	cup granulated sugar
3/4	cup all-purpose flour
1	teaspoon baking powder
1	teaspoon ground cinnamon
1/2	teaspoon salt
1/2	teaspoon ground ginger
1/4	teaspoon ground nutmeg
3	eggs, beaten
2/3	cup cooked, mashed pumpkin
1	teaspoon lemon juice
1	cup chopped nuts

Filling:

1	package cream cheese, at room temperature (8 oz.)
1/2	tablespoon butter or margarine
1	cup confectioners' sugar
1/2	teaspoon vanilla

Sift dry ingredients into large mixing bowl. Beat in eggs, pumpkin and lemon juice until well mixed. Stir in nuts. Pour into greased 15 1/2 x 10 1/2 x 1" jellyroll pan. Bake at 375°F until a wooden pick inserted in the center comes out clean, 15 to 25 minutes. Remove from oven; loosen cake from edges of pan. Invert on wax paper or kitchen towel sprinkled with confectioners' sugar; let stand 10 minutes. Trim hard edges from cake. While warm, roll cake and wax paper or towel from the narrow end. Cool, rolled up, on wire rack.

Make filling. Beat cream cheese and butter until smooth. Gradually add confectioners' sugar; add vanilla. Unroll cake; remove wax paper or towel. Spread filling over cake; roll up again; store in loaf pan (to hold together). Refrigerate. Slice crosswise to serve. (10 servings)

I started working for the Ranch in 1987 in the Housekeeping Department. I moved on to the Foundation office in 1990 (part-time), and became full-time in 1991. My husband Max and I have two children: Andrea, age 15 and Daniel, age 12. I like to make this recipe at Christmas time. It's Daniel's favorite!

Index

Index 392

Index 394

W

Y

Z

NOTES

Ghost Ranch and Friends ORDER FORM
Ghost Ranch Conference Center
HC 77, Box 11
Abiquiu, NM 87510-9601
505/685-4333

Ship to:

Name

Street Address

City

State/Zip

Daytime Phone   Evening Phone

		Qty.	Total
Payment ☐ Check ☐ Money Order	Ghost Ranch & Friends $15.00 each		
Charge to ☐ Visa ☐ MasterCard	Sub Total		
Account Number			
Expiration Date	NM Deliveries 6%		
Name on Card	Shipping & Handling $2.75		
Signature	TOTAL		